Forces of Nature

*A Memoir of Family, Loss,
and Finding Home*

Gina DeMillo Wagner

RUNNING WILD

Published in North America and Europe by Running Wild Press. Visit Running
Wild Press at www.runningwildpress.com, Educators, librarians, book clubs
(as well as the eternally curious), go to www.runningwildpress.com.
ISBN (pbk) 978-1-960018-79-3
ISBN (ebook) 978-1-960018-33-5

For Alan, and siblings everywhere

Author's Note

In writing this memoir, I've endeavored to be as factual as possible. Some names and identifying details have been changed for privacy. I reviewed old letters, journals, emails, medical records, school documents, family photos, and other personal and historical family papers. I interviewed important figures from my childhood as well as people who were present at many of the events recounted here. I spoke with therapists, social workers, and experts on Prader-Willi Syndrome to expand my knowledge and understanding. Where facts and documents fell short, I turned to memory and reconstructed dialogue and emotional details to the best of my ability.

This is a true story told through one person's eyes. Like a prism held up to the light, if you turn it another way, the colors change. There are disparate layers and perspectives that together form a kaleidoscopic view of what happened. This is my perspective.

Above all, in writing this, I sought to honor my brother Alan and validate anyone who's ever experienced a fraught sibling relationship, family estrangement, or complicated grief.

Your love is real.
Your experiences are real.
Your grief is real.

Part One

Endings and Beginnings

Chapter One

August 12, 2016.

The airplane's wheels touch down in Seattle. I feel light, almost giddy, like I'm getting away with something. On the approach, I marvel as I always do at Seattle, how snow-capped peaks are in such close proximity to the sea. The endless carpet of greenery, the chains of islands, boats flowing into and out of ports along the shore.

As the plane bumps along the tarmac toward the gate, I reflexively reach for my phone and turn it on, eager to text my friends and let them know I've arrived. The screen lights up. It pulses like it's taking a deep breath, and then it begins buzzing and chiming with texts and voicemails, each more urgent than the last:

Please call me.

Call me.

CALL ME.

Where are you?

It's very important you call the minute you get this.

THIS IS URGENT

They're all from my father. I'm unsettled by the sight of his name on the display. We rarely talk, and when we do, it's me who calls him. As I see his messages stacking up, sent minutes apart, my stomach seizes, and my legs start trembling.

I don't have to hear his voice to know what's wrong.

I'm supposed to be on vacation. I left my husband, Kris, and two kids back home in Phoenix, Arizona. It's just for a few days, and yet it's not lost on me that with them, I also left behind the vigilance of motherhood. I said goodbye to my eight-year-old daughter and six-year-old son, who are busy chafing against routines, bedtimes, and each other. The school year has just begun, and the four of us have struggled to regain our footing after a spacious summer with lax rules and schedules. This trip holds the hope that I might fall back into myself for a little while, or at least a version of myself I've tucked away but never forgotten. In addition to giving myself a break, I believe I'm doing my family a favor – empowering the kids to rely more on their father, to make their own sandwiches, and to solve arguments without me as a referee. It's good for all of us.

I'm meeting up with two dear friends, women I've known for more than a decade. We met when we were all young magazine editors, before spouses and children, when we traveled around the world for assignments: hiking in New Zealand, skiing in the Alps, kitesurfing in Vietnam. Back home, we'd meet in coffee shops to work on our articles, drink beer in each other's apartments, and read pages from our works in progress.

Through job changes and interstate moves, we held each other accountable to our professional goals and encouraged each other to apply for far-flung assignments or writer's residencies. More than that, though, we made each other laugh. For hours, we'd talk and laugh.

We've rented a farmhouse on Whidbey Island, just north of Seattle in Puget Sound. For the next three days, our only agenda is to relax, maybe drive to the island's cliff tops to watch a sunset or hike a trail. I've been living in the Arizona desert for six years. My body craves trees and billowing veils of wet fog. I imagine ocean breezes, overindulging in seafood and wine, wrapping myself in a blanket, and drinking coffee on the east-facing deck as the sun peeks above the Cascade Mountains.

The plane's taxi to the gate is an eternity. I hear the clack of wheels turning over on the pavement. I feel each bump in my stomach. My hands are shaking as I clutch my phone. I want to call my father, and I don't want to call him. I wonder what might happen if I ignore his texts the same way he has ignored mine over the years. I'm angry that he's intruding, now of all times. There are so many voicemails. I don't think I can escape talking with him.

I stare at the fasten seatbelt sign, willing it to turn off. Once it does, passengers stand up and begin gathering their things. Bodies form a heavy curtain around me. Everyone's moving too slowly. The balding businessman with the unwieldy garment bag. The mother of two toddlers who's balancing backpacks, sippy cups, and plastic bags of crackers. A white-haired gentleman stooped over a cane. They're closing in, and I begin to panic. A dull pain is creeping up my chest, radiating in my throat. It's all I can do not to shove people out of the way and claw toward the cabin door.

I rest my head against the seat in front of me and do my best to breathe in through my nose and out through my mouth. I tell myself the texts might mean nothing. I try to imagine other reasons my father needs to reach me so urgently, but I can't. I clutch my thighs to stop them from trembling. I wait, breathing in and out until people clear the aisle. When they do, I grab my bag and run for the door.

The terminal isn't better. Swarms of travelers consume every available space with backpacks and roller bags. I look for a pocket of quiet, any open place to sit down and return my dad's call out of earshot, but there isn't a vacant seat anywhere.

And so, I stand there in the middle of the concourse, people rushing around me. I focus my gaze on a vertical window on a far wall, where sunlight is coming in, creating stripes on the stone floor. I stare at the light, and I dial my father, and I listen to him tell me what I already know: My brother is dead.

My mind somersaults. For as much as I imagined this happening – since I was five, I've imagined my brother dying – I am shocked and unprepared. "How? I don't understand," I whisper into the phone.

My Dad tries to explain what happened, but it's clear he's not sure. "It was sudden," he stutters. "I don't really understand how he got away from them so quickly." Them, the doctors? Or them, my mother and her husband?

Alan had been living with my mother in Boulder, Colorado, and like me, my father hasn't communicated with her in years. My estrangement from my mother is long and complicated and fraught. It's been made tenser by my desire to stay in touch with Alan. Over the years, I've found detours around my mother in order to maintain a relationship with my brother. At times I've felt like I was participating in a covert operation, or maybe an elaborate deception. Alan loves to check the mailbox several times a day, and so I write him letters, knowing he'll grab them before my mother sees. I call the house during the hours I think she'll be away at church or running errands, or I have Kris make the call, then pass me the phone once Alan is on the line. Kris will arrange visits with Alan, or sometimes I'll try to arrange them through his respite care-givers. I ask them for updates on how Alan is doing instead of asking my mother. In this way, I have felt connected to my brother, though I've always longed for more contact.

I wonder if my father had his own ways of keeping up with Alan without having to interact with his ex-wife. I wonder if he was thrown by her name on his phone's caller ID in the same way I was thrown by his call. I wonder if my father hadn't called me how long it would have taken for me to hear that Alan is dead.

Dad tells me that my mother delivered the news but offered few details. "Something about an asthma attack and possibly a seizure. His heart stopped beating in the ER," he tells me. That's all he knows. It happened last night. My mother had waited until the next day to tell him. I ask him what I should do. "What's happening? Do I need to get back on a plane? When's the funeral?"

"I don't know," he says. "I don't know what the plan is."

"Are they doing an autopsy?"

"No. His heart stopped. He died, Sweetheart."

I bristle. "Sweetheart" isn't something I've heard from my father since I was a little girl.

I turn off my phone, tuck it in my pocket, and begin to wander the airport. I spend long minutes staring at the signs directing passengers to various terminals and ground trans-portation, but they don't make sense to me. It's as if the words are written in another language. I have no idea where to go, so I just keep walking.

By the time my girlfriends find me, I'm sitting in a dusty

corner of baggage claim that's under renovation, on a chair that's ripped, my feet resting on the plywood subfloor. It's the only place I could find a seat without people pressing in. My friends sit with me. They ask me what I want to do next. All I can think to say at the moment, my hands shaking violently, my stomach churning and head throbbing: "It's too soon," I whisper.

It is too soon?

"I wanted to see him one more time."

This thought, that I want to see Alan once more, is actually one of several that will haunt me in the coming weeks, months. "Thought" isn't even the right word. Each one is a siren. Intrusive and urgent. A knot that demands untangling. A puzzle that only I can solve.

The first thought hints not so much at regret as it does a missed opportunity, a door slamming closed. I had believed, as sure as I believe the sun sets in the west, that I would see my brother again, alive, at least once. I imagined I would have the chance to sit with him face-to-face, and that as much as he was capable of doing so, we would talk about our complicated relationship and what we meant to each other. Even as I thought this, I knew it was unrealistic, given Alan's intellectual disabilities. Alan spoke in short, fragmented sentences. The list of topics he liked to talk about was short (dogs, food, cars). His attention span was limited. A deep, introspective conversation was not something he was capable of. But I nonetheless fantasized it would happen.

The second thought comes in the form of a question: *Did Alan know I love him?* I told him frequently that I loved him, but on what level did he know? This may seem like an existential problem. Can love be defined? Do the people we love really

8

know that we love them? How do they know? But the thought for me is more than philosophical. Cognitively, Alan was five years old. He hadn't developed the capacity for abstract reasoning. I had little knowledge of his interior world. Was he capable of understanding love? Did he feel loved? Had he developed a sense of object permanence and healthy attachment, the foundations of loving family relationships? Did he know that people who were far away, out of sight, could still love him? Did he grasp the complexity of relationships, that people could simultaneously be angry with him, fear him, and yet also love him? Did he experience the warmth, the bond, the nurturing of familial love, even if he couldn't articulate it?

The third thought. The third thought is one I'm reluctant to name. It's the most urgent, the one that sideswipes me the moment my father says he can't be sure how Alan died. The one that makes my knees buckle. I'll let it gnaw at me, creating anxiety and making me question reality to such a degree that I'll begin to wonder if I'm losing my mind. The thought is: *She did this.* My mother. *It's all her fault.*

I don't yet understand where this third thought comes from or what it means, whether it's born from grief or some deeper truth. I've just received the worst news of my life. I'm in shock. I'm reeling. I'm trying to figure out where to go and what to do next. I search my mind for answers, for clarity, but instead, my mind delivers more bad news. It serves up thoughts and questions perhaps more painful than the phone call. This thought my mind has given me feels like a betrayal. But it also feels familiar. It is so horrifying and so familiar that instead of considering it, I want to exile it, pretend it never entered my consciousness.

I sit in the broken chair at baggage claim, watching luggage slide down conveyor belts and circle the metal carousels. Black and brown roller bags. Pastel-colored plastic suitcases. A few orange and yellow duffels. Around and around they go with no beginning or end.

As far as I can tell, no one else shares my thoughts. No one will ask the questions I will ask, turn over stones. In the landscape of my family of origin, I am the one who pauses, who wonders, who senses, who investigates. This curiosity makes me unpopular. I want more information, to know the inner workings of things. I'll pursue truth at the expense of relationships. A therapist once told me I'm the one who stands up in the boat. Everyone else either screams at me to sit down or shoves me overboard.

I know that thoughts are not facts. Thoughts are just thoughts. I tell myself this. And yet, they loom. In the coming months, these thoughts and questions will surface time and again. The unknowns will torture me. They'll change shape and meaning. As I navigate the dark halls of grief, they will echo from behind doorways. They will loosen their grip on my psyche. I'll feel something akin to relief, and then they'll strangle me again.

For now, I decide to swallow my questions, the unknowns. They sit in my belly quietly, like a precancerous mass.

Chapter Two

From the moment water bubbles up in the desert, before it's even called a river, when it's just a puddle that pools and stretches like long fingers and collides into something – a trickle, a stream – and begins to flow down from the hills and plateaus, there is a fight for every precious drop. The Salt River stretches 200 miles from the White Mountains of Arizona to its mouth, the Gila River. Legend says its salinity is due to the water licking salt deposits along the riverbanks.

As it flows, dusty towns take their share and lakes fill up and power plants use the water to cool their machines. Once it reaches the outskirts of Phoenix, where I live, the flow is barely a trickle. For long weeks, sometimes months every year, the riverbed goes dry. There's nothing left to give.

This is how I imagine my parents' love. It bubbled up from nothing, like the river.

If the origin of their relationship had its own map, its own geographical story to tell, it might look something like this:

Father

Hibbing, Minnesota. 1940s.

A small mining town sits at the crest of not one but two continental divides. This "Triple Divide" or "The Hill of Three Waters" happens where the St. Lawrence Seaway Divide meets the Laurentian Divide. Up close it's nothing special: Two gentle folds in the great northern landscape create a grassy hilltop. But the intersection makes it unique. Depending upon the exact spot it falls, a drop of rain in Hibbing could flow in one of three directions: north toward Hudson Bay, east to the St. Lawrence River, or south to the Gulf of Mexico. It's a place of enormous potential.

My father grew up on this spot with Catholic parents who valued honesty, hard work, and academic success. My grandmother idolized him, her oldest son (my father's siblings are significantly younger than him, so it was easy for him to hold the spotlight). She always told my father he could achieve anything, and he believed it. He moved boldly, almost arrogantly toward his ambitions, whether it was playing ice hockey, practicing the guitar, or competing in math and science. He excelled in school and worked several jobs at once. He also got into mischief, like hopping trains to see concerts in neighboring towns. But his brilliance seemed to outshine any trouble. He could go anywhere, do anything. He was a local prodigy. His photo still hangs on the walls of Hibbing High School among other distinguished alumni. But staying there, perched atop the Triple Divide was never an option. It's unclear whether the drop of rain chooses its path or whether gravity chooses for him. Regardless, it makes its journey down the hillside.

Mother

Atomic City, USA. 1940s.

On a high desert mesa in northern New Mexico, at the end of a single, winding dirt road lies a secret settlement owned by the government. The land here is dry, volcanic, a mixture of dark basalt and white pumice, prone to earthquakes and erosion. The settlement does not appear on any map. Its residents are invisible, like living ghosts. They enter and exit through the town's military checkpoint. Their driver's licenses, birth certificates, and mailing addresses all say the same thing: PO Box 1663, Santa Fe.

My mother was one of four children, packed into a ramshackle government house designed for a smaller family. No one knew what their father did for a living. Until she was maybe ten or eleven, my mother believed her father worked in a popsicle factory, testing all the flavors to make sure they were safe for children. It made sense to her, she says, because her best friend's father worked at the same building sampling ice cream. But it wasn't that simple, of course. He was working on atomic weapons like all the other fathers in town. Even the mothers had no clue.

This is to say, my mother grew up in a town steeped in deception and denial. An isolated landscape where you could lose track of your ability to sort truth from fiction. A place where people easily grew depressed, confused, desperate. Where toxic dust slowly seeped into their bodies and poisoned them.

Atomic particles vibrate under pressure and heat. They look for a means of escape.

Convergence

Los Alamos, New Mexico. 1969.

After it was declassified and given a location on the map, Los Alamos attracted eager young scientists from all over the world. In the summer of 1969, my father, then a graduate student, completed an internship at the atomic labs, studying alongside some of the world's greatest mathematicians and physicists. My mother and her friends were self-appointed town ambassadors. They got to know the summer students. They'd hang out in the evenings and on weekends and show them around the area. Many of them paired off. My father was drawn to my mother's sense of humor and beauty. She was enamored with his intellect and self-confidence.

What began as a summer fling gained momentum. Together, they floated on a current of idealism. The US was fighting in Vietnam. My father had been spared the draft. There was a prevailing sense that life is short, that they should seize every moment. Young people that summer were awash in optimism and marijuana-fueled hope for a peaceful future. Like everyone they knew, my parents wanted something good and stable after years of uncertainty. They wanted their happily ever after, and so they claimed it. They got engaged at the end of that summer and married the day after Christmas. Immediately after the wedding, my father moved her to Atlanta, where he was in graduate school. He thought he was rescuing her from obscurity, from a too-small town, offering her a better life. Years later, he told me he should have known better. The relationship was unsustainable from the start. They fell in love with an idea, he said. A falsehood. A fairy tale.

This was their river. They drank from each other, and then Alan came along, and by the time the love trickled down to me, there was almost nothing left. I coveted those waters, salty as they were. I spent most of my childhood feeling parched.

This wasn't Alan's fault, or mine. A drought doesn't know the damage it causes.

Can a fish fault the people upstream for drinking? For

needing too much? Does he blame the river itself for not having more to give?

January 1973: Alan was here first. It's impossible to know, in the nearly three years he existed without me, how my brother shaped my parents' view of babies and parenting and what might be considered normal. It will be decades before any doctor suggests genetic testing, before my parents hear the words "Prader-Willi Syndrome," providing context for his delays, behavior, and medical problems. These early years, there is no framework, no vocabulary, no diagnosis. All my parents know is that he was born breech, the umbilical cord a noose around his neck. They think perhaps he suffered brain damage this way. He was a floppy baby, my mother says. He didn't cry.

December 1975: I know what I've been told. Because of him and all that happened before me, I am not allowed to be born in the usual way. The moment my mother's belly contracts, I am brought into the world via an emergency cesarean, though there is nothing critical about my birth. On a cold December night, my mother is sedated, and her belly is sliced open. I am yanked from the womb and whisked away. I'm not sure if my mother held me, if I felt her warmth in those first hours. By all measures, I am a normal 9-pound baby who nonetheless spends a week in the NICU for observation, because no one can explain what has happened to my brother and no one can guarantee that it will not also happen to me.

So, for a brief time, because of him, I am alone in a plastic incubator. I am observed, monitored. I am believed to be fragile until the moment I'm pronounced healthy.

In the years before my mother unraveled, I had, presumably, enough. Neurobiology says that the majority of what we come to understand about love and attachment happens during the small window of birth to age three. I was too young to remember, though the fact that I'm alive and writing these words tells me I got what I needed those first few years when my brain was new. Early love, they say, is a protective force against any madness that might follow.

Those first couple of years we are babies together, Alan and me. We learn to walk around the same time – me at age 1, Alan nearly 4. He is quiet and sweet, my parents tell me as they recall those days. He loves to cuddle me and give me toys. He adores me, they say. And I love him. My round face lights up whenever he's near. My cheeks flush. I reach for his hair and try to pull him closer to me. He kisses my tiny toes and my tiny fingers. He gestures and whines to get what he wants – a snack, a toy, or a picture book he can't reach. He loves music and nursery rhymes. Strange, they say, but even before he can speak, Alan knows what time *Mister Rogers' Neighborhood* airs on PBS. Every afternoon as the hour draws near, he will tug at my mother's hem and point to the TV.

Alan has what we call fits or episodes that send my mother into a frenzy. He will be playing quietly or pulling himself up to standing as toddlers do, when suddenly he'll raise his hands into the air, his eyes will roll back in his head, and he'll fall stiff as a board to the floor. My mother scoops him up, and she and my father rush him to the doctor. Someone stays behind to watch me. A neighbor, a family friend. I am sad when they leave.

In the years ahead, as the episodes repeat, I'll notice that sometimes my father is angry when they return home from the hospital. I'll overhear them arguing. My father will insist Alan is fine. *You're overreacting,* he'll say. *The doctors said he was just dizzy. He lost his balance. There's no cause for alarm.*

He's not fine, my mother will respond. *We are not fine.*

Alan has a gentleman's face, creases in his forehead, always curious, his dark hair slick and combed perfectly to one side. His brown eyes are sharp and penetrating. They remind me of a deer. His arms and legs are weak. He experiences bursts of energy followed by extreme fatigue. He sleeps more than other children his age. He naps twice as long as I do. I am eager for him to wake up. It's as if time moves faster for me than for Alan. I feel impatient for him to wake up, to catch up.

How do we measure the passing of time? There's human time and geomorphic time. There's Alan's sense of time and my sense of time. My parents, too, seem to live by their own time-line. Where do Alan and I fall in history, on the journey to happily ever after?

There's a concept forming inside me, a theory taking root. I have entered my family in the wake of something – a bomb, an earthquake. Or maybe it's still exploding. I am surrounded by the debris. I'm lost in it. Or maybe I am the debris. Or maybe I'm here to clean up the debris. I'm collateral damage. And I'm also here to repair it. I'm part of the restoration process.

For me, there's no before-and-after marker in time, no big revelation. But there *is* a before. For my parents, before exists. I feel it. They were different people before. I am in the after.

In my memory, no one ever sits me down and tells me that Alan is disabled. This isn't a word anyone says. Yet somehow, I know. I see it in the sympathetic faces of family, friends, neighbors. I hear it in the hushed conversations. I notice it at the supermarket, the way strangers glance from Alan to me and back to Alan, where their gaze fixates. I see the soft foods and vitamins my mother spoon feeds him but not me. I notice that he wears diapers still, long after I'm in underwear.

My mother is a storyteller. She likes to tell me about important moments in time. She tells me that I was toilet trained in a single day. *Such an easy child. An angel. A prodigy.* When I was two, she says, she bought me toddler panties with pink roses and lace. She put them on me and sent me to preschool with a warning: If I wet my pants, the flowers would wilt and all the other kids would see. They would stare at me like they stare at Alan. She says this motivated me, the fear of embarrassment, of being watched. Fear is a powerful motivator. My panties stayed dry.

When I'm still a baby, our apartment overlooks a freeway in downtown Atlanta where my father, an academic, is busy becoming one of the world's first computer scientists. The place is small, and Alan needs the second bedroom with space for his crib and changing table and humidifier, so my mother fashions a makeshift bed for me in the guest bathtub. She lines the porcelain with soft, hand-knit blankets, and on top of them places a rectangular box with handles, like a Moses basket made of laminated cardboard. I sleep in that box. The bathroom is windowless and positioned at the farthest point from the surrounding apartments. My mother says my sleeping here means I don't bother the neighbors when I cry. Years from now when we're settled into a comfortable suburban home, she'll brag about my sleeping in that box, how resourceful she was, and how I never complained. I'll hear in her voice the sense of relief that I needed so little, that I could be content with cardboard for a bed.

She folds dime-size squares of Scotch tape inside out and uses them to attach bows to my fair, nearly bald head. She dresses me in homemade pink frilly dresses and relishes the attention of strangers who stop to admire me. Mom says it happens all the time. At the grocery store. The bank.

"Everyone thinks you are so gorgeous. You take their breath away," she says. This seems to anchor her. Attention from strangers. Praise for a perfect child being perfectly groomed by her adoring mother. I imagine it also gives her something to do to take her mind off Alan – sew dresses, shop. She starts a collection of porcelain dolls for me that are too fragile to actually play with. For years they sit there on a shelf, posed on little wire stands. Beautiful and off-limits.

My father told me once that his favorite memory was the day my younger brother William was born. It's all just fragments in my mind, pieces of a larger story. A humid summer day in 1978. The azaleas, once electric in their blooms all over Atlanta, have begun to wilt. I am two-and-a-half. Dad takes Alan and me to the hospital to visit my mom. I remember carrying yellow roses. I remember my mom sitting up in bed, wearing a matching yellow nightgown and bathrobe and pink slippers. Her short brown hair was perfectly styled, and she wore red lipstick. Yet the way she sat, curled over herself, holding her belly, an empty sack– her appearance frightened me. I remember her hugging me, tousling my hair, complaining that no one had bothered to comb it. Beyond that, all I know of that day is the story my father loves to tell.

His favorite memory of that time, he says, is when he takes me to the nursery window to meet my new brother. Several babies are lined up facing the glass, neatly wrapped like pink and blue burritos in their bassinets. My dad lifts me up and points to one of the babies and tells me, "There he is. That's William!" He says I looked confused, but then pointed to each of the other babies and declared, "And there's another one William...and another one William!"

Babies. They were all mine.

If not for Will, I could have hoped I was adopted. I am a blond-haired, blue-eyed girl in a sea of dark-eyed brunettes. But there he is, my little brother: fair skin, soft white hair, and gray eyes that will eventually turn blue.

In time, Will will become my ally and my closest friend. The affection I feel for him matches in intensity the affection I have for Alan. But it manifests differently. If Alan is my quiet, mysterious older brother, then Will is my playmate. He is the one I disappear with into imaginary worlds where stuffed animals come alive and talk with one another. He is the one who is able to build complex fantasies and storylines that go on for days, for weeks. Together, we are superheroes, we are explorers, we are rock stars, we are a princess and prince. We slip into and out of those worlds, always able to pick up where we left off. Meanwhile, Alan is on the periphery, able to play in proximity to us – pushing his toy cars or cuddling a stuffed animal – but he's unable to tell stories or pretend. Still, he seems to find joy in watching us.

Sometimes Will and I sneak into each other's room during nap time. We fall asleep together, curled up on the floor. My little brother is the child of my childhood. In the years ahead, he'll remain anchored to this innocence while I am swept into the sea of adulthood.

My little brother is the last link holding my parents' marriage together, and once the newness of a cute baby wears off, we see my dad less and less. Dad is a professor and researcher at a prominent university. He wears what I consider his uniform: tweed sport coat and plaid shirt and corduroy pants and round glasses like Coke bottles. I watch him polish the thick lenses with a handkerchief and comb his mustache before he walks out the door. He is always busy, doing the work that young scientists do. Publishing papers. Speaking at conferences. Teaching. He works late and travels frequently. I don't know the details of this at the time. I only know that I'm sad because he's so often away.

I'm not sure if my brothers can sense it. We're too young to discuss such things, but I am aware that the energy in the house is shifting. I remember when the kitchen used to be warm and thick with the smell of chicken casserole, chocolate chip cookies, and my mother's French perfume. Lately, it smells like menthol cigarettes.

One day I go to the refrigerator for a snack, and all that's there is a brick of Velveeta cheese wrapped in foil. I unwrap it, sink my teeth into it and gag. It's cold and gelatinous and leaves an unpleasant film on my tongue. On the television, *Mister Rogers'* and *Sesame Street* are replaced by soap operas and game shows. *Days of Our Lives* and *The Price is Right* become a sort of soundtrack or background noise. Theatrical laughter and tears. Applause and violins. No one is really watching.

Some nights my mother yanks my brothers and me out of bed and leads us to her car, bundled in blankets. We drive the winding streets of Atlanta looking for my father. My brothers quickly fall asleep in the backseat, but I am awake in the front, counting street lights, trying to read signs that might tell me where we are. I watch raindrops run races across the windshield. Some nights we find him on campus, his car alone in the parking lot, a single yellow light emanating from a thin window of an otherwise dark building. My mother, ranting under her breath, flings her car door open and runs inside, leaving us alone in the car. If I'm scared by this, I don't remember. My attention is on my brothers stirring in the backseat. I tuck their blankets around them and rub their backs to keep them from waking. Other nights we drive for what feels like hours, and we never find him. We go back home, my mother in tears. She goes inside, shuffles to her room, and collapses into bed. I rouse my brothers and lead them back to their beds and tuck them in.

The next day we don't mention it. It fades from our consciousness like a bad dream.

Dad's absences are a vacuum, sucking out all that is certain and safe from between the walls of our house. His homecomings are a flood of warmth and snuggles and presents purchased last-minute from the airport gift shop. The whiplash of this – frequent absences followed by loving reunions – leaves me stewing in a mix of perpetual hope and despair. My father is a shadow. I'm always looking for him to appear around corners; I am also shocked when he does appear and devastated when he vanishes again. Years from now I'll understand that this confusion has nothing to do with me. His ambition is a cloak. He becomes a workaholic to anesthetize himself – against his failing marriage, the heartache of Alan's condition, or maybe against a shattered ideal. I can't say exactly. But I come to understand this: In numbing his pain, he also becomes numb to the joy of us, his children.

My mother is like a mythological shape-shifter, loving and vivacious one day, dejected and out of reach the next. I wonder what she dreams about, what it was she wanted to be when she grew up. If it was to be married and have children, then what comes next? Unlike my father, she never finishes college. She holds a position in the neighborhood Garden Club and sells Tupperware to earn extra money. She is charismatic and funny. She loves to watch Gilda Radner and Carol Burnett on TV. She emulates their style as she tells jokes and stories to her friends, adding her own flourishes and punch lines. They roar with laughter.

One day I'm snooping in our basement's crawlspace, and I find a stash of clothing and costumes, artifacts from another time. There's a giant gorilla suit that would fit my father and a bright yellow dress stitched with brown piping for my mother, a banana. Matching black-and-white striped prisoner jumpsuits with plastic balls and chains. Cardboard party hats and noise-makers. There are white rubber go-go boots and sparkly high-heeled shoes and sequined dresses that I've never seen my mother wear. Also, luggage etched with golden letters, her initials, for trips I've never seen her take. I grab one of the dresses and pull it over my head. I slip my feet into the glittery shoes, and I start to dance around the house. *Look at me!* I shout. *Look at me!* My mother is in the living room watching television. She looks up at me and laughs, a spontaneous expression of joy that fills me with pride for having been seen. *Where'd you find that?* She asks. When I tell her about the crawlspace, the costumes, the boots and luggage, her expression falls. I've reminded her of something painful. *Go put it back where you found it,* she says.

Some mornings I watch her in the bathroom mirror applying bronzer to her porcelain skin, fluffing her curls, and shellacking them with Miss Breck hairspray. The chemical smell hangs in the air, making it difficult to breathe for several minutes. I watch the curious way she applies lipstick, holding the red wand still and maneuvering her puckered lips around it. She folds a square of toilet paper in half and kisses it. So beautiful, I think. She looks perfect. And yet, when my father is traveling, she stays in her bathrobe all day. Her curls wilt. Her face is pale. No lipstick. She sleeps a lot. Some days there will be nothing to eat because no one has shopped or cooked.

Then, Dad is home again and suddenly there are trays upon trays of food. They're having a party, hosting my father's colleagues for drinks and finger sandwiches, or having several couples over for a dinner buffet. Silver trays piled high with crudités. A wreath of Melba toast surrounding pimento cheese dip. Roasted chicken. Red Jell-O molds with chunks of fruit suspended inside. Warm pans full of homemade brownies, cut perfectly into two-inch squares. I reach for a gooey middle one, and my mother smacks my hand away. *You can have this*, she says and hands me the crispy edges that she has cut away, too overdone for the guests but fine enough for children. She makes me stand on a stool and lean over the sink to eat them so that the crumbs won't hit the freshly waxed floor. I develop a taste for burnt brownies, so much so that into adulthood, they are all that I crave.

When the guests arrive, they mingle in our formal living room – an airy, white-carpeted space at the front of the house where light pours in through a giant picture window. They sit on my mother's Ethan Allen furniture, the silky floral sofa and plaid chairs my brothers and I are not allowed to touch. The living room is a home's first impression, my mother says. It's the face we show to the world.

We can pop in to say hello. My father beckons me to his side and asks me in front of his guests what a prime number is. I know the answer because he taught me. It's a number that can only be divided by itself and one, I tell him. Three. Five. Seven. Eleven. His face lights up, and he hugs me closer. I run my fingers across the ribbing of his corduroy pants. *She's smart like you*, his colleagues say. I am smart, I think. I am like my father.

This idea, that I am like my father, will become a point of pride and anguish for me. It will become my ambition and my curse. In the years ahead, it will help me stand in relief against my mother. If I am like my father, then I must be unlike her. It's an archetype that will bind me to my family and one that will eventually set me free.

After I show off for my dad's colleagues, my job is to take my brothers away to their bedrooms, read to them, tuck them in, make sure they don't disturb the adults downstairs. All night I hear laughter drift through the house, voices murmuring, glasses clinking. Someone plays a few bars on the upright piano. I smell my father's tobacco pipe burning. I weep in my bed, wishing I could be downstairs. I want to experience my parents in this way too. Laughing. Happy.

Around this time, Dad is reading *Alice in Wonderland* to me, chapter by chapter. I am four years old, maybe five, and like so many girls, I want to be Alice. Each night we journey down the rabbit hole, and I am entranced by the fantasy world where little girls grow and shrink and turtles sob and sneezing babies turn into pigs. I am frightened by it and ask him repeatedly, "Is it real?" But Dad never gives me a clear answer.

"Do you think it's real?" he asks. "What is real?"

Or, he tells me, "It's a metaphor."

"What's a metaphor?"

"It's hard to explain."

As things deteriorate between him and my mother, he starts skipping nights and skimming chapters until finally I lose track of the story, and he sets the book aside for good. In my mind, Alice remains suspended in Wonderland, lost in the madness. I wonder if she ever got out.

There is a dance my parents begin to perform. My father pulls away, leaves the house, comes back, threatens to leave again. Meanwhile, my mother pushes, pulls, uses Alan as a sort of lure, an offering. She calls Dad at work. Alan is sick. *Come quick.* "What's wrong?" my father will ask. And she'll reply, "It's Alan." It's her siren. Code red. Come home.

She reminds him of Alan's intense needs, though he knows. Of course, he already knows. Alan had an episode. Alan fell down. Alan needs his medicine or his special food. He needs more diapers. He's sleeping too much. He's sleeping too little. Alan needs to see another specialist. Look at him, can't you tell he's sick? Touch his cheek. Does he seem feverish to you? He needs attention. You're not taking this seriously enough. *How could you leave at a time like this?* The doctors say they don't know what's wrong with him. But he's sick. Very, very sick. Anyone can see he's fragile.

What none of us can see, not clearly, not yet, is that my mother is also sick. Her anxiety – about Alan's health, about the fate of her marriage – has grown horns and teeth and is swallowing her whole. Her siren – *Come quick, it's Alan* – masks something darker and deeper within her. Depression, yes. Desperation, certainly. But something else. A strange sort of martyrdom or mania. Her nervous system is misfiring.

Atomic particles vibrate under pressure and heat.

One day we are watching cartoons, and I hear my mother on the phone. *Oh yes, he's in bad shape,* I hear her say. *He's vomiting. Very pale.* I look over at Alan. His cheeks are pink. No vomit. He's giggling at the coyote chasing the bunny on the screen. *You better come home quick.* By the time the show is over, my father is here. He rushes in, scoops Alan up, places a palm on his forehead. Alan wriggles out of Dad's grip and returns to the television. *He seems alright now,* my dad says. *Maybe it was just something he ate?*

"You weren't here," my mother screams. "You didn't see how bad it was."

I watch Dad's eyes dilate and settle unfocused upon her face as she winds herself up to a frenzied state. She is wild, furious. I can see him calculating whether it is ok to leave. Of course, Alan looks and acts differently. But is he sick? I mean, like *really* sick? No one can say. Except my mother. She can say. And she does say it, repeatedly. He's sick, and we should all pay attention to him. And by that she means, we should all pay attention to *her.*

This is the result: Decades from now, when I'm sitting on an airplane in Seattle with a dozen missed calls and texts from my father, I won't need to ask the question, "What's wrong?" I'll know then, as I know now, it's Alan.

It's always Alan.

At age four or five, I can't yet articulate that I want it to be about me. I want my dad to stay for me. I want my mother to cook for me, to celebrate me, to pay me the level of attention she gives to her party guests.

Who I am and how I fit into the complicated puzzle of my family is still unclear. Does anyone see me? Do they care about me? Do my words and actions have the same sort of power over my father as my mother's do? Am I my parent's child, my brothers' keeper, or another adult?

Sometimes, after he's been away for a long while, Dad will bring Mom a bouquet of yellow roses, and he'll hand me a single bloom on a long stem. Other times, nothing. I learn not to get my hopes up. From the moment I am born and it's determined I am a "normal" baby, I am preordained to not need anyone or anything. If Alan is a special needs kid, then I am to have no needs. And yet, I do. I can learn to deny it, but the truth is I need to be seen. I need parents. I need my Dad to stay, to right the ship.

For a young child, there is no such thing as manipulation, no deceit. There are needs, and there are myriad ways to get these needs met. At first, I make up elaborate stories. I want to captivate my dad the same way I've seen my mother captivate him. One night after dinner, as my father is packing his briefcase to go back to the office, I start telling him about a terrible accident on the playground at preschool. How the monkey bars collapsed on top of a group of children. *Those poor kids,* I say, my lower lip protruding. Dad stops packing for a moment. He's looking at me. His eyes widen. *They tried to run but couldn't escape*, I tell him. The tall metal frame crashed down, crushing their bodies, and five ambulances had arrived. *Yes, five.* Hadn't he heard the sirens?

It's working, I think. He's listening. He puts a heavy hand on my shoulder, gives it a soothing rub. Then, the spell is broken. "Sounds really dramatic," he says with a chuckle and turns back to his briefcase, picks it up, and walks toward the door. "Let's talk more about it when I get home."

"I won't tolerate a liar," my mother whispers into my ear, her breath hot. The left side of my face is on fire. The moment my father's car pulled away, she dragged me away by the elbow and slapped me. "You're pushing him away with your crazy lies," she says.

I'm confused by this. I'm not pushing my father away. I'm trying to get him to stay. Am I not just doing what I've seen her do? I don't argue with her, however, for fear she'll slap me again.

I often think about the hospital, that mysterious place they take Alan. I fantasize that medical people are all that is safe and loving and warm. My mother reveres doctors. She lusts for the hospital, for their support of her and of Alan. I think about the story she tells me again and again about my first week of life, how I spent a week in the incubator, nurtured and protected. It's a safe haven, isn't it? A building for people with needs. I understand the sequence of events. Alan might be playing happily or watching TV, and then he'll begin to cough, to stutter, to walk unsteadily. My mother sounds her alarm. I sense the mood in the house shift. No matter where they are, whether they're in the same room or opposite ends of the house, my parents come together, and they act. They fuss over him. Someone hurriedly packs a bag with blankets and extra clothing. I watch my mother run to the phone, call the nurse, call a neighbor to come over right away to watch me. The hospital is the place they disappear to, cradling my brother in their arms, leaving Will and me behind.

One day I slam my arm repeatedly against the post of my canopy bed. I want to break a bone, snap it in half like a stick. I want a plaster cast and all the attention and sympathy that goes with it. I imagine dozens of loopy signatures on my arm, visual evidence that I am loved, that people care what happens to me. Mom would have to comfort me then, wouldn't she? Her daughter crippled with just one healthy arm? Maybe Dad will be so worried he'll come home and stay for a while. Maybe someone will cook my favorite meal: grilled cheese sandwiches and tomato soup. *They'll feed me the soup.*

After four or five hits, the pain is electric. My arm is red and swollen and the outline of a bruise is beginning to form. And yet the bone is still intact. I've failed. I'm devastated not only by this failure but also the realization that no one is here to comfort me. I collapse in bed and cry myself to sleep.

My one real hospital encounter leaves me with a souvenir, a scar in the center of my forehead. I can't see it, but if I rub my finger across it, it's there. Slightly raised and bumpy and sensitive to the touch, like a fault line, a third eye. You can see it if I've been crying... a white jagged silhouette set against my rosy face.

In my memory, it is one of the last weekends my dad is home. Not just in the house, but *home*. With us. Interacting with us. Kicking around and fixing things and watching TV the way fathers do.

My parents' cars are parked evenly, side-by-side in the carport. It is dusk, and my mother shoos me out of the kitchen while she cooks an enormous pot of spaghetti. When dad is home, my mother cooks for an army, even if it is just us. She pours three packages of pasta into her largest stockpot and browns two pounds of ground beef, then smothers that with three jars of Ragu. Sometimes she opens a can of white mushrooms and throws them in the sauce. Then she piles mountains of the smothered pasta on each of our plates and shakes grated Parmesan on top like snow. We'll slurp enthusiastically, sopping up the red sauce with slices of buttered Wonder Bread. Whatever we don't finish, she'll scoop into Tupperware containers and stash in the freezer to be thawed and reheated a few weeks later.

I love being out of the house. The allure of quiet, the deep cleansing breaths of fresh air. Being alone. As the heavy smell of tomatoes and garlic seep out of the kitchen, I climb on the back bumper of Mom's gray Toyota, stand tall, balance on the edge like an Olympic gymnast and then leap off onto the ground. The sound of my tennis shoes smacking the concrete echo in the carport. I am tall, invincible. And so, I climb and leap again and again, trying to gain more height, thinking I can hang mid-air just a little bit longer.

I glance over and notice that the bumper to my dad's red Volkswagen Rabbit is a few inches taller than the Toyota. *Can I jump higher from there? Maybe do a spin or kick my heels up more?* I climb up and then crouch into a low squat, ready to explode from the edge. Ready to fly like Nadia Comăneci.

I'm not trying to get hurt this time. It's just that the Rabbit's bumper, unlike the Toyota's, is not flush with the car. It is a black rubberized bar that frames the red metal, but it's not fully attached. The gap between the bumper and the hatchback is just wide enough for my toe to get caught there, which is exactly what happens when I try to jump. I leap, my foot gets wedged, and I flop headfirst into the concrete. I see a flash of white and then everything goes dark and quiet.

When I can see again, my cheek is pressed into the ground, and I taste copper pennies. I sit up and see a puddle of red on the gray concrete. I don't remember feeling pain, but the blood terrifies me, and so I scream.

"Jesus!" My dad throws open the back door and runs toward me but pauses when he sees the blood. My mother trails a few steps behind him. The looks on their faces are as neatly matched as the cars; they're horrified. I stretch out my arms, and Dad snatches me up and wipes some of the blood from my eyes with his yellow, cable-knit V-neck sweater.

He takes me inside and lays me down on the kitchen counter like it's a hospital gurney. My head throbs and stings, but I am not crying. I am captivated by the look of concern on my dad's face and then my mom's as they peer over me and examine my wound. I've seen them this worried before, but always about Alan. Never about me.

My mother dampens a washcloth and starts wiping the blood away while my dad contemplates how many stitches I'll need. He holds up his hand and asks me to count his fingers. As cool water floods the wound, I experience a searing pain and start wailing and begging my mom to stop. She says I have a hole in my head and it needs to be cleaned. I tell her I can do it myself, and she hands me the washcloth.

I make my way to the hall bathroom with the washcloth in hand, climb onto the tiled vanity table and peer into the mirror. My blonde bangs are matted with what looks like raspberry jelly. There is, in fact, an oblong hole in my forehead with blood trickling out the bottom. It looks cartoonish. Unreal. I can't tell how deep it is, but I can't see the bottom of it and wonder if my brain will fall out.

Mom wraps a fresh towel around an ice cube and tells me to hold it against my wound to dull the pain. Then she scoops me up in both arms, like a baby, and carries me toward the car. It's rare she holds me like this, so close to her bosom, without it feeling awkward or forced. For a moment, I relax here in her soft arms and relish the nurturing touch.

Sitting in the ER waiting room, my hands start sweating, and my neck feels prickly. Everything is white and green, and people move quickly in and out through gigantic swinging doors. We have to wait. I watch people come and go. Count them. I notice their shoes—tennis shoes, slippers, flip-flops. Grownups are crying. The doctors and nurses are wearing what look like pajamas. I am the only child in the waiting room. I wait for someone to offer me a blanket or toy or show me to my hospital room. I think of the storybook *Madeline* about the French girl whose appendix is taken out. I expect to be tucked into a clean, white bed and given toys and candy. I expect the hospital to open its strong arms and fold me in and hold me for a while. But that doesn't happen. I go largely unnoticed sitting there, except for a few other patients who stare at my blood-tinged washcloth and crinkle their noses.

"I'm hungry," I say. We've missed dinner. Mom roots around in her purse and finds a Dum-Dum lollipop, which I suck on for a while. I paint my tongue with it, trying to cover every taste bud with grape flavor. The sweetness is a nice distraction from the pain.

When I am finally ushered behind the curtain of an examining room, I'm disappointed. It looks nothing like the cozy space I'd imagined. An unfriendly nurse tells me to lie down on a stiff table covered in blue paper. I stare at the ceiling, jealous that my brothers are at home with Dad eating spaghetti.

I need eight stitches, two fewer than Dad predicted. The worst part is the big needle they use to numb my skin. It is longer than my whole hand and sharp, and each poke burns, searing. I lie perfectly still, staring at the fluorescent lights. I am quiet. Tears roll down my cheekbone and pool in my ears. At the end, the doctor tells me I am the bravest little girl he's ever seen. He reaches into his white coat pocket, pulls out two lollipops, and hands them to me.

"You hardly cried at all!" Mom says triumphantly on the drive home. As a result, she says I don't have to share the suckers with my brothers. I deserve both.

It's the first time I remember being rewarded for my ability to bypass pain, to not make a fuss, to endure. Years from now I'll turn this over in my mind, the idea that I suppressed my feelings so skillfully, that I didn't create a scene, that in the midst of a trauma, I was able to be stoic. I'll admire this ability in myself and also loathe it. I'll wonder how many times I could have saved myself if only I had, in fact, made a fuss, thrown a fit, drawn more attention from the adults around me. Because in my ability to be fine, to push through, and to keep quiet in the midst of the abuse that will come, I keep myself unseen. And without being seen, there will be no one to step in and rescue me.

Once we get home from the emergency room, my lollipops still in my hand, the focus turns back to Alan, to my mother, to the bigger crises in the house – that my father, despite my best attempts, is leaving for good.

Chapter Three

August 13, 2016.

I'm receiving all the usual condolences, plus a few unusual ones. Messages from distant family members, old family friends. Some of them are telling me I should feel relieved. I'm no longer burdened by my brother, some people assume. Others say I should be happy that he lived to be forty-three. He could have died sooner.

My aunt tells me he was never supposed to live past age six, something she remembers my mother saying. In the 1970s, doctors knew so little about his condition, yet they felt certain he would die. She internalized this as truth. He was supposed to die at age six, and yet he survived. She says she feels gratitude for all the bonus years he lived. To her, he was a miracle child. But I can't share in her gratitude, because no one ever told me this prophecy.

He died at forty-three.

Fact: If he had died at six, when I was three, I never would have known the harm he'd do to me. I'd never feel the pain of his fist striking my chest, the feeling of pressing my weight against a door, digging in my heels, heart pounding, wondering what I'll do next when he splinters the wood, when he breaks the door down.

Fact: If he had died at six, when I was three, I never would have known the joy, the love. I never would have known how easy it was to make him laugh, how he could string long lines of Matchbox cars across the room and play next to me for hours – silent but content. How once Will came along, the three of us would snuggle and watch movies together. How we'd dance and sing. How we'd use Alan's height to our advantage, teaching him to reach the candy my mother stashed in a cabinet above the refrigerator. How we'd hold his hand and teach him to write his ABCs.

Unknown: If he had died at six, would I ever have wondered if he loved me? Whether he knew I loved him? Would I feel the need to understand the complexity of his condition? Would I have been more accepting of his death?

Part Two

Reentry

Chapter Four

August 13, 2016.

I'm on a plane again, this time hurtling toward a family I've been steadily distancing myself from for years. I'm no longer native to my family of origin, and yet I'm rushing toward them, closing the geographical gap. The mountains and ocean and sailboats shrink behind me as a brown landscape opens up ahead – the rain shadow, that place where the Cascades shield the wind and the moisture. I didn't get to feel the breeze, touch the fog, or watch the sunrise. I didn't get to laugh with my friends.

I close my eyes and sense for the first time the speed of an airplane, my body moving through space and time at 500 miles per hour. I've never been afraid to fly, but at this moment, I am terrified. This is the opposite of a homecoming. I have no idea what I'm heading toward. It suddenly feels impossible that we can stay airborne. The plane is fragile, just metal and plastic, bolts and wires. We're all too fragile. I imagine the window next to me shattering, my body sucked out, descending rapidly to places unknown. I grip the armrests so tightly my fingertips go white. I close my eyes and hang on.

I take deep breaths and try to meditate, to find some peace. Kris and our two children are on their way. By the time I'd called him with the news, he'd already heard from my father. My dad wouldn't say why he was so desperate to get a hold of me, but Kris guessed. Like me, he's imagined this day. He's heard my mother's siren, *It's Alan. Something's wrong with Alan.* I wonder if the facts of Alan's death feel as mysterious to him as they do to me.

"I'll drive up with the kids first thing in the morning," Kris told me last night. He'd already looked at the cost of plane tickets and renting a car and figured it'd be better to drive the fourteen hours from Phoenix to Boulder. "That way we'll have our car. We can come and go as we please and drive home after the funeral."

The funeral.

"I have no idea when the funeral will be," I said, exasperated. "It doesn't sound like anyone's making any decisions."

"They'll have to eventually. Try not to worry about the details too much right now. Just get yourself to Boulder." He assured me he'd be there in a couple of days and help me sort things out.

Just hearing him say this grounds me, soothes me.

Kris has a way of breaking complex problems into manageable segments, like mileposts along a trail. He's somehow able to visualize an entire route with all its turns and elevation changes while focusing his energy on the next best step. It's like he can simultaneously see the forest and the trees.

Our Phoenix home sits at the base of South Mountain, a desert preserve with a fifteen-mile-long rocky spine running along the center, like a geological table runner. The slopes of the mountain are dotted with sagebrush and saguaro cacti.

Pretty to look at but hard to navigate. Ever since we moved here, Kris's goal has been to get the kids to hike every trail on the mountain with him, and there are dozens. Some routes follow a sandy wash as it switchbacks up to a rocky plateau and then pitches steeply to the wide ridgeline. It's challenging for the kids' short legs.

I join them on these adventures sometimes but have noticed that they hike farther when I'm not there. There's something about the tenderness of a child in proximity to their mother. If their legs get tired, they know I'll be quick to scoop them up. I'm too eager to protect them from all manner of discomfort, from hunger to scraped knees.

Recently, Kris took them up a trail called Young Man, part of a trio of routes that, when stitched together, constitute some of the hardest hiking on the mountain. Young Man is just over four miles, moderately difficult. The second route is named Mid-Life Crisis. Mid-Life Crisis is a seven-mile rocky path that leads to Old Man Trail, which ends at the summit (nowhere to go but down from there).

I think about his face beaming with pride when he told me that the kids skittered up Young Man trail, hoisting their bodies over boulders and keeping their balance on sandy slopes. They didn't complain once, he said. In fact, it was Kris, not the kids, who eventually grew tired and decided to turn back. I understood this to mean he'd reached the next milestone, not only in his hiking goal but in fatherhood. He'd instilled in them a drive to explore.

Kris grew up on twenty acres in central Wisconsin. He was what today we'd call a free-range kid, unsupervised and untethered, biking and hiking and fishing local ponds from sunrise to sunset. He wants our kids to grow up with the same sense of wonder that he had. He wants adventure and curiosity to be their lifeblood.

For me growing up in Atlanta, nature was something I craved. It beckoned to me quietly, like pockets of trees peeking out between skyscrapers, like the creeks that wound through neighborhoods. I savored my time playing in my wooded back-yard. I loved to stand outside in the rain, to feel drops hitting my skin, to smell the air scrubbed clean. Every spring, I plucked a few dogwood blooms and put them in glasses of water. I climbed magnolia trees, so sturdy and thick you could get lost in the canopy. The few times my dad took me hiking in North Georgia or when I'd experience being outdoors with friends – on field trips or visiting their vacation homes – I felt a visceral pull. To pay attention, to soak it all in. I think I understood on some level that nature could hold me, could comfort me, could teach me something deeper about the world, about myself.

As I travel toward my family of origin, this is the perspec-tive I want to have, that of being held, of climbing a trail. I want to know that for all the effort ahead of me, for all the rocky ledges and blind corners, that I will be safe, that the summit will beckon. That there will be a reward, a 360-degree view.

I look out the plane window and visualize the world beneath me as a map, me a game piece moving across it, inch by inch. I imagine Kris and the kids as another piece, moving toward me. Soon, I hope, we'll all cross over the desert. We'll crest the Rockies and descend toward Colorado's foothills, where my brother had been living with my mother. Where he died.

It's both the longest and shortest flight of my life.

I had a moment at the Seattle airport, running toward the gate with twenty minutes to spare, clutching a paper bag full of warm scones that my friends handed me as we hugged goodbye.

What's the rush? I wondered. There's no deadline. No plan.

I asked my dad when people were arriving, when the funeral might be, what he needed me to do.

It's up to your mother, he said. *I don't know anything.*

He posted something on Facebook, a medium he typically uses for work, to post his latest research, to stay relevant. It seemed like the quickest, easiest way to let people know, he said. Just a few sentences accompanied by a photo of Alan, me, and Will as kids. Alan is maybe twelve, wearing a gray flannel blazer and bright red tie. I'm wearing a white and blue polka dot dress with a Peter Pan collar and a ribbon across my waist. Will is in plaid, his navy clip-on tie only reaching halfway down his chest, his shirt buttons straining against his toddler belly. We're all wearing the pained expression of siblings who have been told to stand too close to one another and smile.

We lost our boy, Dad wrote. *My oldest child was forty-three.*

A hundred comments pile up. People want to know how it happened, where they can send flowers or donations, if everyone will be gathering in Boulder. Should they send food there?

Tell us what to do, we all beg him.

As the patriarch of the family, it seems he should guide us.

I stare at the screen, waiting. I am the girl in the polka-dot dress and ribbon, hoping her dad will right the ship, take charge, and guide us all toward safety.

I refresh the page.

Refresh.

Refresh.

He never replies.

Chapter Five

In the 1830s, before Atlanta had its own identity, it was just a dot on the map nicknamed Terminus. Terminus, meaning the end of the line. A dot near the southern tail of the Appalachian Mountains, framed by foothills and granite outcroppings to the north and sandy coastal plain to the south. It's part of a geography called the Piedmont, a sort of liminal space between the coast and the mountains. The soil here is a distinctive red clay, high in iron and indelible. It stains like memory. Above ground, the landscape is rolling and lushly green. Beautiful to look at and easy to travel.

Nothing much was expected of the place except that it would be the endpoint for the Western & Atlantic Railroad. A transportation hub at best, a stopover on the way to the places people really wanted to go, west or north or farther south. But as one building became two and two became three and people began to settle here, the name was changed and the place developed its own identity. Atlanta, a feminine form of Atlantic. The name itself was a reinvention. By the 1850s, it was a bustling gateway and supply center. After the Civil War, when

Union General Sherman burned the city down, it reinvented itself again. The New South. And again it was reborn in 1917 after a warehouse fire spread and burned nearly 2,000 buildings, displacing 10,000 people. And again as an epicenter of the Civil Rights movement, the place Dr. Martin Luther King, Jr. called home, a place where he hoped to rewrite the script, the place where he is buried. Revision after revision, each time the city becoming a better version of itself.

It's a metropolis that is at once crowded and spacious. A city that is impossibly green and also laced with gray concrete highways. Its pace is both fast and slow. Serene creeks wind through urban centers. Swaths of forest nestle between skyscrapers. Gazing out an airplane window, you don't immediately see the buildings because the trees are so dense. Even when city developers built an eight-lane circular highway to define a metro area, what locals call the Perimeter, Atlanta couldn't be kept small. It's a place that refuses to be contained or defined, physically or culturally.

I like to think Atlanta is a place that had to burn in order to survive. It had to defy history, outgrow its container, disrupt societal norms, press forward in the face of adversity to become what it is today. It's a place of resilience, of beauty being born from ashes.

· · ·

One spring evening, when I am about six or seven, we are out with my mother, piled in her sedan, running errands. Spring in Atlanta is a burst of color and fragrance, even within the concrete frame of the city. Dogwoods bloom overnight, and hydrangea bushes unfurl thick green leaves and balls of flowers like pompoms. Every surface is coated in a fine yellow powder. Pollen, but I call it fairy dust. The weather is warm, but not yet humid, and the sun sets around eight o'clock, so evenings are the perfect time to be out and about. Usually, I hate the monotony of running errands with Mom. But this night, sitting in the backseat with the window rolled down, wind in my face, I don't mind it so much.

After buying cigarettes at the Food Lion, Mom thumbs through her cash and calculates that we have enough left over to stop for dinner before heading home. Before the divorce, Dad often joked that Mom had a hole in her wallet. "Everything I give her slips right through," he said. After the divorce, she has the same problem; only he isn't around to complain about it. He sends child support checks. She cashes them. Within a few days, we are broke again.

She seems determined to maintain the upper-middle-class lifestyle she had before, to push back against the landslide of loss she feels since Dad left. But she's losing her footing. Mom knows she can't afford the house we live in. The five-bedroom split-level she and my dad bought when I was a toddler is her dream house. It has all the hallmarks of 1970s kitsch—orange shag carpet in the den, brown and tan linoleum in the kitchen, faux wood paneling on the walls, and the exterior siding is painted the color of mint ice cream. While my parents were still married, my mom had taken great care in decorating and filling it with designer furniture, custom drapes and upholstery, and Native American pottery she collected on her trips to New Mexico where she grew up. We have a formal living room and a finished basement, a sloping front yard with dogwood trees, azalea bushes, and a thickly wooded backyard that we kids can easily get lost in.

The neighborhood feels suburban yet is within the Atlanta city limits. Our location inside the Perimeter will eventually become one of the most coveted in the city. For now, my dad calls it "up-and-coming." Our street is a well-manicured oasis full of young families with children. But less than two miles away are public housing developments, strip malls, and abandoned office parks. Dad explained to me once that when some of the more rundown areas around ours were gentrified, our property value would skyrocket.

Our house's value does increase, but with it so do our expenses. Between part-time work as a secretary and her side jobs wallpapering and doing janitorial work, Mom makes enough to cover the mortgage most months, but property taxes, groceries, and utilities are another issue. When she is sad, she buys herself new dresses and shoes, arguing, "When I look better, I feel better." Then there are the diet programs: registration costs, monthly maintenance fees, counseling sessions, and prepackaged foods. Her weight fluctuates, which means she frequently buys new business suits in different sizes to wear to work. No one except her seems bothered by her size. She is a tall woman with an angular face, short chestnut hair that she curls with sponge rollers, broad shoulders, and thin ankles. Even when she's at her heaviest, men find her beautiful. So do I. I'm captivated by her.

Still, she's unhappy. She cries a lot. She smokes a lot. The heaviness registers on her face. The divorce settlement hasn't provided the parachute she hoped for. *He promised he'd always take care of me,* she often says. *He told me I'd have everything I ever needed.* I understand this to mean we'll have money, that my dad promised we'd always have all the money we need. But that doesn't seem to be true. Dad sends the support check once per month, and still, we're left wanting for more. More groceries. More toys and books like my friends have. Shoes that don't have holes in the toes.

"Your father cheated me in more ways than one," my mother says.

Someday I'll realize that this is the bigger loss. It's not the money, though the financial insecurity is suffocating at times. It's the feeling of being cheated out of what she thought she rightly deserved. Her agony is wrapped up in betrayal and abandonment. The loss of her ideal future. Of her self-esteem. A loss of hope.

What I can't say to her, not now and maybe not ever, is that I feel loss too. I feel the loss of my father.

We stop at the little Italian restaurant located in a strip mall near our house. It is my mother's favorite place to eat. The owner, a plump, second-generation Italian woman with ropey brown hair, is also a recent divorcee, and though they never socialize outside the restaurant, the women form a bond with their brief conversations at the hostess desk, sympathetic looks exchanged in passing and sarcastic quips about men and money. There is a familiarity between them. They are not friends, but they are part of the same jaded club.

We kids, of course, are more focused on the meal. Alan has an insatiable appetite. As long as he is awake, he is ravenous. We know this about Alan, but we think it is gluttony or bad behavior. At home, he eats whatever he can find. Whole packages of Oscar Mayer bologna. Sticks of butter and handfuls of uncooked pasta. He grabs food from my and William's plates and shoves it in his mouth before we can stop him. He steals food scraps from the trash. My mother slaps his hand away. She washes his mouth out with soap. She sends him to his room and threatens to beat him with a belt if he can't learn to control himself. She starts hiding food in her bedroom. She buys a padlock for the pantry. She says this is temporary, that he will develop restraint as he matures.

I grow increasingly vigilant, always aware of how much food we have in the house and where it's located. I worry if

Alan finds Mom's stashes, that somehow he will eat himself to death. I worry he will be punished. I also worry every time my stomach growls that there won't be enough for me.

Even in public, where my mother demands our best behavior, Alan descends on food like a lion to its kill. As a result, Will and I have developed quick reflexes. Food is something we compete for, not something that brings any pleasure or nourishment. We snatch our dinner and swallow it, barely chewing, to ensure we get our fair share. We don't yet understand that it's part of Alan's genetics, that he lacks the neurological cues that tell him when he's full. Sitting at a round table with a red-and-white-checked oilcloth cover, we devour pepperoni pizza slices, two baskets of garlic bread, and guzzle giant plastic mugs of soda. Other patrons glare at us, or maybe just at Alan. I can't be sure. I'm used to people staring at Alan. Adults and kids. In stores. On playgrounds. I scowl back at them until they stop. I want to tell them to mind their own business. I want them to understand that Alan can't help the way he is.

When there is nothing left but crumbs, we grab handfuls of pastel-colored butter mints from the hostess stand and make our way back to the car. My mother turns the key over and the engine starts, putters, and stalls. She tries again, and it is silent.

"Fuck," she mutters, staring at her gauges. "Out of gas."

"Fuuuck!" Alan repeats, slapping the window with his bare hand.

We all sit silently for a few minutes while she considers what to do next. I know she's just spent the last of our money, save a dollar or so in change, on dinner. The closest gas station is about a half mile or so away. I think about it. No. We can't push the car that far. And even if we could, how will we pay?

"I'll be right back," Mom says. She grabs the change from her coin purse and walks to a payphone by the restaurant. Several minutes later, she returns and sits with us in the car.

She rolls down the window, lights a cigarette, takes a drag, and stares out the windshield at nothing.

My brothers and I are antsy, poking and pinching one another and asking to go home every thirty seconds or so. *What are we doing here? Why is it taking so long?*

"Why's the car broken?" Will asks. "Can I fix it?"

"Don't worry. I've got it under control," Mom says, tapping her long fingernails on the steering wheel. She blows smoke from the corner of her mouth. Like a gray ribbon, it spirals out the open window.

Just then, a red Volkswagen swings into the parking space next to ours. My dad honks the horn twice, then climbs out, walks around to the hatchback, and retrieves a red and yellow gasoline can. He knocks on our windows and waves to us. A smile spreads wide beneath his Tom Selleck mustache but fades as soon as he greets our mother. Our noses and hands are pressed against the glass—curious, eager, a bit confused. My heart jumps in my chest. It feels too good to be true, like I am watching a movie of my father.

When Dad moved out, I assumed he was gone. Not forever gone. Not dead. But, in a way, it felt like he didn't exist anymore, at least not in any permanent way. He has visitation rights, so we see him every few weeks or so, depending on his travel schedule. Sometimes we sleep over at his apartment and watch movies and eat popcorn. Other times he takes us for an afternoon to a park or the mall or a baseball game. Once, he took us to his office and let us draw pictures all over his chalkboard. But in between these encounters, I have no sense of where he is and when (or if) he'll be back. He exists in another dimension. If he calls the house, I'm not aware, and I don't remember ever asking to call him. One minute he is there with us, protecting us, and then he just *isn't*. I miss him, but I don't question it.

Now, here he is. My mother needed him, called him, and he showed up. How could that be? We roll down our windows and chat with him for a few minutes while Mom pours the gasoline into the tank. He asks about school. We tell him about the pizza we just had for dinner. He mentions he bought a box kite and wants to try it out next time we visit him. The whole while I am waiting for him to scoop me up and put me in his car and drive away.

And then, just as casually as he arrived, he kisses us good-bye, climbs back in his car, and drives away. Gone again. The realization sweeps over me, and my arms and legs feel impossibly heavy. I let him leave without me. I let him get away.

I wish I could say Dad bailed us out again, that he was the force that would keep us from slipping underwater. Time and again, I imagined his red VW Rabbit gunning up our steep driveway, him jumping out, spreading his arms wide, and yelling for us all to pack a bag and come live with him.

But aside from an occasional postcard in the mailbox, long-distance phone calls, or him slipping me a wad of cash to enroll in softball or Girl Scouts, there was no rescuing. Our lives remained separate. Mom apparently had one get-out-of-jail-free card, and she used it on a tank of gas.

Chapter Six

August 13, 2016.

Before I leave Seattle for Colorado, I call my mother. I wasn't sure if I still had her cell phone number. It's been six years since I've called her. But thumbing through my contacts, I find it under her married name.

I need to know. Not only what happened, how exactly he died, but I need to know the answer to at least one of the questions that has been circling my head from the moment my father told me the news.

My mother's voice is remarkably the same as it's always been. Polite. Melodic. Like a receptionist, which she was for several years. It's how she supported us after the divorce, a piecemeal of part-time secretary jobs and temp positions. She could answer phones and type sixty-five words per minute at the same time without making a mistake. When she answers my call, her voice is a little scratchy and faint. She speaks to me as if I am a distant relative or acquaintance she hasn't heard from in years. In a sense, I am.

"I'm so glad you called."

I ask her to fill in the blanks for me. "Dad said something about a breathing problem. Cardiac arrest?"

"He was having an asthma attack – at least I thought it was an asthma attack," she explains. "He was wheezing really badly. I gave him his breathing treatment, all his medications, but it didn't help. He's the one who decided he needed to go to the emergency room."

"*He* decided?" I'd never known Alan to have this kind of agency. My mother made all of his medical decisions. She made most of his everyday decisions, too. When he slept, what he ate, what clothes he wore. From the time we were young, there was an understanding that, because of his condition, Alan couldn't be trusted to take care of himself or clearly communicate his own needs.

"He didn't have the words to explain the pain, but he knew it was bad."

She goes on to describe the scene in intricate detail as if she's described it many times already. It's a short drive to the hospital, less than two miles. She pulls up to the ambulance bay, throws the car in park, and runs inside screaming for help. Alan is having what she thinks is a seizure in the front seat of her car. He's slumped over, his head on the dash. A team of doctors and nurses pull him out, which requires great effort. He's over six feet tall and more than 250 pounds. They lift him onto a gurney and rush him inside, behind glass doors. Before long, they're doing chest compressions. They insert a tube down his throat. They shock his chest.

"What caused the seizure?" I wonder out loud. "And his heart just stopped?"

"I don't really know. It all happened so quickly."

"What about the wheezing? You sure it was asthma? Was he allergic to something?"

"I don't know, Gina."

"So, then..." I stammer.

"So? So, then he died." Her voice takes on a sharpness. She sounds impatient.

I can close my eyes and picture the hospital in Boulder. It's the same one where my kids were born years ago, before we moved to Phoenix. It's a place that already felt significant to me, holding within its walls two of my happiest memories. The three-story building is full of windows and positioned so that almost every room faces the picturesque peaks that flank the town of Boulder. The birthing suites look like luxury hotel rooms, and the nurses are the kindest, most nurturing I've ever met. I walked through the Emergency Department in the middle of the night when I was in labor. It seemed so quiet then. Boulder is a college town. Many of its emergencies are auto accidents or alcohol poisoning or bicycle crashes. Some drug overdoses. I imagine the chaos that probably ensued the moment my mother pulled up to the entrance with Alan and began screaming.

She says she just watched it all through the glass, like a television medical drama. It didn't seem real, she says. Until later, maybe twenty minutes? Maybe thirty? A doctor emerged and asked my mother if they should keep going.

She told them they could stop.

"He was gone," she says. "It was obvious he was gone."

As she speaks those words, I am silent. I try to catch my breath. I don't want her to hear me crying. I can't be the vulnerable one. It's my job to stay strong.

There's so much still unanswered. Did the doctors say what caused it? Will there be an autopsy? Why did she wait until the next day to tell anyone he died?

I experience a familiar tightening of my chest, the anger and confusion I so often feel toward my mother. I think about all the times she called me over the years to say that she couldn't handle Alan alone, that he needed too much attention. She needed help. I think about how I pushed back, how I pleaded with her to move him into a group home that offers professional care. According to her, he was always medically fragile, one seizure or asthma attack away from dying. But I hadn't believed this was true. For as many times Alan was in crisis – the "episodes" he had when we were little, the trips to the hospital, the times he ate until he was sick – there were just as many times my mother had cried wolf. Times she used Alan to lure my dad home. Times she rushed him to the doctor in a panic only to be told nothing is wrong.

After I left home, I began to see my mother's pleas and complaints as attempts to reel me back to caretake my brother, to relieve her of the crushing stress and loneliness, to share the parenting load. Maybe in this way too I am like my father. The more she begged me to come home, the more I wanted to pull away.

Whether it was the mystery of Alan's condition, a projection of my mother's anxiety, or overt manipulation, the result for me was all the same: confusion, skepticism. I struggled to accept her words at face value.

But there was another reason to be skeptical: the evidence of Alan. Whenever I spent time with him, I dismissed any notion of his fragility. To me, he always appeared strong and healthy. Perhaps too strong, given his violent tendencies. Despite his disabilities and developmental delays, he was my big brother. To me, he was invincible.

Of course, this doesn't matter anymore. Alan's gone. Had I been there, could I have saved him? Could anyone have saved him?

"What I really need to know," I finally say, "I mean, I'm wondering... do you think he knew that I love him?"

"Oh, I'm sure he did." She answers quickly, and then she exhales into the phone. It sounds like a gust of wind. "You hadn't seen him in a while, Gina. He talked about you. He missed you a lot."

"You mean he thought about me?" Alan's thoughts tended to get caught in a loop, like his mind was stuck on one channel. He might have talked obsessively about me one day, then the next day talked about the dog who lived down the street or his favorite clerk at the grocery store or a car he admired. He fixated on a handful of people, places, and things he liked. We couldn't be sure what emotions, if any, were attached to those fixations. For him to talk about me didn't necessarily mean that he missed me, though I hope that he did.

"Yes."

"Well, I thought about him too," I say. "I missed him too."

After that, there is a heavy pause. I thank her, say goodbye, and hang up. I am afraid of where the conversation might veer from here, into the territory of my mother's and my relationship. I don't want to know whether she misses me or thinks about me or loves me. And I don't want to say that I have not missed her. I do think about her often, but I can't say that I love her, because I'm not sure how I feel about her. I can't lie, and I can't be cruel.

• • •

There's a throbbing pain behind my right eye. It began the moment my father called me and has spread its grip across my forehead. I stare out the plane window, like a portal to another life. I close my eyes and lean back in my seat. I want to sleep, to escape. I want the restful vacation I had planned, though I know it's selfish to want that. I can picture myself on the ferry with my friends, bound for the island and the oysters and the wine and the sunsets. I feel the ocean breeze in my hair.

I don't even realize I've fallen asleep until the plane's wheels touch down hard in Denver and I'm jolted awake.

This time, as the plane bumps along the tarmac and the jagged purple outline of the Rocky Mountains come into view on the horizon, I don't reach for my phone because there's no one to call. All I can think of is Kris. I feel so alone. I want him here with me. Kris knows how this all might go. He knows the pull of my family, the way boundaries blur, and before I know it, I'm sucked in and unable to breathe.

In the fifteen years we've been together, Kris has witnessed my becoming my own person, awakening to my own needs, creating my own version of family. It was a process that began before I met him, but in many ways, he was a catalyst, the missing piece. From the earliest days of our relationship, under his gaze, I felt known and desired. I felt seen like I never had before. His self-assurance created a safe space where I could step more fully into myself. His vulnerability and strength helped me understand the nature of interdependence. I am my own person. He is his. We can lean on one another without becoming enmeshed or consumed.

When my childhood history bubbles to the surface, he also reminds me that my sense of self is durable. He's shown me by example that it's possible to engage with my family of origin on some level and then separate cleanly. With them, as with everyone, he's compassionate and smart and funny, but he doesn't take any bullshit.

On our wedding day, my mother hid in a bathroom for hours. It had been a battle to get her to even show up. She didn't want to sit within ten feet of certain family members like her sister, whom she hadn't spoken with in years, or my stepmother, whom she often blamed for the demise of my parents' marriage. Once the seating arrangements were settled, she obsessed about how the guests might treat Alan.

"They're good people, Mom," I'd reassured her. "Everyone will love him."

"But what if he acts out?" she asked. "You'll hate me for letting him ruin your big day."

"Nothing can ruin it," I said because I truly believed it. "If he misbehaves, our friends will understand."

As it turned out, Alan was a perfect gentleman that day. He seemed to love the novelty of wearing a tuxedo, complete with shiny shoes and flowers on the lapel. *Look, Gina,* he squealed, pointing to himself in a mirror, as if he couldn't believe the reflection was really him. He spent the morning with the wedding party posing and smiling for photos. Then Kris gave him the task of handing out programs for the ceremony. Alan relished the opportunity to shake our guests' hands. He talked with them about his dog and asked them what kind of car they drove. He seemed proud to have a job to do, proud that Kris had chosen him. Every guest treated my brother with compassion and respect.

Even so, immediately after the ceremony, my mother sent Alan away with a caregiver and then she retreated to the ladies' room. Later, she complained that Kris hadn't bothered to dance with her.

"You forgot about me," she told him. "It's the groom's responsibility to dance with the mother of the bride." She announced this at a crowded dinner party months later, her hand clutching her chest for effect. Maybe she felt safe provoking us in a setting where we'd feel compelled to respond politely. She glared at Kris. "I was so disappointed. Why didn't you dance with me?"

"I looked for you," Kris replied. "Several times."

"Well, you didn't look hard enough."

Kris calmly set down his wine glass and reached for my mother's hand. "Let's dance!" he offered. She tried to pull away. "You weren't available then, Sharon, so dance with me now." And right there, though she squirmed and tried to refuse, he twirled her around the dining room.

He'd called her bluff. I laughed and clapped, knowing without a doubt I'd married the right man, one who is confident in himself and how to handle my mother.

· · ·

My kids are always up for an adventure. I imagine their excitement the moment Kris presented them with the idea of a road trip to Colorado. For them, the Rocky Mountains are their second home, the place we escape to every summer when the Arizona heat is too much to bear. The wild rivers, snowy peaks, and wildflower-filled meadows are a perfect counterbalance to the desert landscape. After months of living in the dryness, our bodies soak up the moisture and greenery. Nature, in every form, is our favorite playground.

My hope in exposing the kids to different landscapes is that they'll come to understand something deeper, something I didn't fully grasp until I was an adult. Different geographies and geological features – Phoenix, Boulder, Atlanta, valleys, deserts, mountains, rivers, hills, urban parks – reflect different aspects of ourselves. A mountain offers perspective, a river allows nourishment and peace, a valley or desert provides space for introspection and solitude. Even urban parks and green infrastructure remind us we are resilient, that we can persevere. In the midst of concrete and chaos, we can thrive. Sometimes, nature can meet our needs in ways that humans can't.

My son Miles is six years old, the age my aunt says Alan was supposed to die, and also a year older than Alan was thought to be intellectually. "Intellectual age" was something Alan was assigned by doctors over the years based on milestones he reached, such as reading and writing, plus fine motor skills, like tying his shoes. It was an imperfect measurement, but the only reference point we had.

I struggle to remember Alan at age six, not because I was three, too young to remember much, but because Alan in a sense was always five. While William and I transformed and matured, he was frozen in time. His intellectual age was an invisible barrier he never crossed, even as his body grew.

I do have one clear memory: Atlanta, Georgia. Summer of 1979. We are underwater. The voices of neighborhood children drift above us, muffled. We exist in a sea of chlorinated blue. I am treading water for the first time without my "swimmies," those inflatable armbands that keep toddlers afloat. I am dunking my body down and clawing my way back to the surface. I am proud of this achievement. Nearby, Alan is diving to the bottom of the pool, collecting shiny pennies that my dad tossed in as a game. He lines them up evenly on the concrete edge. My mother is lounging on a plastic chaise in the shade, far enough away that our splashes won't dampen her freshly set curls but close enough to watch us swim. Baby Will is asleep next to her on a striped beach towel. The air smells like burnt hot dogs and cocoa butter.

Alan is confident and graceful. He is upside down. He is spinning. He is pumping his legs and propelling his body through the water. He is pushing off the bottom and breaking through the pool's surface like a torpedo. He's unconcerned with the rivulets of water flowing down his thick brown hair, over his forehead, and into his eyes. He refuses to wear goggles. He is laughing and squealing with delight.

I am in awe. I want to do this too. Swimming is something Alan does better than me, and not just because he is six and I am three. Swimming is something he will always do better than me, like a superpower.

My parents are watching us. They are smiling. They are clapping every time Alan breaks the surface. They're looking around the pool deck at other parents, making eye contact as if to say, *Do you see the miracle happening here?* They are proud of me, sure. But more than that, they are amazed at their son who is limited in so many ways – speech impaired, lacking balance and muscle tone – and yet so strong and graceful in the pool. It's like the water washes away his disability.

Underwater, I observe my brother in slow motion. He is suspended in space and time. Alan is unafraid. I am unafraid. And so, for a moment, my parents are unafraid too. For a moment, we are tethered by our devotion to Alan, our sense of pride, the notion that maybe things – Alan, their marriage, the future – will be okay after all.

In my memory, this is the closest I've been to reverence for an older sibling, the closest I've felt to intense longing to be able to do something as well as he can. I'm too young to articulate it, but this experience instills in me a hope that will sustain me later in life when I need it most. A belief that things can be better, that family can be a source of love, of safety and happiness. Not just fear, embarrassment, or pain.

Growing up, we adjusted our expectations around Alan's cognitive age, but it wasn't until I had kids of my own that I really began to understand how narrow a definition that is, how it fails to encompass the myriad behaviors, emotions, and developments kids display at a given age.

I think of Miles, his round blue eyes and platinum hair, the way he leaps over cracks in the sidewalk, spins around, walks backward so that he can talk with me. *Mom, guess what?*

He is curious and smart. He wants me to know everything he knows. Every fact is a revelation. *Mom, did you know ...*

... snakes don't have eyelids?

... there are fourteen bones in the human hand?

... camel humps don't have water in them?

... every odd number has an 'e' in it?

Yet, the things Miles knows and does at six are different from what my daughter Bronwynn knew at age six. She rattled off facts about mythological creatures. She rescued worms after rainstorms, picking them up off the pavement and placing them safely in the grass. She struggled with math yet knew how to write fluidly in looping cursive. She enjoyed photography at a young age. Watching my kids grow, I've learned that there are benchmarks and typical achievements, but there's no cookie-cutter standard for what a five-year-old knows and does versus a six-year-old.

Fact: One thing has been consistent for my kids at every age. From their preverbal infancy until now, I've never questioned whether they love me or whether they feel loved. I know in many ways that they do love me. They say the words. They've said the words since they could speak sentences. But it's much more than that. They track me. They know that I'm tracking them. When they feel happy or sad or afraid, they look to me like a beacon.

Fact: Their bodies relax in proximity to mine. They hold my cheeks in their chubby hands and stare at me with an intensity that would frighten me if it was anyone except for my children. I know I love them because I would die for them. I know they love me because they would die *without* me – maybe not literally – but they certainly would be lost. There would be scars as deep as our connection. I know this, in part, because I remember how it felt when my father left me.

Unknown: Is this love or attachment or both?

It is the complexity of the parent-child relationship.

They also possess complex love for each other as siblings. They yell, they tattle, they compete for Kris's and my attention. They also cuddle up next to each other while watching movies. They get lost in imagination together, sometimes for hours. They sneak into each other's bedrooms and whisper stories at night. They cheer for each other when one learns to ride a bike or master a game. They use their piggy bank money to buy one another gifts. They are rivals, and they are allies.

Kris and I observe them quietly and soak it in. Every time, we're amazed and delighted by the depth of their bond. This is how I wish my siblings and I could have been, how we might have been if Alan had been different or if my parents could have held us together. We had fleeting moments – cuddling, pretend play, shared secrets. But it never felt consistent or durable. Too often, I was more of a parent to my brothers than a sister.

I know whatever happens this week, even if I get sucked back into the vortex of my family of origin, my kids will be okay. Bronwynn will engage my mother with her curiosity and empathy and ask where she might find some colored pencils and paper. Miles will pretend he knows how to play the piano and impress all the adults with a few chords. They'll eat the casseroles and cuddle Alan's dog and play with his toys, and if they begin to whine or act restless, Kris will take them on a hike and cheer them up the way he always does.

I wish they were here already. My people. The family I have chosen.

Chapter Seven

Boulder, August 14, 2016.

Entering my mother's home feels like a walk back in time. The moment I step onto her front walkway, I feel my chest constrict. My leg muscles twitch. My skin is electric. I am once again a child – vigilant and weighted down by responsibility, afraid to speak, afraid to be seen. I'm five-foot-ten, but I appear shorter. Since I was a girl, I've walked with my shoulders turned inward, my posture slightly stooped. My mother called it laziness, an unwillingness to stand up straight. "You'd be so much prettier if you sat up tall." I think now that I made myself small. It wasn't a choice. It was survival.

I stop at the doorstep, take a deep breath, and steel myself. *Remember who you are*, I think. It is a mantra I've practiced over the years when I notice the pain of my family creeping in, when I feel the young parts of me breaking through to the surface. *You're safe now.* While it is true I am Alan's sister, I need to remind myself I am also my own person. An adult woman, wife, mother, writer, friend, traveler. I like to run and hike. I am strong and capable. I have muscular legs and lean arms that are always slightly pink from the sun. My voice is clearer and louder than it used to be. I wear some makeup now, a rosy gloss on my lips, highlighter on my cheeks, and brown mascara that enhances my blue eyes. I tie my hair up in a high bun so that people can see my face. I want people to see me.

In order to enter my mother's space and love my family of origin, I first need to remember I am separate from them. I need to maintain the space I've created. The space I fought for.

I open the door to discover a crowd of people who ordinarily wouldn't speak to one another packed tightly in the living room. I glide in quietly. I didn't ring the bell.

The gathering is livelier than I imagined and civil. Over in one corner, my mother's husband Mike is leaning casually against a wall, talking with my stepmother. Across the room, my father is chatting with an uncle who has been on the outs for years. My half-sister Emma—my dad's daughter with my stepmother—is talking with my mother, perhaps for the first time ever. There are several people I don't recognize – neighbors, maybe, Alan's part-time caregivers, or members of my mother's quilting group. No one's laughing, but the conversations are flowing, a steady buzz coming from all corners of the room. There are no tears, I notice. No one appears comfortable enough with each other to cry.

My mother's house in Boulder has a veneer that reminds me of my childhood home in Atlanta. There's a formal sitting room with billowing silk drapes and stiff wingback chairs and collections of antique pottery and silver trinkets arranged symmetrically on dust-free shelves. Books are arranged by size and color. The hardwood floors are polished. The wall art is impersonal, except for one portrait my mother commissioned of my brothers and me when we were toddlers. In it, I'm wearing a high-neck white lace dress with poofy sleeves that extend past my wrists. My brothers are in pale blue suits with pointed collars. Our faces are stiff, our smiles frozen. I remember how much I hated it – the dressing up, the lace and hairbows, the posing.

The house looks staged, ready for a magazine photo shoot. Anything messy is tucked away, out of sight. Beautiful woven baskets hide Alan's toys. Stacks of magazines and catalogs are stored in cabinets. The kitchen countertops are bare. The bedrooms are far removed from the center of the house – up a winding staircase, down long narrow hallways – so you can almost forget that people live within these walls. *Everything is in order here*, the house says. *Everything is fine.*

What the guests don't see is this: The people within the house are not fine.

I think about the blind idealism that drew my parents together without them ever really knowing one another. The parties they put on that made people think they were happy while their marriage was falling apart. How my mother dressed me up and showed me off, her perfect child. How William's birth was supposed to mend something, but no one could say exactly what or how. The way my parents both felt slippery and unknowable. Out of reach. The sense that things had been different once, better maybe, but that I'd never know for sure. I think of Alan. The before and the after, of all the debris. How could things ever be fine? There were too many feelings unspoken, too much lurking beneath the facade.

Alan is here. I smell him, the musky scent of the store-brand deodorant that he always slathered on too thickly. The mint of his toothpaste. My mother was always asking him to brush his teeth. Four, five times a day. He was a mouth breather. His breath quickly grew stale.

Peeking out from a basket on the entryway table, I see one

of his baseball caps and a stack of customer loyalty cards – for pet shops, mostly, but some for grocery stores or warehouse clubs. He carried them like credit cards and had memorized all the discounts and cashback points he'd earned with each one.

If ever there was a customer who deserved a loyalty card, it was Alan. As kids, we had to hide the phone book because he would scroll through and call all his favorite businesses: Dominos Pizza, the Buick dealership, Blockbuster Video. He booked himself haircuts, signed up to test drive cars (he wasn't eligible for a driver's license, let alone a car loan), and ordered pizzas without having money to pay for them. He'd call random homes and ask people whether they fed their pets Iams or Science Diet. (He hated Purina). He quizzed everyone on their shoe size, their height and weight, and wrote it down on a yellow legal pad. He could categorize the people in his life based on their sizes.

I don't know if he ever fully understood the purpose of the loyalty cards or that they weren't actually money, but he insisted on stuffing them in his back pocket. Every pair of his jeans had a faint rectangular outline where the stack wore through the denim fibers. I grab one card off the top and slip it into my palm, tracing the smooth edges with my thumb like one of those worry stones, hoping some of his energy, his wide-eye wonder and delight at the littlest things, might transfer to me.

No one seems to have noticed me come in, so I slip upstairs to his room. I sit down on the foot of his bed and take it all in. His picture books and photographs. His clothes. His toys. Something feels off. The room smells sanitized. His Matchbox cars are lined up neatly on his dresser, smallest to largest. Stuffed animals are arranged symmetrically against his head-board as if he's just out for the day. He'll be right back.

A quilt my mother made is folded in thirds at the foot of the bed. I run my fingers across the tight seams where the perfect little squares and triangles meet. I wonder if his bed was already made the night he died or if someone has been in here since then to clean. Alan didn't care if his room was tidy or not.

I can see his hands, his fingernails chewed down until they're bloody, an anxious habit my mother tried for years to break. We understand now that it was more than a bad habit. It was a compulsion. Obsessive-compulsive behavior is a hallmark of Prader-Willi Syndrome. The most common obsession is food, but many people with Prader-Willi also pick their own skin or bite their nails until they become raw and infected. It's as if Alan turned his anxiety and confusion against himself. A form of self-harm that was also self-protective, an outlet for his inner chaos.

Long before we had a medical framework to explain it, we knew Alan to be obsessive, tireless, myopic. He liked to talk about dogs, about movies, about cars, about food... and not much else. Along with loyalty cards and legal pads with phone numbers and shoe sizes, he was also extremely attached to his toys and liked to have them all visible in his room. Remote-controlled sports cars. A collection of stuffed Snoopy dolls. His portable music player and stacks of CDs. My mother saw this as clutter, an annoyance. I think to Alan, it was soothing. He needed his things, his fixations, like he needed air to breathe.

His obsessions could also be endearing. His ability to memorize everyone's shoe size was something of a party trick that Will and I showed off to our friends. His passion for dogs meant that he watched movies like *Lassie* and *Old Yeller* on repeat for hours, sometimes whole days at a time. He'd laugh every time a dog bounded onto the screen and fast forward the VHS through any sad parts. With one glance, he could identify the make, model, and year of almost any automobile. He'd repeat jokes he heard without understanding the punch line just to hear other people laugh. Because Alan's speech was slurred, I served as his interpreter, translating his questions for strangers, speaking on his behalf.

I close my eyes and see him now with his favorite toys strewn across the room. I see him clutching a stuffed bear like he is still five years old. *Gina, look*, he squeals, *He's so cute. Want to kiss the bear?*

When I open my eyes, he vanishes. I look around for him. Something's not right. The space is too perfect, even by my mother's standards. I move from Alan's bedroom to his bathroom and start opening all the drawers and cabinets. My heart rate climbs. I'm looking for something, but I can't be sure what, so I keep searching. There's toothpaste and shampoo and an electric shaver. I open the medicine cabinet, but it's empty. I want to see what medication he was taking when he died, but I know my mother wouldn't have kept it here within his reach. I draw back the shower curtain. I look in the trash can. Nothing. I'm disappointed, though I can't say why.

My phone vibrates in my back pocket.

Are you here?

Will's text flashes on the screen.

Mom's looking for you.

I make my way back to the center of the house, where the misfits are mingling. My mother, in the middle of this constellation, is stalling. I recognize it on her face immediately, her mouth a thin line, the crease between her eyebrows deepening. The way her voice takes on a tone that doesn't match her expression or the mood of the room.

"Oh! Gina is here," she says, approaching me and leaning in for an awkward side hug. Her shoulders are rigid. Affection never flowed naturally between us. She asks for my help pulling a serving platter off a high shelf, then turns her attention back to the guests.

"Nothing's getting done," Will tells me in angry whispers when I find him in the crowd. "Look," he points to our parents. "They're talking with everyone else except one another because they can't agree on anything," he says. It's been nearly four days, and no one has scheduled the funeral. We've all flown in from across the country to say goodbye, to get on with the complicated business of grieving. We ask them when the service will be. We're all here now, so what can we do to help?

Will tells me he heard them arguing earlier about what to do with Alan's remains, whether he should be embalmed, if the casket should be open or closed, or whether it's better if he's cremated.

I feel bad that Will has been left alone to witness this – the tension between our parents, their avoidance, the heavy questions of what to do with Alan's body. I want to tell him to walk away, to get some rest, to eat something. I want to assure him that it's not our obligation to intervene and fix everything. But if I'm being honest, I still feel the tug of obligation too. I rushed to Will's aid when he texted me, didn't I?

My mother contradicts. She delays. She offers us bowls of chili and homemade chocolate chip cookies that she keeps in the freezer for those times when company drops by and you have nothing to serve. She almost seems happy to have an excuse to thaw them out and entertain guests. We're all here, the way she always wanted.

I can't remember the last time we were all in the same place together. And so peacefully. I watch my mother and my step-mother standing shoulder to shoulder at the sink washing dishes, the lemon scent of Joy dish soap wafting over them as if this is what they have always done, as if Mom didn't ever threaten to call the police if my stepmother so much as set foot on our driveway.

She starts offering up Alan's belongings. She cannot decide when to hold his funeral or what to do with his body, but would I like to have his collection of DVDs? Do the kids want his toys? Here, take this. Have that.

It's too much. The lightness. The good behavior. The social graces. I don't know what I expected, whether I would be more satisfied to see my family in shambles. But I think it would feel more honest than this.

As a child, I could deny. I could swallow my pain, shutter it away, bury it. I could smile, placate my parents, step in, and make decisions when they floundered. I could do that then. But continents drift apart and become their own geographies. The physical distance I've gained over the years has created an emotional shift, a fault line. Those buried parts of me have begun to rise to the surface, creating rivers, mountains, and valleys. What allowed me to survive back there no longer serves me. I'm a citizen of a different country.

I feel the tears welling up, and I excuse myself. I walk out the front door and as far away from the house as possible to a cluster of aspen trees. I want to shriek, to shake the paperwhite trunks and pound my fists. Instead, I swallow it all down until my stomach churns. I weep. My body heaves. I drop to my knees and vomit. I wipe the corners of my mouth with the hem of my shirt and stand up straight.

On my way back inside the house, I bump into my father. He pulls me aside and puts a hand on my shoulder. *She's not being reasonable,* he says. *Can you talk to her? Can you and Will try to talk some sense into her?*

"No. I don't think I can," I tell him and walk away.

As I see it, this is their final act of parenting – to be in the same room, to sit down and decide what should happen to their son now that he is dead. To figure out what they want as his mother and father, how they want to honor him.

What I don't say is this: *I will not parent for you. Not again. Not anymore.*

Chapter Eight

Atlanta, 1982.

The first time I hear my mother say she wants to die, I'm six years old. She is in the kitchen, slamming cupboards open and shut. Will and Alan are in bed, and I am supposed to be too, but I can hear the banging and can't sleep. I creep down the hallway and to the bottom of the stairs where I have a direct view across the den and into the kitchen. I sit, pull my knees to my chest and hug my legs tightly. She never knows I am there.

She rifles through the cabinets, looking for something to eat and cursing. Earlier in the day, Alan went on a binge and ate most of what we had in the pantry—bread and peanut butter, potato chips, cereal, and crackers, plus Mom's stash of freeze-dried diet food on which she had splurged with her last paycheck.

"Those goddamn kids," she curses through clenched teeth. "I should never have had those goddamn kids."

This is something I've heard her say before, under her breath, or in anger to my father, but with a *we*, as in "we shouldn't have had these goddamn kids." As if the kids were the problem all along and not simply the magnifying glass through which all my parents' issues were amplified. But this feels different. What she is saying now has a darker, more desperate tone. I shiver and hold my legs tighter. I can't make sense of it at this age, but I am afraid.

She bangs the last cabinet shut and crumples into a heap on the linoleum floor, buries her head in her hands, and sobs. "That fucking bastard left me with no money and three goddamn kids," she wails. "I should just die. I just want to die. Please, God, let me die!"

My heart races. I want to help her get up off the floor but don't dare speak or move. I can see her there, her hands shaking, her back heaving as she cries. The sounds that emerge from her are guttural, bellowing. I don't understand how it could happen, but I believe that if my mother wills herself to die, she will die. Right there in the middle of the kitchen floor, she will stop breathing and just disappear.

It is like watching a porcelain vase fall from a ledge, knowing that no matter how quickly you spring, you can never catch it in time.

She is shattering. All I can do is watch and wait and try to help her hold the pieces together a little longer.

• • •

Boulder, August 14, 2016.

Back inside the house, I tap my mother's husband Mike on the shoulder. I'm depleted. I want to leave the gathering and take a hot shower and go to sleep until Kris and the kids arrive, but it continues to nag at me, this notion that, left unattended, my mother will self-destruct, that she needs to be saved from herself. It's an old feeling, one that should have expired long ago.

People say you develop more compassion for your parents once you have your own children. I'm a mother now. I understand overwhelm, the feeling that you'll never be able to juggle it all. I understand wondering if you've lost pieces of yourself forever. Your youth, your independence. I understand fleeting moments of despair. I know about tedium, apathy. I understand wanting to close your eyes and sleep for days. I also know that these feelings are fluid, temporary, that they won't consume me, that the joys of parenthood outweigh the pains.

I have a good friend who suffers from bouts of major depression and suicidal ideation. She has never harmed herself, but in her darkest moments, she told me, she's imagined in vivid detail a dozen ways she could die. The morbid images comfort her, she says, like a back door she can slip through to escape her anguish. I asked her once, where does it come from, this idea that you might be better off dead? She told me it's the lie of depression. The illness whispers in your ear and tells you that you are so awful, so broken that the world would be better off without you. Suicide is not an act of selfishness, she said. It's desperation. A cruel fallacy. It's your mind tricking you into believing you'd be doing everyone a favor.

I've used my friend's words, held them close in an attempt to empathize with my mother. But my mother's depression seems more nuanced, more confusing to me. Her moods are erratic, unpredictable. Her despair has a different tenor. Growing up, I never heard her say we'd be better off without her. It was more like she believed that her kids were slowly killing her. It was our fault. We ruined her. Her dreams were destroyed, and she wanted life to be over already. My mother talked about dying so frequently and with such intensity that something shifted within me. In my mind, she began to disappear, to wither. I felt powerless to stop it.

From a young age, though I don't remember exactly how or

when, I grieved the loss of my mother. My letting go may have started when I was a toddler, when I realized her attention was focused on Alan and my father. But the bereavement amplified as I grew older and watched her disappear into herself. This was the paradox: Even as I fought hard to ease her burden and keep her alive, I resigned myself to her dying. At some point, she was gone. She became dead to me.

As an adult, I can sympathize with my mother's position – divorced, alone with three children (one with special needs), working odd jobs, trying to hold onto a house she really couldn't afford. I sketch a scene in my mind, close my eyes, and walk into it briefly, and I feel constricted, trapped. I feel a surge of sadness, of compassion. But I struggle to put myself in the next scene, the one in which she repeats these phrases like a daily prayer: *I have nothing to live for. You're killing me. This is the end of me. I can't go on anymore. Not one more minute. It's all your fault.* She said these things in relation to my father leaving. She said it every time her paycheck ran out. When Alan ate the last of our food. She said it when she lost her job, when a friend snubbed her, when a boyfriend dumped her, when her car wouldn't start, when bill collectors called. She said it when I moved out, and when I refused to come back home.

I just want to die.

Alan's death feels so much bigger than all the previous grievances that drove her to the edge. I can't be sure that there's not still something inside her that would make her finally tumble into the abyss.

"Can I talk to you?"

Mike follows me into the hallway, out of earshot of the guests.

"Keep an eye on Sharon," I tell him.

I started calling my mother by her first name in my early teens. It was practical. By then, with Alan's incessant begging for food, she'd learned to tune out the word "Mom." Calling her name worked. Later, I continued to call her Sharon because I realized she did not feel like a mom to me. Our roles had long been reversed.

"She seems ok," Mike says. "I'm not sure I can do anything. She doesn't want to talk much about it."

"Just," I stammer. "Just be careful. Don't leave her alone." I look down and walk away. I don't want to see whether his face registers confusion or recognition or concern. I don't know what he's seen, what he knows. I don't want to learn the inner workings of their marriage or how he handles her periods of darkness. I just want to know that someone other than me is responsible for pulling her back from the edge this time.

Chapter Nine

Atlanta, 1984.

At eight or nine years old, I'm not consciously thinking about lightening the burden for my mother. I'm not capable of being a martyr. I am a kid. Alan is almost twelve. William is six. We're all kids.

I'm aware that my mother wants to be dead sometimes. I am aware that she needs to sleep off the darkness, that she can't find the energy to prepare meals or clean or bathe my brothers. But these things need to be done. Someone needs to do laundry and feed us. So, I help where and when I can.

To be clear: This is a role I enjoy.

Picture it. A young girl is playing house. She is the mommy, and she gets to be in charge. Not just for a short time, like after school or on a playdate, but all day, every day. Her brothers are willing players, allowing her to read to them, to tie their shoes, to feed them, to tuck them in and gently kiss their foreheads goodnight.

This is me. I have seen a need, and I have willingly stepped into position. It's as if one of the fantasy worlds that Will and I imagined with our stuffed animals has come to life. In the beginning, I relish it.

Where is my mother all this time I'm taking care of my brothers? I can't always be sure. She's in bed resting. She is "out." She is on a date. She is running errands. She is crying on her friends' couches. I notice that her appearance changes. She's in her bathrobe and curlers. She's wearing fancy shift dresses and red lipstick. Her hair is curly and then straight. She buys a home perm kit and makes it curly again. Then the dresses are gone, and she starts wearing tracksuits with an elastic waist. She is earning extra cash cleaning bathrooms at the local church. She is sitting on the floor of her shower, her round body enveloped in a cloud of steam. She's standing on the bathroom scale and crying. She's attending weight loss classes and singles clubs. Sometimes she is driving around Atlanta, touring smaller houses we might move into to save money on the mortgage, though we never actually do. She asks me to lie when people call the house and tell them she's not home. Sometimes I lie and tell them she is there when she isn't because I'm afraid of being alone.

I teach myself to use the Hoover self-driving vacuum. I push my bangs over to the side and secure them with a plastic bunny-shaped barrette. I kick off my Kangaroo sneakers and place them neatly by the front door so as not to track in more dirt. And then I practice making long, even lines across the carpet with the vacuum the way I've seen my mother do on her happier days. I dust the tables with lemon-scented Pledge and water the houseplants to keep them alive. I cook toast and scrambled eggs. I like it when the jam on the toast touches the eggs and makes them sweet, but my brothers prefer their food to be separate. So, I separate it for them.

Before he left, my dad taught me how to crack an egg so that the shell doesn't fall into the bowl. He showed me how to stir in a little milk. "Just a splash," he said. "It makes the eggs fluffier." A little salt and pepper. "Don't overcook them," he said. "Turn off the heat while they're still glistening."

These are some of the closest memories of my childhood. I channel my father, all the warmth I remember from before he left. I become the mommy I wish my mommy could be. My brothers are my babies.

Will is a sweet kid. He has fair skin, almost translucent, that flushes red when he's angry or sad. He has a baby doll named Ralph that he cradles and kisses on the cheek when he thinks no one is watching. He collects caterpillars in a wooden box and gingerly feeds them blades of grass. He is tender-hearted, not just at home, but at school. He's not good at base-ball or soccer. He can't catch. He's afraid of the ball flying toward him, and so from an early age, other boys make fun of him. If he cries, they tease him even more. They call him Mama's Boy and Cry Baby.

On sunny afternoons, I march my brothers into the backyard and tell them we're playing a game I call "Explorer." It's loosely inspired by *Peter Pan* but also by the glossy photos in my dad's *National Geographic* magazines. We are explorers in Africa. Russia. South America. India. Australia. Alan's job is to draw a treasure map. I hand him a box of Crayola crayons and a stack of construction paper. He starts scribbling. Will's job is to fend off intruders. I hand him a broomstick. I play lookout, using old binoculars to peek at our neighbors through the trees. We build lean-tos out of downed tree branches. Alan fetches our rations, sleeves of graham crackers or bags of potato chips, eating most of them himself. We attempt to dig holes to

China with Mom's garden trowel. We fight off pirates with rakes. At dusk, we collect fireflies (Tinkerbells) in old peanut butter jars.

Once, on a day my mother has been in bed for hours, after she yells at us for being too loud and making a mess, I find a length of nylon rope and tie Will to a tree trunk, declaring him the enemy. "You're a spy," I tell him. "You can't be trusted anymore."

He whimpers as I cinch the rope tighter. I'm aware I might be hurting him, but I don't care. I'm angry at something, at someone, but I can't articulate what or who. I wrap the rope around him one, two, three times. The rhythm is satisfying.

"Ow!" Will screams. "Stop it! I'm a good guy!" I ignore his pleas until I'm done tying the ends of the rope in a fat knot. Then I walk around the tree and look at his face and see that he's bawling. He's tied so tightly to the tree trunk that he can barely move his arms. My sense of triumph evaporates. I feel a gut punch of guilt and start bawling too. "I'm so sorry," I say, my breath stuttering, my hands scrambling to loosen the rope.

Alan, hearing our cries, starts sobbing too, which makes me feel even worse. "You're not in trouble, Alan. It's my fault." I free Will and hug him and Alan close. I run my hands up and down his arms, which are red with rope burn. *What was I thinking?* "I won't do that again. I promise."

From then on, I vow to protect Will. From my anger and confusion. From our mother's sadness. From all the bad guys he might encounter in the world.

One day I see him weeping on the playground during recess. He's alone on a swing, his head slumped forward, his feet dragging back and forth, carving lines in the sand. I rush over and pat him on the back. I squat down to his eye level, pull him close, and whisper in his ear, "Save all your crying for after school. You can cry with me, and I'll hug you." I use the cuff of my sleeve to wipe the tears from his face. "Out here you have to be strong. Pretend like you don't care what they say."

What I don't tell him, but soon will realize, is that we also have to hide our tears at home. Home is where we really have to be strong.

By taking care of my brothers, I also take care of my mom. I believe I can ease her burden and make her well. While she is in a tailspin, I can be calm. This is my strength.

I am the helper. I can quiet my needs and nurture others. It makes things easier for everyone.

Those mornings after her bad nights when she says she wants to be dead, I sneak her address book into my backpack and carry it to school. I grab loose change from her dresser, and I go to the payphone by the attendance office. I thumb through the book until I reach a name I know, her friend Karen or maybe Leanne. I call them and tell them she's feeling sad and ask if they will check on her today, maybe take her out to lunch?

Around this time, Alan's behavior is still manageable. He's not reached puberty yet. Or maybe it's just starting. Sometimes I think I see him start to change. He has what I call "the fits." His face is slack, calm. He's watching television next to me or playing with toy cars on the coffee table, driving them back and forth, back and forth. His arms are fluid, moving with ease. Then I see it, his left hand slowly drawing to a fist, his biceps tightening. He's winding up. He pounds the table, just once, but hard. The toy cars jump. Magazines slide to the floor. I recoil. I ask him if he's okay. I ask him what's wrong. He doesn't answer. He stares at me. His forehead scrunches, eyes cross, then his whole face relaxes again. He resumes playing as if nothing happened.

I think about how it might feel to be inside Alan's body. I look at my own body. My brain tells my arm to move. My arm bends and straightens. My brain tells my legs to cross and uncross. My brain tells me to stand up. Tells my feet to stay firmly planted on the floor. I'm not sure how, but my brain also tells me when the atmosphere is tense. Maybe I detect the smell of adrenaline, pheromones. The smell of instability, like sweat and musk. My brain tells me when it's best to stay still, breathe slowly and wait for the tension to clear.

I wonder what Alan's brain tells his body. Does his fist operate independently? Does it strike the table on its own? Is it an involuntary muscle movement like breathing? What does his brain tell him when his eyes look down and see the mess his fist created?

He thinks I'm older than him. He calls me "Big Sister." In a few years, he'll understand that I'm not, and he'll start to wonder why I can do so many things that he can't. He'll rage against me. But for now, he just accepts things the way they are. He likes it when I make dinners of canned corned beef hash, toast, and eggs. He licks his plate and asks for more. If I don't watch him, he'll eat until he's sick, and then he'll eat even more. He doesn't know when to stop. Our refrigerator is often bare. He sneaks food at night. He cries, "My tummy hurts, Gina, make it stop." I rub his belly in a circular motion, something I watched one of the doctors do. He cries when his belly is empty and cries when it's full.

He asks me to comb his hair. It calms him. I wet the comb and drag it across his dark brown bangs. Again and again until I see his shoulders relax. His hair is very fine; it goes where I ask it to go. Alan's eyes are big and brown, like a puppy or fawn. They stand out against his pale skin.

Sometimes I sing him a song. He likes nursery rhymes but also songs from movies like *Annie* or *Chitty Chitty Bang Bang*.

"Sing louder," he tells me. "No, louder!" he insists. He likes things to be big and loud. Sometimes I dance too and make him laugh. I am proud that I can make him laugh. I feel powerful, like I have the ability to take his pain away, to make us feel like normal kids, even if it's only for a short while.

Chapter Ten

August 14, 2016.

"We're in Colorado. You have options," I say, taking a sip of my beer.

We're sitting on the patio of a brewery, William and I, nibbling on a rubbery cheese pizza and drinking craft beers with names like "Rascal," "Two Hearted," and "Mothership." It's a typical summer afternoon in Boulder, maybe eighty degrees, but it feels much hotter. The altitude makes the sun feel more intense. I'm keeping an eye on the mountains to the west of us, looking for dark clouds. Throughout the summer, thunderstorms will gather behind the ridgeline all morning, dropping rain or sometimes hail by mid-afternoon. As quickly as the storms appear, they dissipate, and the sun blazes again. This gives rise to a saying by the locals: If you don't like the weather, just wait five minutes.

I'm thankful to have this distraction. The sunshine. The scenery. The beer. Time with Will. He and I try to talk on the phone every couple of months or so, but summer has kept us busy. We're overdue for a visit.

I poke at the orange slice floating in my glass and watch it bob and sway like a life raft. We're killing time, waiting for our spouses and kids to arrive to support us in whatever this week holds, waiting for someone to tell us what we're supposed to do next. We're existing in a cloud, a gap, the space between what has already happened and what happens next.

Things are okay and not okay. Will is in pain.

He's been updating me on his work, his wife, the latest house projects he's been dreaming about but will probably never complete. He wants to renovate his kitchen, replace the tile countertops with stone and repaint the cabinets. I try to imagine this, my scrawny little brother wielding a hammer or paintbrush, dipping a sponge into a bucket as he wipes away grout from tile. He's smart, but not handy. He told me he once ventured up to his attic and fell through the ceiling into his living room, nearly landing on his wife who was watching TV on the couch. Turns out all his broken dishes and botched chores from our childhood weren't just an act to shirk responsibility. He really is clumsy around the house.

Still, it's something to talk about, like the weather. Not important, but safe, a topic that has nothing to do with Alan or our parents or the funeral they haven't planned.

I'm due some vacation, he's telling me. *I have to take time off this fall.*

He stops and grimaces, clutching his jaw, hunched over and unable to speak for a full minute.

"Sorry," he says, straightening up and wiping his mouth with a napkin. "It comes out of nowhere." It's like a jolt of electricity, he says, when he's speaking or chewing. He thought at first it was a toothache, but every dentist he's seen says his teeth are fine. It's something else, a nerve in his jaw, or maybe a muscle spasm, going off like an alarm several times a day. No obvious trigger.

"I've been popping Advil like candy," he says. "It doesn't really help."

He's worried about getting through this week – the funeral, delivering a eulogy, all the long conversations with relatives we haven't seen in years.

He doubles over again. His anguish might as well be a mirror for how we're feeling inside. But *this pain,* I think, *at least this kind of pain has a remedy.*

"We can fix this," I tell him.

"What do you mean?"

"I mean drugs, Will. Pain relief. We can buy you some weed."

Once he sees that I'm not joking, he considers the idea and dismisses it. "I'll be fine," he says. "I don't want to regret anything I say or do this week."

"That's bullshit," I say. "I think you get a hall pass."

Will has always been a rule follower. One reaction to the chaos we experienced growing up was to overachieve, to be as perfect as we could be, to make up for every one of Alan's limitations. In high school, a friend gave me a six-pack of Zima and asked me to keep it safe for her. I stashed it in the back of my closet for two days until the guilt overwhelmed me, and I finally carried it downstairs and presented it to my mother, *Here take these. I don't want them.*

With Alan gone, the balance feels weighted to my side. Any sense of responsibility I've felt has evaporated. I finish my second beer and order another. I hate being drunk. I don't like feeling out of control. But something inside me is breaking. Alan is dead, and I didn't get to say goodbye. The thread that connected my big brother and me was hard for anyone to understand, but it was real. Our relationship was real. And now it's over without warning. I'm tired of being careful. A part of me wants to unravel. But I don't know how, and I don't want to do it alone.

"You can just try an edible, and if it helps, great. If not, then you can stutter your way through the funeral in agony," I say, finally. He looks at me as if he's trying to read my face, like he's not sure whether to take me seriously.

My head is throbbing and Will and I are still bickering an hour later when we meet up with my dad for coffee.

Meeting up with Dad feels surprisingly normal. Over the years, our relationship has been breezy, episodic, not unlike the visits we had with him after the divorce. I see him when he comes to Phoenix for conferences, during layovers, when he has a few hours or days to spare. He takes Kris and me to dinner. We sip wine in the lobby of his hotel. My kids swim in the pool. They play games on his iPad. He snuggles them and reads them books in much the same way I remember him reading to me.

The secret to loving my dad, I've learned, is not to expect too much. I savor the moments I have with him, even if they're years apart. With every encounter, I gather pieces of my father and try to fit them together like a puzzle. I try to see the full picture of who he is today and who he was before—before he met my mother, before Alan was born, before I came along, before the family imploded. What I know: He's still an academic, stoic and rational, but he also rides (fancy, Italian) motorcycles, participates in civil rights protests, and makes pasta from scratch. He listens to classical music, 70s rock, and bubblegum pop like Katy Perry. He still loves to read. We share book recommendations now. I know that his face lights up when he sees Will and me walking toward him. What I don't know: Whether he has regrets about leaving us, about leaving me.

I collect memories of him. I always have. The day he left my mother, I hid in the coat closet and memorized the coarse texture of his tweed blazer. I ran my index finger along the rim of his wooden pipe, recognizing the oily feel, the warm, sweet smell. Tobacco. I was five, too young to know what it was called.

I remember him in his green recliner, the way I used to tuck under his arm just so, my head on his chest, his heart tha-thumping in my ear. I remember how strange his voice sounded when he shouted, the slam of a door, the vibration of picture frames on the wall, the putter of a diesel engine as he drove away. And later on, his voice again, muffled through the phone's receiver. He was never close or loud again.

"What's worse, Dad? Being slightly stoned at a funeral or doubling over in pain, unable to speak?" I ask.

"Are we speaking hypothetically?" In every situation, Dad is a professor first, inquisitive, analytical. But I think I see a glint in his eye, like a 1960s pot-smoking idealist inside him is shining through.

As if on cue, William clutches his jaw and moans.

"I want to buy Will some weed," I say. "Want to come along?"

My father nods. "Uh, sure," he says as if I'd just asked him if he wants to go see a movie.

Before long, we're scrolling on our phones, reading online reviews of marijuana dispensaries. According to the map, there are three within a mile radius of where we're standing.

"This one gets four stars for customer service," I say, "and it's only two blocks away."

The dispensary is located above a Mexican restaurant. My dad holds the door for us. We climb a flight of stairs and enter a vestibule that has a tall desk, like a bank teller's. The air is warm and heavy with the smell of skunk and tacos. A man, maybe early thirties, is behind the desk and greets us warmly.

"Welcome! First time here? I just need to see your IDs before you can go in."

We hand over our driver's licenses. The guy examines them closely and then studies our faces.

"You all related?" he asks with a smirk. "Is this like a family field trip to the dispensary?"

"Yeah. Something like that," my dad says.

"Great! I'll be your budtender today."

"Budtender?" I stifle a laugh.

The clerk leads us into the shop, a square room that's framed with glass cases, like a deli or bakery. Inside the first case are trays of dried green bud labeled with botanical names and places of origin. Short descriptions read like wine-tasting notes: Earthy. Floral. Nutty. Smooth. Burnt. Potent.

Inside the next case are chocolate bars, hard candies, and gummy bears. Beyond that are rows and rows of cookies, energy bars, syrups, taffy, and granola. There are pre-rolled joints and small glass bottles of oils, waxes, and extracts. One shelf contains beautiful hand-blown glass pipes with vibrant multicolor swirls.

"It's cash only," the guy says, pointing to a sign that says CASH ONLY in big green letters accented with a sketch of a pot leaf.

We begin to look around awkwardly at first and then start browsing with more confidence.

"The edibles have a wide range of potency," he explains. "If you tell me what you're looking for, I can suggest some products."

Will proceeds to describe the pain he's feeling and the relief he'd like to feel. He doesn't want to be so numb that he can't function, he says, but could use a little something to take the edge off. The clerk suggests a lollipop or hard candy. "They offer a slow, steady release."

While Will gets situated, I'm staring at a tin of honey-flavored lozenges called Chill Pills. The label says they're great for anxiety. They're also organic, which somehow makes them more appealing.

"Those are perfection," the clerk says. "They're made with CBD and a strain of Indica that's really smooth. Plus, they're low dose and not very psychoactive, so you won't feel high. Just really, really chill."

I turn the container over and over in my palm.

We make our final choices, and my dad offers to pay, as if he's buying us ice cream cones at the fair. It's endearing and awkward at the same time.

That night, as I walk up the sidewalk toward my mother's front door for a second time, I pop a Chill Pill in my mouth. I feel rebellious. Kris and the kids will be here soon enough, I tell myself. I just have to get by until then. The Chill Pill tastes strange, like sour honey. I maneuver it under my tongue and sense the effects kicking in.

I ring the doorbell, confident that for at least a little while, I won't have to feel much of anything.

Dinner has been laid out, a buffet of cold cuts, veggie trays, and casseroles. For a moment I worry about Alan with all this food out in the open. *He won't be able to control himself. He'll make himself sick.* I look around to make sure he's not in danger. Then, I remember. He's not here.

My mother greets me briefly. No hug. Instead, she directs me to the buffet.

I haven't eaten much the past few days, and for the first time, I notice I'm hungry. I walk the length of the food table, loading my paper plate until it almost buckles. I grab a fork, find a quiet corner, sit down, and scan the room as I eat.

My mother's friends circle around her. It's like a strange dance. They pat her back and squeeze her arms. They tend to her needs. Mom looks at ease, as if she's rehearsed this. She smiles weakly. She laughs a little. They laugh a little. She offers everyone more food. For a moment, briefly, over the rim of my wine glass, I catch my mother staring at me with contempt. Her eyes bore into me, her lip curls. She doesn't want me here, I think. Maybe she's angry with me. Maybe I'm a reminder of something she's trying to forget. The look is quick, a flash, but it sends a jolt of electricity through my body. Did anyone else notice it?

My eyes feel especially sharp like I can see everything that's happening in the room, even behind me.

Her friends. What do they know? Do they know I haven't seen or spoken with my mother in years? Do they wonder why? What has she told them about me? About us?

For a moment I consider that my mother is a very different person to them than she is to me. I can see it. She is a good friend. She is generous, kind, funny and supportive. That is true. Their experience of her is true.

But their experience has not been my experience. She is not the same person to me that she is to them. Their friendship may be real, but it does not compensate for or erase the mother she was to me and my brothers growing up or the woman she has been to me as an adult. My experience is also true.

In a split second, in a sideways glance, I make the decision to let this go. Part of me wants her friends to confront me so that I can tell them my truth. Tell them to be careful. Tell them what I know about this woman they adore. Another part is relieved that no one asks.

Everyone is polite. I feel eerily calm. I smile the placid smile you smile after someone has died. I hold their gaze warmly for the tiniest of moments, as if to say, I see you.

I accept you being here in your role, as a support for my mother.

But I know they don't see me, not fully. How can they? There's so much they don't know. So much I'm sure my mother would never say.

Chapter Eleven

Atlanta, 1986.

By the time I am ten or eleven, I spend several nights a week cooking dinner for my brothers and nagging them to get their pajamas on and get into bed. Even on nights my mom is at home, she is too exhausted to care for us. She asks me to help out — doing dishes, folding laundry, cleaning the bathroom.

It's no longer a game.

William keeps to himself. He likes to read chapter books and create imaginary worlds in his bedroom, assigning roles to each of his action figures and stuffed animals. I hear him through his closed door, acting out intergalactic wars or recreating scenes from J.R.R. Tolkien's *The Hobbit*, which he listens to on cassette tape. My dad mailed us the whole set. At eight, Will is too young to help much with chores, and when he does, he often creates more work – putting dishes away in the wrong cupboards, jamming the vacuum cleaner by sucking up pennies, pouring too much soap in the washing machine so that it overflows. He also has a TV in his room and falls asleep with it on most nights. He mostly stays out of the way, and that is fine by me.

Alan, on the other hand, doesn't understand why his younger sister is in charge. He stands at least a foot taller than me now and seventy pounds heavier. A teenage surge of testosterone has given him round biceps and broad shoulders, but his mind is still five years old. If I tell him to go to bed or remind him he can't have candy for dinner, he responds with a five-year-old's temper tantrum. At first, it isn't anything I can't handle. He throws himself on the floor or storms off to his room crying, and I let him be. Eventually, the more I enforce the house rules, the more defiant Alan becomes. He cries and shoves me away. The threat of my telling mom is enough to stop him at first, but more and more, Alan grows bold and violent. I follow through on my threats and tell Mom when Alan hits me or shoves me. But she often dismisses my fears, saying that we'll have to work it out ourselves.

"It's just a phase, Gina. I don't have time to referee," she says. She doesn't yet know that violence is a symptom of Prader-Willi, that left unmitigated, the surges of testosterone will overload Alan's brain like a circuit board. The inability to regulate hormones is part of the condition. Once Alan reaches adolescence, that fuse will blow. Over and over again, he will continue to explode.

Alan begins to understand that he isn't being punished for hitting me, and so he becomes brasher. If I block his way to the refrigerator or try to change the channel on the television or catch him sneaking food – or, most often, if I step in to prevent him from hitting William – he lashes out at me. He punches fast and hard. I am quick and can dodge most of the blows. But sometimes he grabs my arm and pulls it backwards, or he picks up the nearest book and throws it at my head. Most of the time he misses. But not always.

One night, I pass him on the stairs and remind him to brush his teeth before bed. His eyes are on me, and I immediately think better of saying anything. He has been grouchy all afternoon and evening, saying he misses Mom, and he has refused to do anything I ask. Will even stepped in to help me several times – trying to gently persuade Alan to do what he was told, helping him pick out his pajamas, and clearing his dinner plate for him. None of it seems to diffuse Alan's mood, and part of me knows it would probably be best if I just locked myself in my room and let Mom deal with the situation when she gets home.

I am so entrenched in my mothering role, however, that I don't always know when to back off. I don't like the chaos of no one being in charge. So I persist with the bedtime routine.

Alan's shoulders twitch, and before I can move, he reaches out and grabs my hair and pulls me to the ground like a dog on a leash. My cheek bounces off the thick shag carpet, and a warm pain creeps across my temple and scalp. He's pulling harder, and I begin to feel my hair ripping out, strand by strand. His shirt collar is in my hands, and I yank it until the seam rips. I beg him to stop and reach up to brace my hair, pulling it back to relieve the tension. It is a brutal tug of war.

As quickly as it began, it is over. He drags me several feet, then drops me and kicks me in the ribs, knocking the wind out of me.

Years later I'll try to remember how I felt in this moment, ribs bruised, scalp bleeding. I'm vaguely aware that my brother can kill me if he wants to – or even if he doesn't want to. He's capable of beating me to death. Someday, that realization will make me weep. But for now, I'm numb. I'm surviving. I'm disoriented and confused. Because, despite his rage, Alan is often unaware of his own strength. So when he looks down and sees me cowering and crying, he immediately tries to hug me, saying "I'm sorry. Don't cry. I'm sorry." His remorse is genuine.

I scramble to my feet and run to my room, lock the door, and collapse in bed shaking. *Why is he like this? Why can't I stop him? Where is Mom when I need her?* I look over at the row of porcelain dolls lined up on my bookshelf. Smiling, unbroken, untouchable. I imagine myself grabbing one by her hair, smashing her into a wall.

I long to call my dad and tell him to come get me, but he now lives several states away. Besides, I have often threatened to call Dad when my mom doesn't take my complaints about Alan seriously. She tells me that I am being dramatic, exaggerating. And anyway, if I do call, she says, Dad will stop sending us money, and he'll take us away from her, and she will have no one, and that the thought of being alone makes her want to die.

In other words, to save myself would mean killing her.

Alan's tantrums evolve into unpredictable rage and destructiveness. In a flash, he can go from sitting peacefully watching television to throwing a chair through a plate glass window. I know the term "plate glass" only because my mother explained it to me the first time he broke our sliding glass door. She warned me that people had been killed by sheets of broken glass falling from their frames. So, if Alan were to ever break a window again (which he does), Will and I should stay away from the glass until she gets home to clean it up. She doesn't need any of us losing limbs.

I can't hate Alan, though. No matter how much he hurts me, I know it's not what he wants to do. I am angry. I am exhausted. I am fearful. I am confused by the wild swings in his behavior. But I understand this much: He is no more in control of his body than I am. When he calms down, when he cries and tells me he's sorry, I tell him I'm sorry too.

Chapter Twelve

Boulder, August 15, 2016.

Cause and effect are not simple concepts. This is what I know: Alan died because his heart stopped. But what caused his heart to stop? If I trace the line back through my mother's words, I know that before his heart stopped, he had what appeared to be a seizure. Appeared only to her because she said it happened in the car on the way to the hospital. Did the doctors witness any of it? Did they think it was a seizure? And if I trace the line back further, what caused the seizure? An asthma attack, according to my mother. The asthma attack came first and then the medication used to try to stop the asthma attack and then the seizure and then the heart stopped and then death. But something had to have triggered the asthma attack. So, what is the cause and what is the effect? Where does the chain of events begin and end?

My dad once spent a year teaching computer science at the University of Padua in Italy. Founded in 1222, Padua is known for being the fifth oldest surviving university in the world. It's the place where Galileo was a professor of mathematics around the turn of the 17th century. Galileo used mathematics to demonstrate cause and effect relationships for all sorts of phenomena, such as how quickly objects of different sizes and weights fall through space and time. It's here where classical science latched on to the principle of causality. The law of cause and effect also has roots in Greek philosophy, Hebrew belief, and Buddhism. My dad taught me as a young child to question everything, to examine every theory, to think critically, to look for the root cause.

If I am like my father, why isn't he asking the same questions I am? It puzzles me that he's not more curious about Alan's cause of death. Is this not what he taught me?

"His heart just failed," he told me, as if the heart is also an experiment, an object that falls through the cracks of space and time.

According to the Centers for Disease Control and Prevention (CDC), a natural cause of death is anything that isn't a non-natural cause of death. By this definition, it's easier to define non-natural causes, which include accidents, homicide, suicide, accidental poisoning, and drowning. Under "natural causes," the CDC reports nearly fifty categories of diseases and ailments with dozens of subcategories. I can imagine that many of the "natural" causes feel very unnatural to the family members who grieve the loss: Sudden Infant Death Syndrome. Cancer. Influenza. Heart defects.

Unless someone dies peacefully of old age, you could argue that no death is really natural.

It's not unusual for people with Prader-Willi Syndrome to have other medical problems. The most common issues stem from obesity since those with PWS struggle to control their food intake. Diabetes and high blood pressure are common. If left unchecked, this can lead to heart disease. Studies show a high incidence of psychological problems among Prader-Willi patients too. Specifically, they tend to suffer from mood disorders, obsessive-compulsive disorder, or psychotic episodes. In all my research, I haven't found a correlation between Prader-Willi and asthma.

In the past seven years, Alan has been hospitalized five times that I'm aware of, possibly more. My mother used to include me in the group emails she'd send to family and friends detailing his latest medical crises. He choked on some food. He developed pneumonia. He reacted poorly to new doses of medication. A caregiver gave him Claritin-D instead of the Claritin he typically takes, and it interacted poorly with his other medication. He had a seizure. He had a cyst. He needed exploratory surgery.

Come quick, it's Alan.

The outpouring of sympathy and support is generous. People offer to visit, to bring meals, to do all the things people do when a loved one is ill. I respond to the emails with curiosity. Can you tell me more about what his doctor said? What caused the seizure? Who changed his medication? How did he choke? Can I talk with Alan directly? I'd love to see him, I say. I send Alan letters and photographs. I forward Sharon's emails to my father and ask him, *What do you think of all this? Can you call the doctors and find out more?*

What I really want to know but am afraid to ask: Which of Alan's medical issues are preventable? And which are inevitable? Choking? A missed dose of medication? Pneumonia? What categories would these fall under? What is natural, and what is unnatural?

At some point, Sharon stops copying me on the emails. There are additional hospitalizations that I'm only aware of because Will or Dad tell me about them after the fact.

What I do know: My father has remained passive in Alan's care. Over the years, he laments this to me, saying my mother shut him out of any decision-making when it comes to Alan. He tells me that he feels like he's not getting the complete story, that he wants to talk directly to Alan's doctors and caregivers, but he can't because he has no legal rights. Sharon is Alan's legal guardian. She has power of attorney.

So, when Dad tells me he is certain Alan's death was natural, that there's no need to perform an autopsy, I can't help but question.

I remember as a young kid sitting in the waiting rooms of lawyers' offices, of therapists' offices. I remember my parents disappearing behind heavy wooden doors for hours. I could hear their raised voices – the tenor of my father, the soprano of my mother. I saw her swollen eyes and his furrowed brow as they emerged. I remember receptionists offering me and my brothers coloring books, Highlights magazines, and bottles of Coca-Cola, telling us not to worry, it would all be over soon.

This refrain, *It will all be over soon*, became a part of my survival strategy.

In a way, it feels like my parents are reenacting their divorce in the wake of Alan's death. They're bickering over assets, except the assets this time are Alan's body, planning rights, and control over what will happen next. They each have their own ideas of what the funeral should be like, how to best honor Alan. My mother wants it to be Christmas-themed. My father wants something more traditional. My mother insists that the service include Holy Communion. Dad thinks that will drag it out too long. I'm keeping my distance, partly because I know my opinion won't impact the outcome.

Someone called a minister to guide them, to mediate. He

will sit down with my parents in much the same way I remember them sitting down with therapists when I was little. Someone will help them navigate the path forward through this difficult thing they must do. But instead of negotiating custody and child support and visitation schedules, it's caskets and pallbearers and headstones – and whatever elements of Christmas feel appropriate to include at a funeral.

This is how I imagine it will happen: The minister will take my parents' words, their distant, shimmering ideas for how this event might go (an event they may or may not ever have anticipated) and shape them into something concrete. He is a referee. A tour guide. A party planner. A keeper of checklists.

Will they bury him? It's not clear. They decide to have him cremated. Maybe. But they'll do an open casket first so everyone can say their goodbyes.

"Okay, so that's a wake and a funeral," the minister might say. "Have you given any thought to flowers?"

"Poinsettias?" Sharon may ask.

"I'm not sure we'll find those this time of year," the minister replies.

He might steer them away from the question of Alan's remains, the paralyzing issue they can't agree on. My father wants to bury him where he grew up, in northern Minnesota. My mother wants to take him to New Mexico where she grew up. The looks on their faces as they each state their wish, as they each lay claim to Alan's body – it's an intensity I haven't seen from them since we were small. The room feels electric, the air buzzing with unspoken truths, unnamed pain. Whose child was Alan? What landscape does he represent? To what geography does he belong?

They plan the funeral. Just the funeral for now. It will take place in three days.

Part Three

The Wake

Chapter Thirteen

Boulder, August 17, 2016.

A warm afternoon. I'm on the couch, my son Miles draped across me like a blanket. My daughter Bronwynn nestled under my arm. Their freshly shampooed hair tickles my chin. They smell like candied apples. Kris made them shower this morning, washing off the grit of their road trip. He combed their hair and placed their dress clothes neatly at the foot of their beds. One outfit for the wake, one for the funeral.

"The rest is casual," I tell him. "No one really will care what they're wearing."

They arrived two nights ago, bursting through the door and throwing their arms around my waist. Their little bodies felt like an anchor, tethering me to the ground. Kris approached me slower, gently placed his hand on the back of my head and pulled me toward him for a kiss. Without any of us letting go, the kids start rattling off details about their two-day drive.

"I brought my Pokémon cards and watched three movies," Miles says. I can feel the pent-up, six-year-old energy vibrating through him, his eyes lighting up. "And last night we stayed in a hotel, and we walked to this place that had hamburgers THIS HUGE, and Daddy let us get milkshakes!"

"I made Miles sleep on the bed with Daddy, so I got the whole other bed to myself," Bronwynn says with a hint of pride. "I slept diagonal, like this," she gestures, "with my blanket and bunny. And today, we got gum at the gas station. I have a whole pack. Want a piece?" Her voice is quiet, cautious like she's not sure whether it's okay to talk about such happy things.

I once heard a podcast about people who can physically feel what they witness other people feeling. If they watch someone stub their toe, their foot hurts. If they see someone cry, they feel intense emotional pain. The experts called it mirror-touch synesthesia. For some, it's so intense that they shutter themselves away in their homes so they are never exposed to anyone else's pain.

There are mild versions, though, too. It's a spectrum. Some people are just highly sensitive, deeply empathic, able to read everyone's feelings in the room. Their nervous system alights easily, but the feelings aren't debilitating. In fact, they can be beneficial. They connect with people more easily. They sense danger before anyone else. They read body language and can tell when someone is lying.

Sometimes I think Bronwynn falls into this group, the highly sensitive person category. She is the barometer for our family, the first to show the world outwardly when things are not okay.

I had a therapist tell me once that Bronwynn inherited some of my childhood pain, a concept that Bessell van der Kolk describes in *The Body Keeps the Score*. His decades of research shows how trauma and stress over time can alter a person's brain and body, including their DNA. This means that certain survival traits like hypervigilance can become written into our genes and passed down from generation to generation. A neurobiological ripple effect. Though she herself has not suffered violence or neglect, though Kris and I have worked to provide the most loving, safe, and nurturing environment, my daughter retains my family trauma on a cellular level. She's alert. She feels things more deeply than any other eight-year-old I know. On one hand, the smallest injustices can crash over her like an ocean wave, leaving her in a heap on the floor. On the other, she can sense from across the room when someone needs a friend, a smile, a hug. It's a blessing and a curse, the therapist said. She will be a deeply intuitive, creative adult. But she also might become burnt out unless she learns to set boundaries. Kris and I call it her superpower – a gift she can use for good or for evil.

I watch her now, and I wonder: If trauma can be written into our DNA, then did she also inherit the ambivalent feelings I have toward my brother, her uncle? Is she, like me, fighting a tangle of feelings so tight they may never unravel?

My brother is dead. The thought repeats itself, like my brain won't let me forget. Even in this peaceful, happy moment. My brother is dead. My children are here. This is not a dream. I'm safe. I'm relieved to see them, to touch them, evidence of the healthier family I created.

My brother is gone.

My children are here.

The chasm between my old life and this one is closing.

The sensation of their little bodies next to mine, hearing their voices, I feel my chest relax for the first time in a week, and I let out a sob. I don't realize I've been holding it in.

• • •

This morning a dear friend surprised me with a text:

> I've booked you a massage at the St. Julien Spa at 3:00. Go if you want to or ignore if you don't. It's paid for.

I go, and I cry through the entire thing. It's therapeutic in more ways than one, laying there open, naked except for a sheet, vulnerable, and letting a stranger nurture me for an hour.

"Your shoulders and neck are full of knots," the massage therapist says. "It's where you're holding all your stress."

She presses her thumb into each knot until it melts away, a sharp pain followed by radiating warmth.

"Things happen that leave a mark on the body," she says. "They leave marks in space and time."

I think about the marks Alan has left on my body. The ghosts of bruises he inflicted. The thin white scar on my thumb, sliced open when I was cleaning up jagged glass after he broke a window. The spots on my scalp where he pulled my hair out, and it never fully grew back. And other scars no one can see – the constant ache of always wondering if he's safe, if I'm safe, if William is safe, if my mother is safe. The ache of wanting everyone to be happy. Scars on my nervous system: I flinch at the slightest sounds. I'm rarely able to sleep deeply or fully relax; I'm always vigilant, ready to respond to whatever crisis comes next. Scars on my heart from where it burst with jealousy over the attention Alan received and I didn't. The quiet pain of always wanting more than he or my parents could give.

As this woman skillfully dissolves every knot, I secretly hope she finds and melts away those other marks too.

At the end, she mists my face with lavender oil and gives me a steaming washcloth to wipe away the tears. She excuses herself so I can get dressed. I lay there for what feels like a long time, letting my body sink into the table before I finally take a deep breath, sit up, swing my legs over the edge, and put my feet on the cold floor.

I rise, get dressed, and walk back into the harsh sunlight.

Chapter Fourteen

"Do you think he'll wake up?" Bronwynn asks from the backseat as we drive to my mother's house.

"No, honey. It's just called a wake," Kris says. "Two words: A. Wake."

"Yeah, but do people hope he'll maybe wake up, just maybe?"

"He won't even be there, babe. His body is at the funeral home."

We crest a hill, and the Flatirons come into view, five sheer, sandstone faces jutting toward the sky. Named for their resemblance to irons that pioneers used to press their clothes, the Flatirons are part of what geologists call an uplift, an overlap between two fault lines. A 60-million-year-old jagged seam. In this case, a seam that fastens the smooth, rolling plains to the sharp edge of the Rockies.

A part of me wonders what I might say to Alan, given the chance, if he were to wake up. Would I tell him what he means to me? Would I ask him what went wrong? I know I'd hug him one more time. His hugs were fierce and heavy. He'd wrap his whole upper body around you and refuse to let go. I'd want to look him in the eyes and tell him, unequivocally, that in spite of everything, I truly love him. That none of it was ever his fault.

But this isn't a wake in the literal sense, I explain to the kids; it's a spiritual one. Some religious traditions hold that you should sit in the home of the deceased and be in their presence as they make the journey from this life to the next. Call it a wake, or a vigil; it's what some of us think we're doing the night before the funeral when we gather for the third time at my mother's house. Others of us believe we're simply gathering for dinner.

The invitation had gone out by text. We'll meet at Sharon's house, my aunt said. Just family. Nothing formal.

By the time we wander through the door, it appears the adults are gliding along in more of a dream state—here but not present. My mother has arranged on her countertops a mosaic of comfort food she's been given by friends and neighbors over the past several days. There are giant bowls of pasta salad, ceramic dishes of green bean casserole with crispy onions on top, bubbling lasagna, crock pots of soup, trays of sandwiches, and so many baked goods.

The kids immediately dig in, snatching dinner rolls and heaping scoops of creamy casseroles onto their plates. I make sure they grab a few raw veggies too. I grab a carrot for myself and nibble as I scan the rest of the spread, considering what I might eat. My stomach has been tight all week, and I haven't been able to take more than a few bites of anything without feeling nauseous.

I watch everyone relax and serve themselves, unconcerned about hiding the food, measuring portions, or keeping a close eye on Alan to make sure he's not eating too much and making himself sick.

"Buffets are Alan's best friend and worst enemy," my mother often said.

The sight of a spread like this would have made him giddy. I look around and notice that she's removed the locks she kept on the cabinets to prevent Alan from gorging in the night. The buffet is unguarded. His place setting with the special no-spill water bottles and plates is gone. I'm struck by how soon after his death my mother eased her protections. Does she feel a new sense of freedom or relief? Or is it simply too painful for her to see any reminders of Alan? It's been more than twenty years since I lived with Alan, and I feel hardwired to worry about his safety around food. Locking kitchen cabinets is part of my muscle memory. When my kids were babies, childproofing felt easy, familiar, almost soothing. But somehow, Sharon seems to have erased her memory overnight. I'm saddened by this. It feels like in a way she's erasing Alan too.

When we finally sit at the table, plates full of food, Kris looks around and notices that Sharon's husband isn't there. Technically Mike is my stepfather, but I never think of him that way. I was twenty-two when they got married and had already been on the outs with my mother for years. At the time, her request for a traditional wedding ceremony seemed confusing to me. I wasn't the only family member she had been estranged from. Her life was a constant push and pull as people entered and exited. On some deep level, she might have known that she needed people to love her, to support her, to keep her alive. But for as long as I can remember, she sabotaged relationships, forcing people away. Mike was kind of a loner, a widower, passive and introverted. They had known each other for years and had recently reconnected. He seemed unfazed by my mother's mood swings, and for his part appeared to enjoy having a companion by his side. Their wedding invitation, letter-pressed into crisp white cardstock, might have come as a relief to some. She'd finally found her person. She may finally experience the joy she so deserves. But to my twenty-two-year-old mind, the wedding plans felt like an attempt to draw people back to her, me included. I imagined Mike would have been happy to elope.

"I need you to be my maid of honor," Sharon said to me. "I don't have anyone else."

It was a fall wedding, held at a small, historic chapel a couple hours south of Atlanta. She picked out a black velvet dress for me to wear, not unlike the one I'm planning to wear to Alan's funeral. She asked me to write and deliver a toast at her reception. "Something poetic," she said. "You have such a beautiful way with words." I can't remember anything I said as I raised a glass of champagne toward my mother. I remember the feeling I had, a swirl of resentment and relief. Resentment for what I felt was a charade, me standing by my mother's side as though I'd been there all along, under her wing. Relief that I could finally pass the baton to someone else. She was Mike's responsibility now.

After the wedding, she and Mike moved with Alan to northern New Mexico, where they both had roots, and placed Alan in a group home. This was supposed to be their happily ever after: Alan would be lovingly cared for at the home while they started a new life together. But within a few months, they received a late-night call. A social worker at the home had caught Alan stealing food from the kitchen. When she confronted him and attempted to take the food away, Alan punched her. She sounded an alarm; a police officer came and restrained Alan until a doctor could arrive to sedate him. There were no second chances. He was a danger to the staff and other residents, they said, and would have to move out immediately.

For the next several years, the cycle continued this way. Alan enjoyed stints at group homes all over the U.S. but always wound up back with Mom and Mike. Eventually, the three of them moved to Boulder to be closer to me and Kris and to access a large network of daytime caregivers and part-time programs for special needs adults. Boulder is known for its inclusion and the care and acceptance it provides marginalized people. There was an array of experts who could handle his behavioral issues, who understood that his violent tendencies were driven by hormones and insatiable hunger and not a malicious intent to hurt anyone. This would be a safer, more nurturing place for him to live.

When he wasn't with caregivers, he was home with Mom and Mike. He became their grown-up child. Mike had never had children of his own and always said it was because he didn't have the patience for them. But over the years, from what I observed, he learned to care for Alan like he was someone close to a son.

"Did Mike run to the store?" Kris asks.

"No. He left," my mother says, casually.

"What do you mean he left?" Others at the table have put down their forks and are listening intently, mouths agape.

"He had a business trip previously scheduled," she says. "I told him he should go."

"Does he know the funeral is tomorrow?" My father asks.

"He's not coming to the funeral," she says. "Go on, everybody. Eat up while it's hot!"

None of us can eat. We're too shocked. I try to imagine how that conversation might have gone. Did Mike try to weasel out of going to the funeral, to avoid the sadness and discomfort of it all? Or had my mother convinced him to leave? What business could he have that is more critical than his stepson's death? I study my mother's face for some hint of the rest of the story, but her expression is eerily blank.

The blankness, the absence of emotion gives me more anxiety than an outburst would. I could say that my mother deals with loss and pain in a reserved and quiet manner. I could say she keeps feelings close to her chest. But that would be a lie. Loss and pain, resentment and anger simmer in our family. It festers. It remains dormant like a volcano – who can say how long – until it finally erupts.

For my mother and Mike, it looks something like this: Day after day, Alan acts like Alan. He asks repetitive questions. He hugs people too hard. He hangs on Mom's arm and asks her every five minutes when his next meal will be and what can he eat. His mood veers unexpectedly from exuberant to angry. If he gets too hungry, he becomes defiant, sneaky. He digs through the trashcan for leftovers or scraps of discarded food. My mother sets a timer and sends him to time out in his room. She redirects his attention away from eating, tells him to go watch a movie or listen to his music. When he persists to the point of violence, when he begins to shout at her and Mike, she takes away his favorite things. No dessert, she says. No music. No trips to the pet store with his dog. With every privilege she revokes, Alan becomes more combative until he finally collapses in a 250-pound heap, sobbing. Mike observes all of this from the sideline, Mom explains. Over the years, she calls and tells me this over the phone. "He's no help at all." Day in and day out, it's the same.

Newlywed and living near Boulder at the time, Kris and I go to their house for dinner. We bring gifts for Alan – a new set of colored pencils or a CD we think he might like. We walk into a perfectly clean space and the smell of chili simmering on the stove. The dining room table is draped in linen and set with placemats and the good china. Alan laughs with joy when he sees us. We hug him, letting him squeeze tight. We play fetch with his dog. We ask him what movies he's watched lately. My mother asks us what's new, how's work, how's the house? Mike opens the fridge and offers us drinks. Beer or soda? They're holding everything together tightly, but we can see immediately the exhaustion on her and Mike's faces. Over the course of an evening, the stitches start to unravel: As the small talk fades, Alan obsesses over dinner. When can we eat? He wails when he's told it's not quite ready. Mom chases him out of the kitchen. She gives him additional doses of medication until he's subdued. Sometimes he sobs so deeply that he can't catch his breath. She gives him water and rubs his back until he settles down. Then she allows him to eat the food he so desperately wanted in the first place. He eats quickly, then he slumps back in his chair. Soon, he falls asleep.

Sometimes, Mike steps in and tries to redirect Alan's attention and save my mother from the stressful pattern of punishing and medicating him. Mike gives Alan a task, like folding cloth napkins or filling glasses with water. Alan's hands shake as he pours water from a pitcher into the glasses. He knocks one over, water spills and pools on the tablecloth. My mother tells Mike through gritted teeth to back off.

"I'm just trying to help," Mike says.

"You don't know what's best for him," she snaps. "Here, make yourself useful," she gives Mike a grocery list and sends him to the store. Then she smiles at Kris and me. She tries to laugh it off like it's nothing. No big deal. Just another day in the life with Alan, right? "Never a dull moment."

But we see it in her face, the impatience, the festering. It's as heartbreaking as it is familiar. I've seen this double-bind play out before, not just between her and Mike, but with anyone who steps in and tries to help. She tells people she's drowning, she needs more support for Alan. But when real assistance is offered, she pushes it away. It would be easy to dismiss this as martyrdom. She has sacrificed herself, her freedom, for Alan, and she wants everyone to know that she is suffering.

I believe it's bigger than that. She has also sacrificed her sanity. And without her accepting professional help, she may never get it back.

This is the curse of mental illness left untreated, a short circuit in the mind. She believes she is utterly alone because in the past she was alone. My father left. Neighbors and friends distanced themselves from her, the single mom with the disabled kid. She felt overwhelmed because life was over-whelming. She was unequipped to handle Alan's needs alone, unable to feed him enough or fix his violent outbursts, or even keep up with the bills so that the heat would stay on.

Decades have passed. She is no longer alone. It's as if, all these years later, she still hasn't come up for air. Her brain is clinging to the belief that things are hopeless, that nobody cares. Life is difficult, to be sure. Alan is still Alan. But today, at this moment, she is not alone. She has access to people and organizations and financial resources that didn't exist when we were kids. When people genuinely offer support, she is unable to recognize it, let alone receive it.

Like the little girl growing up in the atomic town, she's unable to decipher fact from fiction. Something unseen is poisoning her slowly from the inside out.

In her book, *Maybe You Should Talk to Someone,* Lori Gottlieb references a classic cartoon drawing of a prisoner shaking the bars of his cell. He's frantic, desperate. But to the right and left, the jail cell is open. No bars. "All the prisoner has to do is walk around," she writes. It's easy to feel completely stuck, trapped in our emotional cells, she explains. "But there's a way out – as long as we're willing to see it."

Alan starts crying again. "I sorry," he says. "I so sorry." He assumes he's in trouble because of the spilled water. Kris and I try to distract Alan. We suggest going for a walk or playing with his toy cars. We sit down and draw pictures with him. Give everyone a chance to settle down. Until Mike returns from the store and my mother discovers he's bought the wrong brand of milk or salted butter when she wanted unsalted. It's the proverbial straw. Her eye twitches. Her cheeks turn bright red, her brow furrows, and she unleashes a torrent of rage. "Can't you get one goddamn thing right?" she screams. "Nothing in my life can ever go right." She storms out of the room. Mike throws up his arms in defeat, grabs a beer, pops it open, and leaves – back outside or downstairs to his study. We don't see him again all night.

Those early years, Kris and I would intervene. We'd try to mediate. We'd defend Mike to my mother and my mother to Mike. We'd offer to take Alan out to eat so they could enjoy some time alone. We'd change the subject, try to lighten the mood. But after a while, we realized the problem was much bigger than us. The more we inserted ourselves into the drama, the more discontent we became. The negativity worked its way inside us, like inhaling toxic fumes. It caused Kris and me to bicker in a way that threatened to undo us like it had undone my mother and Mike. I'd look at Kris and wonder if it was just a matter of time before he left me the way my father had. Any benign request he made—could I fold the laundry? Would I mind picking up some dinner on the way home?—began to echo my family's neediness. *Would I have to parent my husband now too?*

Though I knew intellectually that this wasn't the case, on a cellular level I feared I was being dragged back into my childhood, and I was taking Kris with me. But I no longer belonged there. I could no longer assume the role of peacemaker and caregiver without cutting off the part of myself that wanted something different. I had to make a choice between my new life and my old one.

These are some of the reasons I stayed away for so long. Once I had my own children, I didn't want them exposed to Sharon's red-faced rage or Alan's unpredictable violence. I wanted them to know all the good parts of Alan, his unbridled joy, his tenderness toward animals, his love of cars and movies. But I couldn't give them a road map or set of instructions for how to navigate these waters, how to tell when it is safe and when it is not. When my mother was stable and when she was not. So I kept them away.

Now, with Mike having mysteriously disappeared the night before Alan's funeral, I wonder if he really had failed in his role as a father figure, or if he had never been allowed to try.

I also wonder what Mike knows, what he's seen. Maybe he holds some of the answers to my questions.

We all stare at my mother, waiting for further explanation. She stares at her plate and pushes the food around with her fork. "It's a church funeral, and Mike isn't into religious stuff," she says after a minute of silence. "It's just not his thing."

And with that, the conversation is over. No one wants to dig deeper and potentially uncover a landmine.

• • •

Religion may not have been Mike's thing, but I couldn't really say it was our thing either. It is just something we'd done for as long as I can remember. Everything from baptisms to confirmations to weddings—and yes, funerals—had to be conducted under the banner of religion in some way or another. It's one of the threads that held the family together, no matter how tenuous.

My parents intended to raise us Catholic. They were married in a Catholic church at Christmastime. My brothers and I were baptized Catholic, wearing long white gowns, bonnets, and white leather shoes, surrounded by godparents I never really knew. We attended mass and Sunday school. I memorized the prayers and rites. There was even a special education class for Alan where he colored black and white photocopied images of Jesus and the Virgin Mary. The teacher once gave him a package of communion wafers, quarter-size disks of rice, so he could practice the sacrament ritual with my mother. The wafers hadn't been blessed by a priest yet, so they weren't considered sacred. Alan would cup his hands under his chin while my mother repeated, "The body of Christ, given for you." She placed a wafer in his palm. He was supposed to say "amen" and delicately transfer the wafer from his hand to his mouth and let it dissolve on his tongue. My mother encouraged him to keep his lips closed so he wouldn't drool.

Instead, Alan crunched the wafers loudly, and when my mother wasn't looking, he'd grab several more and pop them into his mouth. The sheath of wafers was gone in minutes. Will and I thought this was hilarious. Watching Alan outsmart an adult and get what he wants was entertaining. When Mom noticed what was happening, she threw up her hands. "Fine. You'll all go to hell. See if I care."

My interpretation of religion was a little different. I was drawn to the people, the sense of community. I liked the songs and the soothing smell of incense and candles flickering on the altar. I cut up rosaries and fashioned the beads into pins and bracelets and gave them to my friends at school. At mass, when my mother wasn't looking, I doodled on the pages of the hymnal and put candy in the offering plate because I figured Jesus might like to have some treats. I don't remember what spiritual beliefs I held as a child, but I did enjoy a good story, and the Bible is full of stories.

The more I heard about Mary, the more I wanted her to be not just a blessed holy mother, but *my* mother. In my bedroom growing up, I had an airbrushed plastic nativity scene that was meant to be a lawn decoration. It was about thirty percent life-size, and it lit up when you plugged it in. I had begged for it one year when my parents were still married. It was on display at the local hardware store, and the moment I saw it glowing – Mary's face so lovely and peaceful – I just had to have it. I pleaded with them, clutching at the hem of my mother's skirt, tearfully looking up at my father as if my life was at stake until they gave in and bought it for me. But they refused to display it in the yard. It was tacky, they said. So, every year at Christmastime, I set it up in my room and plugged it in. The warm blue glow of Mary and Joseph soothed me to sleep. It was like I wasn't alone. Sometimes, I took Baby Jesus out of the manger and slept with him in my bed.

After the divorce, Mom and Dad were shunned from the church we attended. Divorce was a sin. We still went to mass occasionally, but they weren't allowed to take communion. I remember my First Confession, my dad whispering something to the priest about the divorce and about "Alan's condition" and how I might want to talk about it. I didn't know back then that people talk with priests about topics other than sin. I didn't realize that my father might have been suggesting that I need support around these issues. Hearing my dad say that I may want to discuss Alan's condition, I assumed I had done something wrong, or maybe Alan had done something wrong, that somehow we had caused this crevasse in our family that was so deep and cold that even the church wouldn't cross over it. I assumed that my jealousy of Alan and the attention he received was my sin. My fear of my brother was a sin.

I sat across from the priest on a plastic school chair in a large storage closet, not in a wooden booth like I'd seen the adults disappear into. I looked into the stoic face of the middle-aged man wearing white robes and recited the prayer I'd memorized:

My God, I am very sorry for having offended you. I detest all my sins because I dread the loss of Heaven and the pain of hell. But most of all because sins offend you, my God, who are all good and deserving of all my love.

The priest nodded in approval, so I took this as an invitation to confess. I rattled off a small list of sins as quickly as I could: I'd fibbed to my parents. I had coveted my friends' toys. I'd stolen a peppermint from a jar on my teacher's desk and a handful of quarters from my mother's nightstand. And then, a big one: I was sometimes embarrassed to have a brother like Alan.

"Embarrassed?" The priest asked.

"Yes. People stare at him all the time, they stare at us. I get embarrassed. I'm tired of always talking for him. I wish I could hide."

"Hide?"

"Or maybe just fit in. I wish we could be a *normal* family sometimes."

I waited for him to tell me I was a horrible child. I waited for my penance. After a moment, he said, finally, "Your parents are adulterers." He paused, perhaps waiting for me to ask what "adulterer" meant. I didn't. I was too intimidated, or maybe just confused. "And God has given them the punishment of caring for your brother for the rest of their lives. But you can be free from that burden."

I nodded as if in agreement but really felt more confused and eager to leave.

He instructed me to repent for myself and for my family. He told me to pray the rosary for my parents, and I could be released from their shame.

Later when my dad asked me how the confession had gone, I said, simply, "Fine." It would be years before I thought about it again and the weight of the priest's message would fully hit me. If it was true that Alan was delivered to my parents as God's punishment for their sins, what did that mean for me? Was it my job to redeem them?

Chapter Fifteen

In September 2013, an epic rainstorm doused Boulder and surrounding communities with nearly a year's worth of rainfall in less than a week. Weather experts called it a 1,000-year storm. Flash floods washed away entire communities in the foothills. The water tore roads and bridges in half. In town, manholes turned into geysers, and the typically quiet creeks that course through the city overflowed their banks, overtook the streets, and flooded thousands of homes.

Kris, the kids, and I had moved to Arizona a few years prior. Kris was offered a job that would double his salary and also conveniently draw a geographical boundary between my mother and us. It was a fresh start, and we jumped at the opportunity.

As we watched the flood coverage on the evening news, I worried about Alan, Sharon, and Mike's safety. It had been a while since we'd been in contact with Sharon, and I wasn't sure if she'd welcome a phone call, so Kris quickly composed an email with the subject line, *You guys okay?*

He received a reply from my mother the next day: "We're

fine. The basement is a wreck. Completely flooded. Carpet and drywall have to be replaced. We lost a lot of stuff we had stored down there. It looks like Gina's box of childhood keepsakes is ruined. The boys' boxes miraculously survived. Insurance should cover most of the damage."

I should have felt relief to know they were safe, but as Kris read me the message, my cheeks burned. How was it that only *my* keepsakes had been ruined? I'd asked her for that box nearly ten years prior when Kris and I got married and bought our first house. It contained my baby photos, childhood drawings, a few of my first toys that I had hoped to pass on to my kids, a clay imprint of my tiny hand. It also had some of my first published writing—a fifth-grade essay that earned me a state literary prize, short stories I'd written and published in high school.

"I'm not sure where it is. I'll look for it," Sharon had said back then.

My mother is what I'd call an organized hoarder. On the surface, her home looks cluttered but clean. Collections of southwestern pottery are arranged neatly on shelves, magazines and books stacked and organized by size and color, throw blankets folded in thirds and draped over the backs of chairs. Everything is symmetrical and dust-free.

Open a closet or peek in the cabinets, and you'll discover fifty tubes of toothpaste stacked neatly on a shelf, stockpiles of shampoo, box upon cardboard box of clothing with the tags still on, piles of quilting fabric several feet high, and cases of canned goods and bottled water. She is anxiously preparing for something—a new sewing project, for guests, or maybe for disaster.

During the first couple of years of my marriage, I asked her frequently about my stuff and got the same response. "Haven't come across it yet. I'll keep an eye out!" I offered to help her look, but she refused.

Eventually, I resigned myself to the idea that the box was missing but not forever lost. I imagined someday my mother and Mike would move and clean out the basement, and it would surface. Or in the distant future, they'd die, and Will and I would clean out their house. My history was in there, somewhere, like gold buried in the mountains of my mother's junk. Someday I'd find it.

Whether I could articulate it or not, rescuing that box meant reclaiming something bigger. These were my artifacts, my memories. Proof I'd existed, that I was important. The flood felt like a reversal, an erasure. To hear that my stuff was completely destroyed, and my brothers' keepsakes had been spared? I was bitter. Jealous. Confused. Had she known where the box was all along? Why didn't she give it to me? How is it that nothing was salvageable?

I'd been largely absent from my mother's life for several years, but now it was official. A storm of biblical proportions had swept in and washed me away.

The night before the funeral, after an uncomfortably quiet dinner, we all gather in the living room and my mother brings out stacks of photo albums and shoeboxes overflowing with images, mostly of Alan as a child. She hands them out, and we all begin thumbing through them. There's a tiny manila envelope with locks of Alan's baby-soft brown hair from his first haircut. The black and white outline of his newborn hands and feet stamped with ink. A page titled "Baby's Firsts" full of my mother's handwriting in faded blue ink. So many of his firsts – smile, words, steps – had come much later than expected. Deeper in the stacks there are photos of Alan on a carousel, at a petting zoo, blowing out birthday candles on a cake shaped like a firetruck. There's a photo of Alan and me as toddlers sitting on my dad's lap. Alan sitting next to my mother, his head resting on her shoulder. There's Alan and me smiling in front of a Christmas tree. Another photo shows Alan, William, and me in homemade Halloween costumes. Alan is a lion. I am a nurse. Will is a mouse.

I suppose this is the "wake" part of the wake, our time to remember Alan, to share stories. And if it's true that his spirit is still hanging around, this is the time to let him know it is safe to pass on to wherever or whatever is next after you die. I can't say I sense his spirit here at this moment, but I sense his dog, Clyde, a clumsy gray and white standard poodle who is nosing under my elbow repeatedly in a bid for me to pet him. I reach down, cup my hand under Clyde's chin, and look into his glassy eyes, hoping to see Alan. I lean in close and whisper into Clyde's ear, "I love you. I'm so sorry." Just in case. He licks my cheek.

I always imagined I might feel some measure of relief if Alan died before my parents. For selfish reasons. Because I did not want to face the prospect of caring for him into old age. But also because I knew what a profound loss it would be for Alan if my mother died first. One that he could not comprehend and would grieve so deeply that no one could touch the sorrow. He depended on her with the blind trust of a toddler. She was his source of everything—food, comfort, medicine, care, safety.

I continue to stare at the old photos of Alan, his arms wrapped tightly around my mother's neck, him holding his pet dogs, his wide grin as he stands with my father. There are even a few studio images of Alan, Will, and me. We're sitting in front of a fake wooded landscape or mottled blue backdrop, wearing crisp dress clothes in matching colors. In every image, Alan is smiling the biggest of all. The way he bonded with people, the way he seemed to love us unconditionally was remarkable, like nothing I've ever seen. As much as I can remember, Alan never met another person or animal he didn't like.

I wonder, had he died when he was six and I was three, like my aunt said he was supposed to, would I have felt Alan's deep affection? Would I have felt the loss? At forty, I feel tremendous loss. I feel unrelieved. I feel ripped apart, like there's a gap in the universe. I feel disoriented and strange. It occurs to me that loss cannot exist without having gained something. They are two sides of the same coin, like joy and sadness.

I am sad to think of my keepsakes destroyed, my early memories erased. But page after page, looking at my brother's albums, I realize photographs never tell the complete story. Like my mother's carefully decorated home, like the dresses and bows she dressed me in, we show people what we want them to see. I'd wanted that box to give me some deeper truth about myself, about my family, about Alan. I thought it would help me reclaim my childhood, piece it all together in a way that makes sense and brings some comfort or closure. But I realize now that even before the flood, the keepsakes were fragile. They only hinted at the story.

Alan is a lion.

I am a nurse.

Will is a mouse.

A photograph will change shape, shift loyalty, reflect a different history depending on who is holding it. As long as my keepsakes were trapped in my mother's house, they were never really safe, never really mine.

There's no way in the aftermath of the flood we could have predicted that Alan would only live three more years. Despite his genetic abnormality, we had no reason to believe he wouldn't survive into old age. Whatever death sentence the doctor had given my parents in the 70s when Alan was an infant had proven not to be true, so my parents had dismissed it. They kept the prophecy from me, so I assumed Alan would always be with me.

If I had known then what was to come, if the universe had somehow given me a choice—destroy my keepsake box or my brother's instead—I would have sacrificed my own. It feels now like a fair price for the freedom I've gained, for the ability to walk away from a story that was never really mine in the first place. At this point, I figure I can keep longing for my old stuff, or I can accept that my memories were never really contained in that box. They're alive, with me, in my bones, my nervous system, my blood.

I close my eyes, place my hands on my belly and breathe. In through my nose, out through my mouth. Those thoughts and questions that plagued me in the moments after I heard that Alan had died are still here, but they're changing shape. Maybe the question isn't whether Alan knew I loved him, but rather how he interpreted that love, or his capacity to hold onto love as memory, like an emotional keepsake. Maybe the larger question isn't about what we had as brother and sister, but about what was lost when he died. Like the flood and its aftermath... in relationships, can we catalog what was destroyed and what remains? Can I file a claim?

I feel my chest rise and fall. With each deep exhale, I begin to wonder if the question of what happened to Alan is a proxy for the question of what happened to me.

Chapter Sixteen

Atlanta, 1988.

There is a brief, magical time when we imagine Alan won't always be dependent on us. He'll live his own life apart from my mother. Maybe with a roommate or part-time caregiver checking up on him. Maybe in his own place. Maybe someday I won't have to worry so much about him.

When I'm twelve and Alan is fifteen, he attends a special education school that focuses on life skills. No one knows enough about Alan's condition to tell if he will ever mature enough to live independently. There are no benchmarks to compare his progress to. So, for a while, my mother chooses to assume that he can be independent.

The school looks like just about any other, a sprawling single-story cement block building with long rectangular windows. It's flanked by basketball courts and playgrounds on one side and a circular driveway on the other where parents pull up to drop off their children. But there's also a long wheelchair ramp leading up to the front door. On the playground, there's a special swing that looks more like a car seat with a five-point harness. Inside, many of the doors and cabinets are protected with child locks.

My mother volunteers with the PTA. She organizes holiday parties and makes cookies for bake sales and brings her camera to the school and photographs the children and creates slideshows that the principal shows at fundraising events. My brothers and I often tag along, walking the halls after hours while Mom sets up decorations or stuffs letters into envelopes.

At his special school, Alan learns how to count money and how to write a check. He shops in a pretend grocery store using a list he has written himself. He fails to understand the value of money. If a loaf of bread costs one dollar, he assumes that a new Oldsmobile will cost about twenty dollars. At one end of the building, a few classrooms have been renovated to resemble a real apartment where students can cook and make beds and clean. They practice what to do when a visitor knocks on the door. This part comes easy to Alan, who is social and trusting of everyone. He invites people in. He offers them a glass of water and a cookie. He offers them a seat on a frayed yellow corduroy couch, then starts interrogating them about their shoe size, their pets, and what brands of products they buy.

This place is much better than all the other schools Alan has attended. The teachers are patient. They decipher Alan's speech patterns with ease. They love the students. You can tell by looking at their faces, the way they smile at them. While I roll my eyes at Alan's relentless questions, they respond. Even if they've told him their shoe size several times already, they tell him again. And then, they gently suggest new questions he might ask. They teach him how to take turns while talking, how to listen. They show him what it means to be a good friend.

I used to feel intimidated by Alan's classmates. Some of them sit in imposing robotic wheelchairs. Some of them wear helmets to protect them when they have seizures. The school is noisy. Kids cry. They scream. They flap their arms and kick their legs. Once, I watched two teachers restrain a boy who tried to beat his head against the concrete block wall. I was afraid because I didn't understand what was happening inside their bodies. I was worried I could catch their disabilities like a cold. No one ever told me that's not how disability happens.

But the more time I spend at the school, the more the kids start to look like regular kids to me. I begin to see past their chairs and devices. I see their faces, their personalities, their senses of humor and wonder. One day when I'm visiting Alan's classroom, I notice a new girl sitting in a corner in a wheelchair. She's slumped over to one side, her brown pigtails askew. Her eyes are tightly closed, but it looks like she's smiling. Her mouth is open, and her lips are upturned. It's like she's in her own world, listening to music no one else can hear. I'm instantly intrigued by her. Her hands are clenched on the tray of her wheelchair, and I notice she's holding something that looks like a white plastic chopstick. The teacher notices me staring and nudges me. "Katherine is really sweet," she says. "She's about your age, too. Maybe you should talk to her."

When I approach Katherine, slowly, cautiously, her eyes spring open, and she sits up straight, throws her head back, and laughs. Reflexively, I laugh too. Who is this silly girl, I wonder. I introduce myself, and she nods then takes the chopstick and taps it against her tray. I lean over to see what she's tapping and notice a wide computer panel full of words and pictures – a talking board. After a few taps, a computer voice says, "My name is Katherine. Do you like teddy bears?" I nod, yes. She taps again. "I collect teddy bears." She points down to her chair where two stuffed bears are nestled in her lap under her seat-belt. "Want to play?"

Over the course of several visits, I learn that Katherine also likes to watch television. We both like The Cosby Show. She listens to music and she takes swim lessons in a heated therapy pool. She lets me try out her talking board, and I tap out a few nonsense sentences, which makes her laugh. "You're a terrible talker," she tells me, "but I like you."

Compared to many of his classmates, Alan appears fairly calm. His speech is slurred, but his motor skills are pretty good. He can walk and run and throw a ball, though catching is more difficult. He is overly affectionate, hugging every other student and teacher until they have to peel him off. They try to explain boundaries to him, personal space, but the next day he's hugging everyone again.

The school plants a seed in my family, a tiny vision that maybe, perhaps, Alan can live on his own someday. We see it happen for other students. They graduate and go on to become store clerks, work at movie theaters, or assist at animal shelters. With the help of their parents, they live in apartments or group homes. Their families visit them and watch them flourish out in the real world. Not every student enjoys this happy ending, but I think it's safe to say that my mother, Will, and I desperately want to believe this can be our story. My mother begins to talk with Alan about jobs he might like. She signs him up for extra skills classes. Then one day she brings home a driver's training manual and announces that he'll need to start studying.

"We'll have to see if he can learn how to drive," she says. A driver's license, while not required for independence, would certainly make his life easier, she says. "It will be an adventure!"

In some ways, Alan has known how to operate a car since he was a toddler. My mother loves to recount stories of him screaming and pointing from the backseat before he was capable of talking. He'd scream when she'd forget to release the emergency brake. He'd scream when she made a wrong turn. He'd scream when he saw another car running a red light or failing to signal properly.

His ability to navigate streets and memorize traffic laws is like a superpower. So much so that later in childhood, when he is able to speak, he becomes my mother's personal GPS. This is helpful in Atlanta, a city that is not laid out on a grid, where streets often change names, wind aimlessly, and double back on themselves. Still, knowledge of a car and traffic laws doesn't translate into driving ability. Will and I realize this before my mother does.

One day, when I'm maybe nine or ten, my mother leaves my brothers and me waiting in the car while she visits a friend who's been ill. Casserole in hand, she steps out of the car, an Oldsmobile wagon with fake wood paneling that she bought after the divorce. She tells us over her shoulder to stay put. "I'll just be a minute, kids. Don't fight. Sit still and wait patiently."

We watch her approach the front door of the brick ranch home and ring the doorbell. The door opens, and she disappears inside. We immediately unbuckle our seatbelts. We're un-tethered beasts, fiddling with the radio, opening the glove box, and jamming our hands into the cracks of the upholstered bench seats. Will finds two dimes and a Tootsie Roll. I offer to trade him the pennies I found for the candy, and he agrees.

Alan, meanwhile, has climbed from the backseat into the driver's seat and is beginning to fiddle with knobs. He twists the steering wheel from side to side dramatically like he's playing an arcade game.

"Stop that, Alan. You're going to get in trouble," Will warns.

"I not," Alan says. "I the driver."

"You really shouldn't be touching those knobs, Alan. You don't know what they do," I add, gently, trying not to send him into a rage. The windshield wipers start going and stop. He turns on the hazard lights and turn signals. Then, suddenly the car jerks beneath us. He's grabbed the automatic shift and put it in Drive. The car begins rolling slowly down the driveway, toward the front of the brick house.

"Stop the car!" Will shouts. "Stop the car!"

"I trying!" Alan yells, pushing against the shifter. While he seems to understand that it needs to go back to P, he doesn't realize that the gear won't shift into Park without pressing the brake. And his legs are too short to reach the pedals.

The car continues to roll. I start screaming at him from the backseat, "Put it back in Park! Pull up the brake!"

Alan covers his face with his hands and starts wailing, "I not want be in trouble!"

Will opens his car door and tumbles out, sprinting toward the front door, yelling for my mother. I lunge from the backseat, grab the emergency brake and pull it as hard as I can. My hands are shaking. I'm terrified and not entirely sure if I'm doing the right thing or making it worse. The car groans and slows down but continues to creep toward the house.

My mother and Will run outside toward the car. She opens the door, pushes Alan away from the driver's seat, steps on the brake, and puts the car in park. Once we've stopped, I look out the front windshield and see that we're inches away from hitting the house. I let out a deep sigh of relief.

Instead of yelling at Alan, though, my mother whips around and slaps me across the cheek. "This is your fault," she says. "You were supposed to be watching your brothers."

When Alan turns fifteen, my mother decides to test his driving ability in an empty church parking lot. Will and I ask to be let out of the car to observe at a distance. Standing on a curb at the far end of the lot, we watch as my mother switches places with Alan so that he's in the driver's seat. We see her pointing to the pedals and gearshift, explaining to him what they each do. We see Alan adjust the rearview mirror and place his hands on the wheel. The car jerks forward maybe twenty-five feet and then screeches to a halt. Again it jerks and stops. Jerks and stops. Soon, it begins to roll forward slowly and turn left, making a clumsy loop around the lot. The tires squeal against the apex of the turn.

For a minute, it looks like he might be getting the hang of it. He makes one more lap around, pumping the brakes occasionally, but generally keeping to a consistent path. Then, the car stops. My mother motions for him to turn the other way, toward a wide expanse of empty parking spaces.

Will and I are quiet, watching, glued to the scene like a television show.

"I think this is a terrible idea," Will says. "He's going to crash."

"Maybe he won't," I say.

"He definitely will."

Will is a realist. Whereas I sometimes cling to a morsel of hope, some idealistic notion that things will one day turn around, that Alan will somehow become the big brother I've always dreamed of, Will is quietly resigned to a darker truth. Unlike me, he has no memory of a time when things were less broken, when my father lived at home, when we swam at the neighborhood pool, when there were still bedtime stories and lovingly cooked meals – a time when the unknown meant the possibility that Alan could someday recover from his ailments.

William's relationship with Alan is different from mine. He

is Alan's protector, like me, but more in a brotherly sense, not a parental one. When kids tease Alan, Will steps in, grabbing Alan by the arm and leading him away to play elsewhere. When strangers glare, Will tells them to mind their own business. When Alan sneaks food or breaks something at home, Will hides the evidence. I stepped up at a young age to care for my brothers, and in doing so, I gave Will the freedom to remain a child. It also gives him space to observe at a distance. And from that distance, I think he sees some situations more clearly than I do.

The Oldsmobile begins to turn in the other direction, then suddenly speeds up, the engine revving violently, until it reaches the parking spaces. We see brake lights and hear the tires skid, then the car jumps the curb, drives over a grassy median, and narrowly misses a lamppost. It rests there for a moment before Alan and my mother get out of the car and switch places once more. My mother reverses the car back onto the pavement and drives around to where Will and I are standing like statues. She rolls down the window.

"Close your goddamn mouths and get in."

We drive home in silence except for Alan muttering, "I sorry, Mom," every few minutes. "I so sorry."

At school, Alan fails to grasp the life skills he'll need to survive alone. He thinks he can pay rent for ten dollars. He burns food on the stove and tries to put aluminum foil and silverware in the microwave. He leaves the faucet running and floods the bathroom. He's too trusting of strangers. But even if he mastered all those things, there's still his insatiable appetite.

"This is not just a big appetite of a growing teenager," the teachers tell my mother. "It's a much bigger problem." Left alone, he will literally eat himself to death, they warn.

We don't know then that his condition has a name, that people like him with Prader-Willi syndrome can become morbidly obese. We just know that he's missing the signals in his brain or nervous system that tell him when he's full. We accept that he will likely need to live in a food-controlled environment for the rest of his life and that he can never decide for himself what's appropriate to eat and what is not.

My mother buys padlocks for the cupboards and refrigerator. Will and I hide stashes of snacks in our rooms for those times Mom isn't home to unlock them. Alan, aware now that he'll never be able to drive, starts collecting bus schedules and memorizing them. He unfolds dozens of the accordion maps and covers his bedroom floor with them. It's not long before he can tell you how to get anywhere in Atlanta you could possibly want to go.

In several years, when he's twenty-one years old, Alan will graduate high school with an honorary diploma. He'll stand at the podium in a cap and gown and deliver a speech that my mother wrote with words simple enough that he can read them aloud. Not everyone in the audience will understand his slurred voice, but they'll listen intently. My mother will cry as he reads. We'll all beam with pride and forget for a moment the cloud of uncertainty that has followed him around since he was an infant. He will, for a brief time, be just like the rest of us, working toward goals and achieving them, moving his tassel across the cap from right to left, and looking to the future.

After graduation, Alan will try a few different part-time jobs. He'll sweep the sidewalk at a drive-in burger place. He'll stock shelves at the local hardware store. He'll work as a greeter at Kmart. Managers are willing to give him a chance, but in the end, without fail, each of them will call my mother and explain that he costs them more money than he saves. He steals food.

He breaks things. He's more work than help. They're very sorry, but it's a business decision, not personal.

We all settle into the realization that Alan will never live on his own. He will never even be left alone for more than an hour or two. He will always require someone, likely one of us, by his side. To my mother, this is another dashed hope, another shattered ideal, another reason to despair. To me, it feels more ominous. I feel like I've been handed a prison sentence. What kind of life will I have if my job is to care for my family until they die?

Chapter Seventeen

Boulder, August 16, 2016.

I don't know how to grieve. I know how to problem-solve. I know to-do lists. I know how to take care of other people. There's never been space in my family for my feelings, so when they surface, I don't know what to do.

There's a puzzle here, something unresolved. I approach it the way I was taught – as a journalist, as my father's daughter. I research. I narrow the problem to specific questions and then tackle them one at a time. Maybe this way I'll get to a hypothesis, a theory.

There are long, anxious hours to fill before Alan's funeral takes place. I busy myself. I tell myself I'm being useful. Useful to whom, I can't say.

I call the hospital where Alan died. I don't have a plan or a script. I don't know who I want to speak with. I just want answers, details about what happened when he died. Maybe I can get copies of his medical records and begin to fill in the blanks and find an explanation. Maybe there's something the doctors missed, a heart condition or defect. Maybe there was an unsafe interaction between his medications. He saw so many specialists – a general practitioner, a neurologist, a pulmonologist, a psychiatrist for his medications to control compulsive eating and violent outbursts. Did they talk with one another? Compare notes?

I think back to what I was taught in journalism school about which types of records are public information and which are private. As an immediate family member, I know I can request an autopsy be performed, but it has to be approved by the hospital and the county coroner. To get approval, I have to provide a valid reason. At this point, I don't have one. I have discomfort. I have a sinking feeling. I have confusion. I have spotty details from my parents.

When a nurse answers the phone in the emergency department, I calmly explain that my brother died there and that I want to know more about what happened. She takes my information and says she'll have to look up who was on duty that day and get back to me. An hour later she calls back and tells me that she can confirm that my brother was treated and died on the evening of August 11th, but she can't provide any details. If I have legal documentation, such as power of attorney, then they can release those records. Otherwise, they're sealed.

"What about an autopsy?"

"There is no autopsy. The doctor signed off that it was natural causes."

My voice jams in my throat. I want to ask if it's too late to request an autopsy. I imagine she'll ask me why, and I'll say something about his medications, that I'm worried he had an adverse reaction. I rehearse the next thing I'll say in my mind, but no actual words come out.

There's a long pause and a sigh. "The body was signed for and released to the funeral home. I'm sorry for your loss."

I thank her, hang up, grab my laptop, and type "how to

request an autopsy" into the search bar. I learn that if the coroner has already signed off on the death certificate, then my only option would be to hire a third-party company to perform an autopsy. I learn that private autopsies cost $5,000 or more. If the body has already been embalmed, which is likely given that it's been at the funeral home for a few days, then any toxicology findings would be inconclusive.

I weigh the cost of appealing to the coroner and hiring a forensic company – the financial cost and the emotional cost to my family by delaying Alan's funeral. I also consider the price of my own sanity, digging for an explanation that may not exist, widening the chasm between me and the rest of my family. And for what? I can't even say what I'm looking for. Closure? Peace of mind? To feel like I advocated for my brother?

I don't want more drama. I want what I've always wanted, to make sense of the contradictions that plagued my brother's life, his behavior, our relationship...and now his death.

Chapter Eighteen

Atlanta, 1990.

My bedroom door is splintered along the bottom from Alan trying to kick it open. I have to be careful entering and exiting my room in bare feet, in case my toes catch against the sharp wood.

I've learned to read the subtle changes in his moods. I can sense his muscles tensing as the day progresses. I hear the way his breathing becomes shallow. I see the wrinkle that settles into his forehead, the way his eyes glaze over like he's no longer in his body, no longer thinking, just doing what his hormones tell him to do. I can predict when he's ready to explode. I study him like it's my job. At the first warning signs, Will and I can hunker down in our rooms and wait out the storm. Still, about once a week I take an elbow in the stomach or a kick to the shins or a shove into a door frame.

My mom is here, and she's not here. Some nights I find her sitting alone in the living room. The space is dark except for a glow from the tip of her cigarette. She's watching out the front window, waiting for something or someone. I never know what or who. Some nights she's out past midnight. I don't know where. Some nights she doesn't come home at all. One night I startle awake. There's a man's voice in the hall outside my bedroom. *Shh. You'll wake my kids*, I hear Sharon whisper. I hear her bedroom door close and latch. The next morning, the man is gone.

If I tell my mother what Alan has done, if I show her the splinters on my door or the bruises on my torso, one of two things might happen. She will dismiss it with a shrug, *What do you expect me to do about it, Gina?* Or she will punish Alan by hitting him with a leather belt which leaves him wailing and confused and only fuels his anger even more. So, Will and I try not to tell her. It's an unspoken pact. We protect Alan from her, though no one protects us from him.

One particularly bad night, my mother is out on a date. I am cooking hamburger patties for my brothers. 10,000 Maniacs is playing on the stereo. I'm standing in front of the stove, flipping the meat, singing along with Natalie Merchant, trying not to splatter grease on my brand new, yellow fleece hoodie, the one I bought earlier today for twenty-five dollars, the last of my cash. I earn forty to fifty dollars a week from babysitting jobs, sometimes more. A decent chunk of money for a fourteen-year-old, but more than half of it I give to my mother to buy groceries or help pay bills.

Sharon would never say that we are poor. She pays the mortgage and electricity on time most months using her paycheck from secretarial work and my father's support payments. It's the other expenses that she seems to struggle with. The telephone bill. Her car payments. Groceries. Water. Clothes for me and my brothers. I can guess our shortfall each month based on how soon the bill collectors start calling. If it's toward the end of the month, I know we'll scrape by until Dad's next check arrives on the first. But if they call before the fifteenth and start threatening to turn services off, I know we're more than a month behind.

I lie to her about how much I earn, keeping back a few dollars here and there for myself. I stash my money in a zippered pink wallet and shove it deep beneath my mattress. It's not often my mother lets me go out with friends – she needs my help at home – but when she does, I use my cash to pay for things. Movie tickets. Snacks.

This day I went to the mall with my closest friends, Lucy and Stephanie. Lucy I've known since preschool; she is quiet, kind, and generous. She has long, red hair and freckles. She plays tennis and violin and volunteers at her church. She's the kind of straitlaced kid who never gives her parents any reason to worry.

Steph is a poet. She's creative and a little edgy, which I like. Her bedroom walls are plastered with travel photographs and music posters and quotes from writers she admires. She is often the one to introduce me to new books to read and new bands to listen to. Her passion for art is contagious.

We're friends because we're in many of the same classes, and we're friends because they're two of the most authentic, nonjudgmental girls I've ever known. They don't avoid me because of Alan. A lot of kids get shifty and quiet when they meet my brother. He makes them uncomfortable, and so by association, I make them uncomfortable. Lucy and Steph don't treat me any differently. Around them, I feel normal.

Lucy's dad had loaned her his credit card to buy some new clothes. Steph had some cash from babysitting. My friends aren't rich, but they always have enough. Whereas I don't ask my mother for money for fear of her screaming that I'm selfish, reminding me we barely scrape by as it is, railing against my father and how he doesn't pay enough child support to cover all of Alan's expenses – my friends ask freely for whatever they need.

At the mall, we wander through several stores. Lucy purchases a few things: a green striped rugby shirt at The Gap, some berry scented lotion at a beauty store, a new journal at the bookstore. I experience a vicarious thrill every time she hands over her father's credit card, like anything is possible. Steph has torn a hole in her favorite pair of jeans, and so she searches several stores for a new pair, settling on the ones that are marked down fifty percent at Rich's. As she takes them to the dressing room to try on, I peruse the sale rack and notice the bright yellow hoodie. I am drawn to it immediately, partly because of the buttery soft fleece, partly because it is on clearance, but more so because of the embroidered logo across the chest that says *Esprit*, in bold letters. It's a brand I've seen in magazines and emblazoned on the popular girls at school. Though I can't articulate it at the time, I want the hoodie because I want to belong. I want to feel like a normal kid who does normal things like buying name-brand clothing at the mall. And so, though I know I won't have money left over to eat with my friends at the food court, I hand over all my cash to the clerk.

Back at home, as soon as my mother leaves home for the night, I put my new hoodie on. Just slipping it over my head conveys a sense of power. I feel proud that I was able to buy myself something that she couldn't.

I'm in charge. I'm cooking dinner. I'm running my left hand across the embroidery, *Esprit*, and holding a spatula in my right hand when I hear Alan approach me from behind. He's pressing his body against my back and trying to reach around me to grab a hamburger out of the pan. I take a step backward and shove him away with my hip "You'll burn yourself, Alan. Just wait a few minutes." He lunges forward again and grabs my wrist. I elbow him, and in doing so, the greasy spatula smears across my new hoodie. I shriek, "Look what you made me do! Why can't you just sit down and be patient while I cook?"

"I want dinner now," he hollers.

"Tough shit! Now you're going to have to wait longer." I throw down the spatula and rush to the sink to try to wash out the stain, but the water only makes the grease spread.

Behind me, Alan grabs a steak knife from the counter and presses it into my back. I feel the sharp tip pierce my clothing before I fully realize what he's doing. I carefully turn around to see him holding the knife awkwardly at my chest, gripping the handle the same way he grips a pencil. This action, holding the knife to a person's heart, is something he's seen on television, I think. We've caught him flipping through channels late at night, watching cop shows and R-rated movies. I've seen him pantomime holding a gun and firing it. I don't think he understands the real-life consequences of wielding a weapon and using it to harm someone.

He cocks his elbow and lunges at me, hoping to stab, but the handle slips from his fingers, and the knife falls to the floor at my feet. I kick it hard. It slides across the linoleum and lodges beneath the refrigerator. Alan stares at me, his lip quivering. There's no premeditation here. Neither of us knows what he'll do next.

Will runs in from the other room, eyes wide and fists raised, "Leave her alone, Alan!"

"Will, don't. Just get out of here before he hurts you, too." I lunge for the stove and turn the heat off. Alan is standing by the sink, frozen. The fight has disappeared from his eyes. I run out of the kitchen, upstairs to my mother's bedroom, close and lock the door, and call my father long distance.

Dad moved from Atlanta to the Midwest a few years ago for a teaching position at a prestigious university. He's involved in high-profile research projects, traveling frequently and working on computer security projects for the U.S. Department of Defense. We see him every six months. Sometimes less. It's tough to reach my dad on the phone because of his schedule, but I am alone and scared and have no idea how to reach my mom, so I just dial the number and pray. My fingers tremble in the rotary holes. I want him to answer, and I don't. I want him to know what's happening, and I'm afraid of the fallout with my mother if I tell him.

He answers, and I'm so surprised to hear his voice that I tell him everything in a single breath. I can handle the punching and kicking just fine, I tell Dad, but the knife thing is new.

I'm having trouble catching my breath. I've been terrified before. When Alan has broken windows. When he's pinned me to the ground and kicked me. When he's dragged me by the hair. I've felt trapped. I've panicked and cried. But I always knew the moment would pass. His surge of violence would end, and I'd scramble to my feet and recover. *Just close your eyes*, I'd think. *It'll be over soon*. But tonight feels different, like his rage has reached a whole new level.

"I really think he could have killed me this time," I say to my dad and start to sob.

"Where's your mom?" he asks.

"I don't know. She's out. She might not be back until morning."

"Did she leave you a number to call?"

"No."

He sighs and mutters something under his breath. "Okay, put Alan on the phone."

I call downstairs to my brother and tell him to pick up the phone in the kitchen. I hear his labored breathing when he picks up and guess that he's scarfed down all the hamburgers on the stove.

"What?" Alan says.

"What did you do, Alan?"

"I not do nothing. I hungry."

"You almost hurt your sister very badly."

"I not mean it."

I listen to my dad's voice, loud and stern, as he lectures Alan. He scolds him, threatens him with punishments I know he can never follow through on from so far away – taking away his music, his favorite toys, confining him to his room. But somehow Alan seems intimidated enough to comply. He hangs up the receiver and puts himself to bed for the night. I hear him stomp down the stairs to his bedroom and slam the door.

I thank my dad. He tells me to gather up all the knives and scissors, anything sharp, and hide them somewhere Alan won't find them.

"I'll talk with your mom about this tomorrow," he assures me. "But the next time he threatens you, don't call me. Call the police."

Chapter Nineteen

Boulder, August 16, 2016.

I've called the police a few times in my life. Once, in college, I dialed 911 when a guy in my dorm overdosed on a hallucinogenic drug and everyone else was scared to call. I called when I witnessed a drunk driver weaving dangerously through traffic. I called in the middle of the night when a vandal threw rocks at my house, breaking a window. Those were easy calls to make. Lives are at stake. Crimes have been committed. It's time to call for help.

In so many areas of my life, I am confident, self-assured. I have a voice. I can advocate for others. But when it comes to seeking support for myself, I'm paralyzed. Despite my dad's admonition, I never called the police to report Alan's violence. I didn't call when he tossed a chair through a window. I didn't call the night he tried to strangle me. I didn't call on those nights my mother went missing, in the era before cell phones, when I had no idea where she was or whether she was alive or dead. The idea of calling for help felt too extreme, too dramatic.

Other people had it worse. It wasn't a big deal. I'd be fine. I was always going to be fine.

And now. Though I know intellectually that I am an adult, that I am safe, that I have options, that my parents no longer have power over me, I still feel the bind. I was afraid then as I am afraid now of bringing other people into a murky situation. I'm afraid of what they might see and what they might not see. I worry that things are so much worse than I imagine or, alternatively, that it's not so bad.

I can close my eyes and hear my mother's shrill voice in the days following my phone call to my father. *How dare you? Don't you know he'll use this against me? Why do you feel the need to dramatize everything? You're making up stories for attention. If you're hell-bent on airing our dirty laundry, you might as well kill me.*

In other words, the cost of my speaking out was her life. Figuratively. Literally. It didn't matter. On some level, conscious or not, I knew that the price to pay for sharing my experience was too high. So, I kept quiet and swapped her truth for mine. And now, I still struggle to know the difference.

I think about the police, whether they would have been any help back then. I wonder if there's any legal recourse now for a sibling who wants access to more information. Alan is dead. He's gone. There's nothing obvious that suggests there's more to the story. Maybe I'm fooling myself, avoiding the emotional pain that's sure to overwhelm me. Instead of facing the loss and regret over not understanding my brother better, I'm busying myself. And perhaps I'm also avoiding some guilt over the idea that I could have done more to help him, to help all of us. Not just in recent years, but back when we were kids.

Fact: As I turn these thoughts over in my mind, I feel very alone. But the reality is I'm not alone. I'm surrounded by Kris, my kids, and my closest friends. They're more than just a support system. They're my family now, and while they can't go back in time and repair my past, they can help me heal from it.

Fact: In a couple of years I'll ask these people what they remember about me in the weeks following Alan's death. They'll tell me that I acted unsettled, that I was withdrawn, brooding. Some will say I was preoccupied with the idea of an autopsy and medical records, but when they asked, I couldn't tell them why. At some point, I'll tell my inner circle the whole story, everything I was thinking at the time. Everything I've uncovered since and failed to uncover. And to my shock I'll find that a few of them were thinking these things too, wondering if Alan's death could have been prevented. Kris will tell me that he was quietly asking the same questions I was, that he too was searching for someone or something to blame, but he was too afraid to tell me. He didn't want me to feel worse than I already felt.

It will all seem incongruous, how I could feel so alone and so afraid to reach out.

Fact: This is the complexity of grief, that it can be lonely, isolating. Yet, it's also universal. If you are a human being who dares to love other humans, you will grieve.

Fact: Some losses are so unpalatable to ourselves and to others that we feel like we have to package them somehow, force them into a shape that we can hold and examine without fear. This process is endless and exhausting.

Fact: Though the circumstances of Alan's death are unique, my sense of loss, my questioning, my confusion is not.

Fact: The weight of grief is compounded by tangential losses. Loss of opportunity. Loss of a shared future. Loss of control. Loss of innocence. Loss of the illusion that we'll ever know the answers to why, to how, to what if.

Fact: Relationships that are fraught in life become no less

complicated after death. The unanswered questions, the unfin-
ished business between you and your loved one don't go away.
If anything, the loss only amplifies the unknowns. The questions become your inheritance.

I'll learn that if I had just spoken up, if I had managed to
somehow reach outside of myself and voice my need for
answers, I would have perhaps discovered that I'm not crazy,
that my questions are valid, that safe people were available the
whole time, waiting, ready to step in, intervene, walk beside me
into the scary unknown.

Chapter Twenty

Atlanta, 1992.

My sophomore year of high school, I am tall and thin. My wardrobe consists of fraying thrift-store Levi's and a collection of white t-shirts, some V-neck, some crew, some tank tops. I wear Birkenstock sandals, the ones my father bought me for Christmas, even when it's cold outside. My blond hair is long and wavy, well past my shoulders. I don't wear bangs.

I'm not a member of any particular social group because I fit in with just about everyone. I like it this way, under everyone's radar. I make good grades, and I have a core group of friends who are kind and genuine. Lucy and Steph are still two of my closest, but I've also gotten to know other kids. High school has given me some space from my brothers. Now when I meet new people, they don't think of me as Alan's sister. I'm just me.

One afternoon as I am leaving school to walk home, Mrs. Ellison, the guidance counselor, intercepts me in the hallway. Except for brief meetings to discuss class schedules and sign up for standardized tests, Mrs. Ellison and I rarely speak. Yet, she is one of my favorite people at the high school. She is warm and nurturing—she wears brightly colored cardigan sweaters and corduroy pants, and her reading glasses always hang around her neck from a silver chain.

There are some mornings my mom has trouble getting out of bed. She can sink into a deep depression overnight. I find her in a fetal position under a blanket, or sometimes crouched and crying on the bathroom floor. Her whole body quakes as she complains how much she hates her job, hates life, hates having kids. No one will ever love her again, she says. We're all damaged, she says. Nobody wants us. It's like for weeks she is standing on the threshold of a dark doorway, and one day she steps through. Disappears. There's no telling how long she'll stay on the other side or if she will ever step back into the light.

Mrs. Ellison speaks in a southern drawl, her voice thick as molasses, and is the soft, friendly face who always lets me use her telephone, no questions asked. When my mom is suicidal, I want to call and check on her. Mrs. Ellison steps out of her office to give me privacy as I call. Though she never pries, she smiles at me knowingly. She offered once to talk with me about my home life, but I politely refused. "Everything's fine," I told her. "I just had to call my mom and remind her I'll be late getting home today. Science Club meeting." I avoided her eyes and dashed back to class.

This day she catches up to me as I pass her office and puts her hand on my shoulder.

"Do you have a minute, darlin'?" she asks.

"Sure! What's up?" I am rarely in a rush to get home after school. Most days, I hang out on the front lawn with several friends whose parents also work full-time. We stretch out on the warm, manicured grass, rest our heads on our backpacks, and talk. We play hacky sack, listen to music, flirt with boys.

Sometimes we read our assigned homework pages until the sun dips behind the rooftop of the gym. That is our cue to go home.

Mrs. Ellison leads me inside her office and asks me to sit down in the armchair opposite her desk. She sits down and places her palms flat on the desktop as if to say, let's get down to business. "Tomorrow, Ms. Jones, the county social worker, is coming for her weekly visit, and I've asked her to speak with you."

"Um, okay. Why?" I don't know much about Ms. Jones except that she shows up periodically and keeps track of the pregnant girls, drug users, and other "problem kids" to make sure they are attending class and on track to graduate. This is a large public high school in the city limits of Atlanta. We have our share of disadvantaged kids.

I'm far from disadvantaged. I'm in the gifted program. I maintain Bs and As in all my classes. There's no chance I'd become pregnant because I don't have time to date, and even if I did, I can't let anyone see the bruises on my body inflicted by Alan. I don't attend parties. I prefer listening to music alone or hanging out with a few close friends. I once stole a mood ring from a gift shop at the mall – slipped it into my pocket and walked right out. I wore it every day afterward, until the cheap metal turned my skin green. Another time, I lied about having a babysitting job so that I could sleep over at Lucy's house. I've smoked a few of my mother's cigarettes, and when she gives me cash to buy her more, I skim a couple extra dollars from her wallet. A few times I've called myself in sick to school just so I can experience the joy and freedom of being home alone without anyone to take care of except myself.

None of this, I think, warrants a visit from the county social worker.

"Well, one of your teachers has expressed concern about you," Mrs. Ellison pauses and seems to be searching for the right words. "You're looking very thin and tired," she says solemnly.

"Oh... Well, I'm not dieting or anything," I say lightly. I tuck my hands under my thighs to stop them from shaking. There are a few girls in my grade, mostly cheerleaders and gymnasts, who are being treated for eating disorders, and I assure her that I am not intentionally losing weight. If it's true that I'm too thin, it's because I am less hungry than most people. I am the opposite of Alan. I need little food to feel satiated.

"Well, it's not just that," Mrs. Ellison goes on. "Your friends Stephanie and Lucy came to see me the other day and told me a little about what's happening to you at home."

It takes a moment for her words to register. What's happening at home? What could she know?

Then, it hits me. A few weeks ago I hosted Steph at my house. It was a Friday. Mom came home early from work buoyant, effervescent. I hadn't seen her this radiant in months. Just looking at her, I felt a rush of energy. She told me she'd just received a bonus at work, and a colleague had asked her on a date. To celebrate, she suggested I invite a friend over. She handed me two crisp twenty-dollar bills and said I could order pizza and rent a few movies.

"I need to pick out something to wear," she said over her shoulder as she dashed up the stairs. "Can you and your friend babysit the boys tonight?" It felt good to see her gliding through the house like this – hopeful and light. I watched her in the bathroom touching up her makeup and curling her hair and was reminded of how she used to dress up like this for my father. I wondered if the cash bonus coupled with a fancy date were omens of better things to come.

The evening started out calm. Steph arrived around 6:00. We ordered two pizzas, a veggie one for us, and pepperoni for my brothers. We served slices onto paper plates, poured tall glasses of soda, and ate huddled around the television. After the movie ended around 9:00, Will disappeared upstairs to his room to read. I told Alan it was time for bed. Steph grabbed his pajamas from a pile of clean laundry on the couch and handed them to me, and I walked Alan to the bathroom to brush his teeth.

"I not tired," Alan said.

"It doesn't matter," I replied. "It's bedtime." I was eager to get him to sleep so Steph and I could hang out, talk, and listen to music in my room.

Alan turned back toward the living room. "I need to hug Steph," he said.

"I'm not sure Steph wants a hug," I said, looking back at my friend. She shrugged as if to say, *It's fine, no big deal.*

He shuffled over to her, arms outstretched, pulled her into a bear hug and wouldn't let go.

"That's enough, Alan," I said. He squeezed harder. "That's enough!"

"I can't breathe, Alan," Steph squeaked, a hint of panic in her voice.

"Alan! Stop!" I screamed, prying his arms off my friend. He let go, and then immediately turned to me, grabbed me by the hair, and slammed my head into the wall. I saw a flash of white light and felt immediately dizzy. As I regained my balance, Steph stepped between us and yelled in an unnaturally deep voice, "Do *not* hurt your sister!" She shook a fist in his face, though he stood nearly a foot taller than her. Alan, seemingly caught off guard by Steph's anger, took a few steps back. It gave us an opening to run.

Steph and I rushed to my room and locked ourselves in. Alan stood outside the bedroom door for an hour, kicking and punching it until he finally kicked a hole in the bottom, getting his tennis shoe stuck in the hollow core. He then sat outside my door sobbing and apologizing.

"Does this happen a lot?" Steph asked.

"No," I lied, "he's just overtired. And the sugar. I probably shouldn't have let him drink soda." I tried to smile as if to say, *Don't worry. It's no big deal.* It happened so often I might have convinced myself it was normal. Except the look on Steph's face conveyed otherwise. She looked terrified.

Lucy wasn't there that night, but I can guess Steph told her what happened. Lucy and I are close. Like me, she has two brothers. In some ways, I think, we are the sisters we each wish we'd had. I once spent a weekend with her and her family at their lake house north of Atlanta, and another time I traveled with them to their beach condo on the Georgia Coast. Each time it felt like they were whisking me away to somewhere magical, like a fairy tale. A sparkling lake framed by forests and mountains. The white beach dotted with sea stars and sand dollars. *Nothing bad can happen here*, I thought. Ensconced by nature and my friend's loving family, I felt safe, protected.

We never talk openly about it, but Lucy seems to intuit when things are chaotic at my house, and she tries as best she can to intervene without making a big fuss about it. Once, when I got my period unexpectedly in chemistry class, Lucy slipped out and called her mother, who brought me a change of underwear, shorts, and maxi pads. Neither of them asked why I couldn't call my own mother for help.

Sometimes after school, Lucy teaches me how to drive her Honda sedan around the student parking lot. She always packs extra food in her lunch, too, in case I don't have anything to eat. And she gives me hand-me-down clothes from her closet.

As I sit staring at Mrs. Ellison, the puzzle pieces start falling into place. On some level, I have convinced myself that I'm hiding something, that my friends don't know the extent of the crisis at my house. I smile. I minimize. I endure. Meanwhile, they not only notice what's happening, but they have quietly intervened.

Years from now, I will ask Lucy what she remembers about my family growing up. She will offer a few recollections, but none more telling than this one: She will say she remembers me calling her one day terrified that Alan was going to seriously hurt me. I had developed an internal seismograph that could predict his violent outbursts with accuracy. I felt one coming on, sensed his agitation building to a breaking point. I felt like I couldn't escape this time, and so I called my friend for advice.

Lucy will recall rushing over to my house and walking in the back door to find my mother sitting on the couch, smoking a menthol cigarette and watching game shows on television. I am sitting in a chair opposite my mother.

"I wasn't sure what you needed me to do, so I just sat there in the living room with you, and we chatted about nothing important," Lucy says. "I thought maybe you felt safer having someone else there."

Suddenly, she recalls, Alan bursts into the room, grabs me behind the neck, and yanks me out of the chair. I scream at him to leave me alone, to sit somewhere else, but he is so imposing. He takes my seat by force.

"Your mother just sat there," Lucy says. "It's like she was there, but she wasn't."

As I sit with Mrs. Ellison, a part of me feels betrayed that my friends would go behind my back and talk with her about me. These aren't their problems to tell. The last thing I want is pity or to be seen as needy. I feel exposed, vulnerable, embarrassed.

Yet, a bigger part of me also feels relieved that someone, an adult, finally knows what is going on and wants to help. When you hold onto secrets too long, they begin to taste sour, like curdled milk.

"Ms. Jones is going to question you about the abuse and discuss options with you for getting some help," Mrs. Ellison says.

It is the first time I've heard that term associated with my situation: *Abuse*. It makes me uncomfortable. It is too extreme a word, I think. A term you hear on those cheesy after-school specials. Life at home is tough, sure, but it isn't abuse, is it? There are kids far, far worse off than me. Yes, my dad is absent. My mom is a single mom. She is lonely and overwhelmed and forgets about me and William sometimes. And Alan gets a little carried away with his tantrums. He is essentially a five-year-old trapped in a grown man's body. He doesn't know his own strength. My family doesn't exactly feel okay to me, but it feels normal because it's all I've ever known.

I tell Mrs. Ellison this, and she just looks at me, quizzically.

"Well, if we can help make things better for you, we want to do that, and Ms. Jones can help." She seems sincere, but still, I am wary.

That night, lying in bed, I wonder what kind of help the school might offer. I think about stories I've read about children being rescued and placed in foster care or an orphanage. I have no real knowledge of these things. The idea sort of glimmers like a mirage in the distance. I'm terrified of what might happen, but I'm also intrigued. I wonder what it would be like to live somewhere else for a change, with another family. I think about Lucy's house or Steph's, where there's always food in the refrigerator and two parents who want to know how you're doing, how school is going, how you feel, what you want to be when you grow up. Or, better yet, maybe I'd be sent to a boarding school far from the city and not deal with family at all. This idea intrigues me the most: Starting a new life on my own, on my own terms, choosing the people I want to spend my time with.

The next day Mrs. Ellison comes to get me from chemistry class, and my teacher looks as if he is expecting her. I wonder if the whole school knows I am meeting with the social worker and what they must think about me. But Mrs. Ellison assures me this is being handled discreetly and no one, not even my mother, will know about it unless some action is taken at a later date.

The walk around the corner to the counseling office feels a mile long. I notice for the first time the mottled pattern of the polished concrete floor and the endless rows of lockers along the walls. My breathing becomes shallow, and I have to focus straight ahead to keep the lockers from closing in and strangling me. The hallway seems to grow narrower with each step.

The door to the office swings open, and there stands Ms. Jones, tall and slender with gaunt cheeks and freckles. She wears a tailored red suit and moves stiffly and doesn't smile readily. She is all business. After initially explaining her role at the school and reiterating what Mrs. Ellison said about my teacher's and friends' concerns, she says she just needs to ask me a few questions. "Don't worry," she says. "Anything you say at this point is confidential."

She wants to know what a typical day is like for me, how often my mom goes out at night, where my dad is living, when did they divorce, how often am I alone with my brothers, what we eat, where we sleep, has my brother ever molested me?

Whereabouts on my body has he punched me, and do I have any bruises currently that she couldn't see? Can I show them to her? It is a laundry list of questions that she fires at me so quickly I barely have time to think.

I hesitate to lift my shirt, but her eyes are on me. I nervously lift the back to show her a fading welt below my shoulder blade, about a week old but still tender. My scalp is sore from Alan pulling my hair, but she can't see that, so I don't mention it.

She jots down notes and asks for more details about particular incidents my friends have told her about and I haven't mentioned.

Then she asks, "Have you ever been to the emergency room as a result of your brother hurting you?"

"No"

"Has a doctor of any kind ever treated you for injuries inflicted by your brother?"

"No," I reply. "Why are you asking me this?"

Ms. Jones just says, "Mm-hmm" and scribbles some more notes.

I sit up tall and pull my shoulders back. I want her to see that I'm strong. I believe at this moment she needs to know that the bruises mean nothing, that I haven't been affected as much as my friends say I have. I want her to see that I'm fine, everything is fine. I don't need her intervention. I don't need anything. Someday I'll look back at this and realize that *this* is the adverse effect of abuse. Bruises heal. But it will take decades to undo the damage that comes from denying my own reality. From being so close to help and not reaching for it.

Ms. Jones puts the tablet down, leans forward, and looks me in the eye. "Honey, I'll be straight with you. In this city, you have to have an ER record a mile long before we'd ever consider removing you from your home."

"I never said I wanted to be removed," I reply softly.

"What is it you want, then?"

"I don't want anything," I say, blinking back tears. *Do I want something? Why does her question feel so painful?* "I'm tired of all this. I just want my mom to be happy and Alan to leave me alone."

She nods. "You have a daddy somewhere, right?"

"Yes."

"And he's never hurt you, right?"

"Right."

She sits back, folds her arms across her chest, and sucks her teeth. "Well, your mama ain't ever gonna be happy," she says bluntly. "If you want to be happy, and if you want your brother to stop beatin' up on you, I suggest you go live with your daddy."

I try to explain that I hardly see my father. He lives out of state and has a new family of his own, and I don't want to move that far away from my life, from Will and my friends. I don't think my dad even wants me anyway, I say.

"Well then, you might start thinking about gettin' a job so you can move away in a couple of years. Go to college. There are scholarships available. Mrs. Ellison can help you apply." She stands up, walks around the desk, pats me on the shoulder, and sends me back to class.

That night, I can't sleep. I keep turning the conversation over and over in my head. I know on some level the social worker is right. My mother might never be happy. No matter how hard I try, no matter how much I step in to help, she may never be okay. And Alan may never grow out of his violence either. Before this moment, I'd never considered a future that didn't include caring for Alan and my mother. The idea is foreign and almost dangerous, but also intriguing, like it's hanging out on the edge of possibility. Every time I go near it, my heart begins to race.

I didn't ask to be rescued, but I realize now how much I hoped I might be. If I was taken from home, it wouldn't be my fault. I wouldn't be abandoning my family. And yet, I'd still be free.

But it doesn't look like anyone will be rescuing me now. If what Ms. Jones says is true, there is no one out there who can take care of me. It's up to me to take care of myself.

I'm enrolled in Advanced Placement classes in my high school. I always assumed college was the plan. But suddenly, I begin to consider what it actually means to pack up my life, move out, and leave my family behind. I imagine myself with a job, with money, with my own apartment and living a life on my own. I picture myself strolling along a cobblestone path at a manicured college campus somewhere, not a care in the world, only responsible for me. It's equally thrilling and terrifying.

Just as I'm starting to drift off to sleep, I am seized by a sharp pain in my chest, like a nightmare, like my heart has stopped beating. I sit upright, sweating. The walls begin to sway.

My brothers. Who will take care of my brothers if I leave? What will happen to them? Can I really abandon them, leave them behind to pursue my own goals, the way my father left us?

Part Four

A Funeral in Slow Motion with Christmas Music

Chapter Twenty-One

Boulder, August 18, 2016.

O Come, O Come Emmanuel.
And ransom captive Israel,
That mourns in lonely exile here,
Until the son of God appear,
Rejoice! Rejoice, Emmanuel

They say an angel appeared to Joseph in a dream and told him that Mary was to have a baby, God's son. The angel said the baby would be called Jesus, Emmanuel, which means "God is with us."

My mother says she had a premonition when she was pregnant with Alan. It was her first pregnancy, but still, she knew he was special. She felt strange, like the baby she was carrying wasn't meant for this world.

By 9 a.m. it's already sunny and warm. I'm wearing a black silk shirtdress. My hair is fastened in a ponytail. Dread settles in my chest so heavy I can't breathe. I can't swallow. I can't speak. Every few minutes, I stare at my watch in disbelief. I have never *not* wanted to be somewhere as much as I don't want to be here.

How many children, in a fit of jealousy or rage, have fantasized about their brother or sister dying? How many have daydreamed about the day when their rival fades away, when the fighting stops, and they are lavished with all the love and attention they ever wanted? I did. In the darkest moments, I dreamed of this day.

It is nothing as I imagined.

As I walk toward the church, my black leather heels clip-clopping on pavement, Kris and my kids disappear from my peripheral vision. They fade from my view, in a dark shadow, waiting, suspended in time until I can come back to them, back from the dark place I am now, this dreadful place. I hear Miles's voice faintly, "What's wrong with Mommy?"

What is wrong?

I see a large wooden door. I grab the handle. I pull. I step inside. A rush of air, thick and cold. The smell of incense burns my nose. A man is waving his hands in my face, trying to get my attention. He's wearing a nametag. He is the undertaker. He's here to take us all under.

Christmas music is playing. Sunlight through stained glass paints multicolored shapes across the walls, across the floor. The undertaker is saying something to Kris and to my uncle about the hearse. The hearse is here, and he needs someone to help unload the casket. His voice is urgent, almost rude. Hadn't we planned ahead for this? The casket is very heavy. He can't be expected to deal with it alone. Where are all the pallbearers?

When I was young, my mother taught me how to wrap Christmas presents perfectly, how to measure the right amount of paper, how to cut a perfectly straight line, how to fold the corners precisely so that the paper is taut, how to place the ribbon, how to use the sharp edge of scissors to create curly bows. It took time. The best things do. And practice. I often had to unfold it all and repeat the steps. But in the end, it was beautiful. People praised the gift-wrapping. *What a work of art. It's almost too lovely to open.*

When Alan wrapped gifts, he used too much paper. He did not fold it neatly. He twisted the paper around and around until the gift was a blob, held together by long, wrinkled ribbons of Scotch tape. Then he'd place a bow on top. *It's wrapped in love,* we would say. It's wrapped in love.

I want this day to be the messy blob of paper, held together by fragile ribbons of tape. Wrapped in love. Instead, everywhere I look it is perfection. Tight. Neat. Too lovely to open.

It came upon a midnight clear,
That glorious song of old,
From angels bending near the earth
To touch their harps of gold:
'Peace on the earth, good will to men,
From heaven's all-gracious King.
The world in solemn stillness lay
To hear the angels sing.

Yet with the woes of sin and strife
The world has suffered long;
Beneath the heavenly strain have rolled
Two thousand years of wrong;
And man, at war with man, hears not
The tidings which they bring;
O hush the noise, ye men of strife,
And hear the angels sing!

O ye, beneath life's crushing load,
Whose forms are bending low,
Who toil along the climbing way
With painful steps and slow,
Look now! for glad and golden hours
Come swiftly on the wing;
O rest beside the weary road
And hear the angels sing!

When I heard that Mike was skipping the funeral, I was angry, confused. Now I am jealous. I don't want to be here. A couple of friends who live in Boulder have promised to come so that I will know someone here, so that I will see familiar faces, so that I will feel some support. I look around now, but I don't see them yet. It's still early.

Another friend suggested I write Alan a note and place it in his pocket while the casket is open. This morning I sat staring at a blank page for an hour. Nothing came to me. I have so much to say and nothing to say.

I sense my children tugging at me, willing me to come back to them, to be present with them. I sense them, but I can't see them. I see a tall wooden podium cradling a guest book. I see people lining up to write in that book. What can they write? They are here. He is not. I guess someday we'll look back and know they were here.

9:15 a.m. The door swings open, a flood of light, chased by a dark shadow. The casket comes through the door. Shiny with brass handles. It looks heavy. It bobs and weaves through the doorway. I hear the men grunt. We move out of the way. They take it (him) back to another room, the small chapel, the original 1920s one-room sanctuary that the rest of the church was eventually built around, large stone walls around a small heart. There the casket will be opened. There the family will gather to say goodbye, in the heart of the church.

Alan is intact in the casket, ready to be viewed. Afterward, he'll be burned, the ashes divided fifty-fifty. What happens to him after that is unclear.

I wonder who does the dividing, how the proportions are determined, who weighs this and decides that it's fair. Who is the cartographer, drawing boundary lines upon my brother? Who decides what geography gets to claim him, my mother's or my father's? Do his ashes go back to the river that created him? Do any pieces of him belong to me and Will? Or will he occupy a landscape that's all his own?

My skin is prickling. My head aches. Red and green flowers adorn the aisles. Everything looks red and green to me, though I'm not sure if this is reality or if I'm seeing colors that aren't here. The fabric draped over the tables. The ribbons adorning the church pews. Plates of cookies are placed on the red and green table. A tri-fold poster board is placed behind the cookies, like a science fair display. On the board are photographs of Alan.

Away in a manger, no crib for his bed
The little Lord Jesus laid down his sweet head
The stars in the sky looked down where he lay
The little Lord Jesus asleep on the hay
The cattle are lowing, the baby awakes,
But little Lord Jesus no crying he makes

My two-year-old nephew, Will's son, is running around as toddlers do, defying his mother, yelling NO. NO. NO. My sister-in-law is chasing him, trying to scoop him up. His arms and legs flail. She looks at me, apologetic. This is not the time or place to misbehave, she is saying. I smile and tell her it's okay. I'm thankful to witness his unbridled rage, like a tiny mirror.

9:30 a.m. Time is moving too slowly. In the heart, that tiny room, stifling hot, Alan's open casket is on display. I had hoped to have a moment alone with him, to say goodbye, but my family is packed into this small room so tightly it's hard to breathe. It feels like all eyes are on each other, measuring each person's response. Are we appropriately sad? Is it okay to smile at the incongruence of hearing Christmas music in August? Does anyone else find this strange? We all sit shoulder-to-shoulder, passing tissues, staring at the casket. No one speaks.

Long lay the world in sin and error pining,
Till He appeared and the soul felt its worth.
A thrill of hope the weary world rejoices,
For yonder breaks a new glorious morn.
Fall on your knees!
O hear the angels' voices
O night divine
O night divine

He doesn't look the same. I knew he wouldn't, and yet I'm surprised to find him so still, so quiet. I could always hear him breathing. No matter where he was in the house, you could always hear him breathing. I can't remember ever seeing him with his mouth closed.

His body is dressed up. It's pumped full of chemicals. There is makeup on his face. He's resting peacefully inside a satin-lined box, antiseptic, neat, wrapped, and delivered like a present under the tree.

Where will they take him from here? My parents did not agree on the burial. This is the compromise: An open casket viewing for the family. A closed casket ceremony for everyone else. Music. Christmas in August. I wonder, but I don't ask, if the casket is cremated with him. How much of the remains will be him and how much will be wood ash and dust? What will remain?

Fall on your knees!
Oh, hear the angel's voices

9:45 a.m. I stare at him for some time there in the box. I watch my uncle place a gold coin in his hand. It's not easy, slipping it under his stiff fingers. I watch him lean in and force it into place. I read somewhere that people will place gold coins on the body of the dead, to bribe the ferryman who carries the soul across the river from this world to the next. Sometimes the coins are placed on the eyes of the dead to prevent the living from seeing their own mortality reflected back at them.

When it's my turn to approach the casket, I face my brother. I notice his eyelashes, like feathers. He always had such beautiful eyes. I notice his hands, his fingernails clean but jagged. You can still see how he bit them down to nothing. I close my eyes and try to focus on what I want to say. My legs start to shake. I open my eyes. I feel embarrassed. I sense everyone's eyes on my back.

9:50 a.m. The undertaker comes in to close the casket and move it into the large sanctuary where the funeral service will be. It begins in ten minutes. He presses a lever, and the lid buckles, and he catches it and guides it down until it's closed. Someone covers the casket in a quilt, a quilt my mother made, the same quilt I saw folded neatly at the foot of Alan's bed after he died. He's in there now, tucked in for the night. Ultimately, I'm unable to say any meaningful goodbye, something I'll come to regret.

Chapter Twenty-Two

Atlanta, 1990.

Alan is sitting in the sitting room. That's what we call it, the sitting room, though it's rarely used for sitting. Some Southerners call it a receiving room, for receiving guests. It's the formal living room at the front of our house with the Ethan Allen sofa and the fancy wingback chairs.

A large picture window lets in the afternoon light. The window stretches floor to ceiling, and behind it is a large empty space that we kids use like a stage for performing. We stand inside the sitting room window and perform for people on the sidewalk outside our house.

Alan is sitting there, in the sitting room with a Sony Walkman clipped to his belt and a fanny pack full of cassette tapes – all Christmas music. He's wearing baby blue Bermuda shorts and knee-high socks and a pale yellow Izod shirt. He's wearing plastic headphones with foam earpieces, playing Christmas music, and singing at the top of his lungs. Singing, for Alan, sounds a lot like shouting. He's shouting the

Christmas music. His voice is so loud that a neighbor walking his dog outside stops and stares.

We're used to it, the Christmas music in summertime and Alan's shout-singing. He shout-sings other artists too. Kenny Rogers, Pete Seeger, Elton John, Prince, Garth Brooks. He doesn't discriminate. He's happiest when he's singing, so we don't ever tell him to stop. Alan's joy, when it appears, is uninhibited. Years from now I'll come to understand that he doesn't have an inner critic. He hasn't internalized "should" or "shouldn't" the way the rest of us have. It is an unexpected gift of his condition, a lack of regard for what others might think of him, the freedom to fully express himself.

I love music too. Before the divorce, music had been a magical force in our family. Riding in Dad's Volkswagen Rabbit, we would listen to cassette tapes of Simon and Garfunkel and Bob Dylan. Dad would press stop in between each song and explain to us its history and meaning. He actually grew up down the street from Bob Dylan (or Bobbie Zimmerman, as my grandmother always called him). Dad bragged about it. He lifted Dylan up as an example of greatness emerging from the dust of a poor mining town. "It goes to show, you kids can be anything you want to be if you work hard enough," he said.

I was probably the only kid my age who knew Dylan's real name or that "The Boxer" was Paul Simon's autobiographical ballad about overcoming loneliness and poverty in New York City.

"There's actually a verse missing," my dad told us excitedly as the chorus reached its crescendo. "It's not here on this tape, but they sang the extra verse on stage during their tour."

When summer thunderstorms pounded our front porch and threw long streams of lightning sideways behind the pine trees in our backyard, my mom sometimes played "I Love A

Rainy Night," by Eddie Rabbitt to ease our fears. I'd run to her with the record album in my hand. "Play it! Play it!," and when she did, my brothers and I would dance and twirl around, jumping on and off the couch.

For a while, we had an upright piano in our living room. My parents aren't musicians, but they owned the piano and a few guitars and liked to memorize catchy songs to play at parties. My dad taught me how to play Chopsticks and a passage from Aaron Copland's "Appalachian Spring." He placed my tiny fingers on the keys at middle C and told me to copy everything he played on the upper register. Over and over again we played until I no longer needed to watch his hands to know which keys to press next.

When I would practice, Alan would slide onto the bench beside me and sit quietly, listening. He'd watch my fingers move across the keys as if studying them, trying to decode the pattern. He wouldn't say a single word, except when I finished playing, and he'd lay his head on my shoulder and quietly beg, "Do it again." Music soothed him then, much the way it soothes him now.

Sometime after the divorce, my mother sold the piano to pay the mortgage, but I never forgot the song or the feeling of Alan sitting so quietly, so content by my side. Years later, I can sit down at any keyboard, close my eyes, tap out the notes, and feel him with me.

The Christmas music is special, though. Christmas is Alan's trademark. Anyone he meets, he asks them what they want for Christmas, and whether they have been good this year. He writes letters to Santa. He writes lists of the foods he wants to eat. He wants turkey and stuffing and sweet potatoes. He wants Coca-Cola in a glass bottle and a mesh bag full of chocolate gold coins in his stocking. He wants new cassette tapes and his favorite movies on VHS and a large tin of flavored popcorn. This is more significant than his other obsessions (food, cars, dogs). He seems to have the ability to channel the joy of Christmastime at any given moment.

And he shares his joy with the rest of us. We all are a bit lighter this time of year. Mom often says, "The best part of having divorced parents is that you get to celebrate Christmas twice." I hear this as a gift in itself. We get two holidays, one at Dad's house and one at Mom's. Two trees. Two visits from Santa Claus. Years later I'll wonder if she and my father were participating in an unspoken competition to see who could give us a better holiday.

Mom spends the last of her cash on an eight-foot-tall, fresh-cut Douglas fir.

"I thought that money was for necessities," I say.

"A tree *is* a necessity," she says.

I watch her hand over the wrinkled bills to a teenager working at the tree lot at a local church. Two tens, two fives, and the rest in dollar bills. "You don't ever want a spruce or a cypress," she says. "They're cheap for a reason. The needles fall off before you even get it home and decorated."

"We don't need a tree, Mom," I protest. A Christmas tree won't feed us dinner.

Alan is crying. He wants a bigger tree, the one that is flocked with fake, pink snow.

"We could get a little tree, like Charlie Brown," Will says.

"This one will look just gorgeous by the fireplace," she says.

We tie the tree to the roof of the Oldsmobile and drive it home. It takes all four of us to haul it inside – Will and I holding the tip, Mom and Alan holding the trunk. Once it's set up, I realize Mom is right. It looks beautiful, almost Rockwellian, so full and symmetrical, standing by the red brick fireplace with our stockings. Mom begins playing Christmas albums. Bing Crosby. Gene Autry. Frank Sinatra. She hangs ornaments and tries to cheer us up by showing us all the hand-made ones we'd given her over the years—a toilet paper roll I'd decorated with markers and yarn so that it vaguely resembled a nutcracker, a wreath made of macaroni noodles painted green and red by Will. A cardboard cutout of Santa from Alan. A paper Star of Bethlehem, wrinkled and yellowed from so many years folded away in a box. She attaches so much sentimentality to our preschool crafts. They are artifacts from an easier, happier time.

Though Will and I no longer believe in Santa Claus, we make a trip to the mall each year for Alan. We stand in line behind the red velvet ropes, the three of us. We wind our way toward the fake winter scene, toward Santa on his throne. We step across the cottony blanket of artificial snow. We wear coordinating sweaters – mine green, the boys red – and comb our hair neatly, the way Mom likes. We smile for the camera. We accept the free candy Santa offers us.

We do this because if we don't stand with Alan, if we don't escort him, he will pester the young children in the line, asking what they want for Christmas and whether or not they've been good little boys and girls that year.

If I'm being honest, we also go with Alan to see Santa because it keeps the magic alive. Mom wants him to keep believing. If he sees that Will and I have lost interest, he will start to wonder. Mom collects the Santa photos each year –the smiling images of all three of us on Santa's lap. The entire time we stand in line, Will and I are embarrassed. We can feel the glares of strangers who sense there is something different about Alan but don't quite understand what it is. Santa asks us to translate what Alan is saying. The whole line of parents and kids stand there waiting, watching, staring. We know we should be more gracious, more patient. But we are teenagers ourselves. We feel self-conscious, uncomfortable in our skin.

And yet, at the end, when the elf hands us the photograph and we study it, when we catch a glimpse of Alan's face, the way he lights up with joy and hope in the fact that Santa heard him, that his wish was received (and will be granted?) Will and I may not admit it, but we can't help but feel a rush of joy too.

Chapter Twenty-Three

Boulder, August 18, 2016.

With each Christmas melody that plays at Alan's funeral, I sense history shifting, remixing. Music is evocative; a few notes can transport you through time to other scenes, other places you've heard the same song. These carols have held joyful memories for me. Not just memories of Alan, but memories of my first Christmas married to Kris when I made us new stockings and ornaments. And later, the Christmases with our children. This music is the backdrop of new traditions we've adopted, the four of us: Kris's famous pancakes on Christmas morning, staying in our pajamas all day, meeting up with friends for hot buttered rum (for the adults) and cider (for the kids). The smell of nutmeg and cinnamon. Going on walks to look at holiday lights. Watching movies and building lopsided gingerbread houses. Licking sweet icing off our fingertips.

But there's an overwriting happening now, and I try to resist it. I try to tune out. I do everything I can to take my mind elsewhere. I have to because I'm already wondering how it will feel next Christmas and the one after and the one after that.

Will I forever associate the holidays with Alan's death? Will I be able to hear a Christmas carol without thinking of his funeral? They are now inextricably linked.

10:20 a.m. Welcome to Holland

"I am often asked to describe the experience of raising a child with a disability - to try to help people who have not shared that unique experience to understand it, to imagine how it would feel. It's like this.

"When you're going to have a baby, it's like planning a fabulous vacation trip - to Italy. You buy a bunch of guidebooks and make your wonderful plans. The Coliseum. The Michelangelo David. The gondolas in Venice. You may learn some handy phrases in Italian. It's all very exciting.

"After months of eager anticipation, the day finally arrives. You pack your bags and off you go. Several hours later, the plane lands. The flight attendant comes in and says, 'Welcome to Holland.'

"'Holland?!?' you say. 'What do you mean Holland?? I signed up for Italy! I'm supposed to be in Italy. All my life I've dreamed of going to Italy.'

"But there's been a change in the flight plan. They've landed in Holland and there you must stay.

These words float over the heads of three dozen people sitting in pews, the mourners. My mother's closest friend is standing at the pulpit reading a poem called "Welcome to Holland." It's an extended metaphor for parents of children with special needs. You wanted Italy? Tough luck. You got Holland instead.

"The important thing is that they haven't taken you to a horrible, disgusting, filthy place, full of pestilence, famine, and disease. It's just a different place.

"So you must go out and buy new guidebooks. And you must learn a whole new language. And you will meet a whole new group of people you would never have met.

"It's just a different place. It's slower-paced than Italy, less flashy than Italy. But after you've been there for a while and you catch your breath, you look around.... and you begin to notice that Holland has windmills....and Holland has tulips. Holland even has Rembrandts."

"But everyone you know is busy coming and going from Italy... and they're all bragging about what a wonderful time they had there. And for the rest of your life, you will say 'Yes, that's where I was supposed to go. That's what I had planned.'

"And the pain of that will never, ever, ever, ever go away... because the loss of that dream is a very very significant loss.

"But... if you spend your life mourning the fact that you didn't get to Italy, you may never be free to enjoy the very special, the very lovely things ... about Holland."

At the third "ever" I hear people sniffling. I get it. It's poignant. There are lovely things about Holland, too. The tulips. The windmills. The adorable wooden clogs. And if you spend your whole life pining for Italy, you might miss those things.

It's a soothing message.

In this moment, however, I am so exhausted, so ready to be done with the funeral, I look at Kris and shake my head as if to say, *I can't do this. I can't listen to this shit anymore.*

All week long, I've watched people's faces as they try to think of the right thing to say in response to my loss, and then proceed to say the wrong thing. I should be thankful that Alan lived to forty-three. He is in a better place. It's hard to understand now, but this is part of God's larger plan. One friend texted, *So glad this weight has been lifted from your shoulders.* Another mourner simply hugged me and said, *I hope you finally have some peace.*

People mean well. They assume Alan's death might bring a feeling of relief. They try to make sense of it, to make the loss more palatable. This is true of every type of loss, every rendition of grief. It's especially true when someone dies young or dies out of turn. It's especially true when your relationship with the dead person was complicated. It's *especially* true when that person has a profound disability and dies suddenly, mysteriously. But platitudes and clichés aren't helpful. They might make the speaker feel better, but not the bereaved.

No manner of rationalizing, of meaning-making, of waxing poetic will make Alan's death okay.

As the Holland analogy drones on, my eyes plead with Kris to let me stand up and leave. He encloses my hands in his and squeezes tight.

While I agree with the poem's sentiment – there are unexpected joys in living with disabilities, and it does no good to dwell on our idealized images of how a family *should* be – the bucolic, peaceful, rolling green landscape of Holland was not our experience either. Is it anyone's experience? I think many special needs families would do better to envision a war-torn landscape, where landmines lurk beneath the tulips. In this place, we are vigilant. We don't know what to expect.

I think about Atlanta, its tumultuous history, and its beauty. The city that was revised by adversity. The city is beautiful in the way a scar is beautiful because it tells a deeper story of resilience. We can make a home here, in these imperfect buildings full of cracked plaster and faulty wiring. But we can never fully relax. You're always looking down the road, peeking around the next curve, waiting for the next obstacle to overcome.

Even then, if we edit the poem, it still doesn't fit because the basic premise, this idea that disabled people are foreign, that "normal" families and disabled families reside in different countries is wrong. It perpetuates the separateness, the otherness, the stigma that makes me (and I suspect many other siblings) feel so dreadfully alone.

At best, the poem is trite and short-sighted. At worst, it is ableism. You can't exile a group of people to another country and then tell them to smell the tulips and be grateful. In doing so, you not only dismiss the complexity of their experience, but you ignore an important reality – that the people you've marginalized aren't all that different from you. We're all human beings, we're all vulnerable and worthy of being known and seen and supported. We too belong in Italy, no matter what our limitations and differences might be.

And if you *really* want to get into it – which I do, anything to take my mind off of my brother in a box – let's consider another problem I have with the Holland-Italy analogy: My father is Italian. He holds dual U.S.-Italian citizenship and has lived in Padua, a university town with cobblestone streets, where every resident is given a clay jug that they fill with the village's own wine.

I glance over at him as the poem is read, trying to see if there's any flicker of discontent on his face. He stares straight ahead, his jaw tight, his face stoic.

My father actually lived in Italy while my mother was in metaphorical Holland.

When we were young, Dad took us there, my brothers and I, which means Alan was in Italy, too. And it was beautiful. Our trips to Italy to visit my father are some of the happiest memories of my childhood. We saw the Coliseum. We gazed at David, that naked marble masterpiece. We toured the Sistine Chapel. We ate gelato twice a day and walked until our feet ached and gorged on seafood and pasta and drank cold Coca-Cola out of tiny Italian bottles.

"Slow down," my dad would say to Alan, who tried to swallow the whole bottle in one gulp. "Enjoy it." He encouraged us to savor everything. Every sight. Every bite. That entire trip, Alan was peaceful, like he knew deep down he was experiencing something extraordinary.

We've been to Italy. And we've been to Holland. So as the poem is read, I cry too, because it seems no one will ever understand.

After the reading, the minister takes the pulpit and gives a sermon. He cautions the mourners not to fall back on clichés. Don't tell the grieving family members that God has a reason for taking Alan away, he says. Don't assure us he is in a better place when we so desperately still want him here. God does have a reason, he says, but it's not one we're meant to know or understand. The pastor, as best he is able, paints a picture of Alan's life. He has a page full of notes, but he forgets many things. When he names all of Alan's family members, he forgets to mention our stepmother and half-sister. He doesn't mention Mike. He asks us all to stand, place our hands on the casket, and pray. We all shift toward the middle aisle and jockey for a position next to the casket. As I place my palm on the box and close my eyes, I get a sad, sinking feeling. I sense Alan is slipping away from me, and it's all my fault. I was selfish in my refusal to help with the funeral. I'd been acting out of pain instead of love. I declined to write a eulogy, and now I wonder if that was the right decision. Alan is in this box, but he's also a vapor, unformed, floating further and further away. I could have been the one to tether him here, to tell people what he was really like, who he really was, at least to me. Instead, with every breath I take, he's drifting. I exhale and push him out into the clouds. He's losing his shape.

• • •

A few nights ago, I awoke suddenly, convinced I needed to remember every good and beautiful thing about Alan. I thought about how Alan made lists on yellow legal pads. I took out a piece of paper and pen and began scribbling my own list. Fragments. Vignettes. Tidbits. The scaffolding upon which I will build him back up into a fully formed being – something I can touch and hold. If I can make sense of these memories, then maybe our relationship will feel complete. He will be whole. I will untangle it all, finally, and make sense of us.

Memories of My Brother, in No Particular Order:

1. When he is not violent, he is endlessly nurturing.
2. Everything I know about acceptance, patience, and what might be considered "normal" stems from my relationship with Alan. Because of him, I am aware that none of us are perfect. No relationship is flawless. We all have our limitations, whether visible like Alan's or not.
3. Alan has a photographic memory. He can name the make, model, and year of any car after seeing it only once before. He remembers the name of any person he meets, even decades later.
4. He loves to swim. On land, his legs and arms are clumsy, but underwater they seem to dance. I watch him, how gracefully he moves, and almost forget for a moment that he has a disability.
5. He is tenacious.
6. His voice is unique. Though it's often a chore, I secretly love that I can understand Alan's slurred speech better than anyone else. It feels like a secret connection that he and I share. Whenever he's speaking and someone looks confused, he looks at me. I step in and interpret for him. I know what he needs.
7. He is both brutal and fragile. Which to me means he's fully human.
8. I wasn't always afraid of him. I used to enjoy sitting next to him when we were smaller.

9. When he laughs, he covers his whole face with his hands, forming a little cave over his mouth, and his laugh echoes in the cave. He laughs at cute animals. He laughs at cartoons. He laughs at small children swinging on a playground.
10. I am so afraid of him and so sad to feel so afraid.

I stop writing and look at the list. I realize I could keep going like this forever, and I wouldn't feel any better. I have dozens, maybe hundreds of happier memories of Alan to counteract the painful ones. But they are just that, memories. No matter how hard I think about him, no matter what I write, I'll never be able to separate out the strands of our relationship. I'll never bring him back.

10:55 a.m. Will steps up to the pulpit. In his shaking hands is the eulogy he has written, the one he volunteered to write when I said I couldn't, when I was too afraid that my ambivalent feelings might burst through, a tangled mess of grief and anger and resentment and love and loss. When I looked around at the crowd of relatives – of strangers – at my mother's house, I realized I could not trust myself to be transparent with any of them.

I admire Will's bravery. He is terrified, and yet he stands, and he speaks. I squeeze his arm as he stands, a gesture of solidarity, a small show of support for whatever it is he has to say. As he begins to speak, it becomes clear to me that he is shaking because he intends to share some truth, *his* truth, which is in part our truth as siblings.

"I'd like to say that I always saw the blessing of having a brother like Alan," he says, "but that's not the case." His voice cracks as he talks about the embarrassments and frustrations he felt having a brother who towered over him and acted like a child. He talks about the experiences with Alan that helped him gain compassion, patience, and a zest for life.

Will dares to say what no one else today will, that to love Alan was often difficult. It was complicated and messy. His words ring truer than any I've heard since the day Alan died, and for the first time all week, I feel like I have an ally in the family. When he returns to the pew and sits next to me, I rest my head on his shoulder and cry. I don't care who is watching.

What happens next feels like a dream, and maybe it was, but I can recall it vividly: When it's finally over, when all the prayers have been said and communion has been administered and the casket is wheeled away and placed into the back of the hearse (the undertaker once again huffing and barking orders) and the people file out into the lobby and eat their cookies, a woman wearing a dark suit and nametag approaches me. She works for the church or the funeral home, I think. She has an official presence, a glow about her. She's holding a folded quilt. It's balanced on her arms like a serving platter. I recognize this quilt as the one that was folded at the foot of Alan's bed. I can see the same squares and triangles I traced with my fingers at Sharon's house a week ago. The woman extends the quilt to me. *We're cleaning up, and I wasn't sure what to do with this,* she says. *It looks special, and I didn't want anyone to put it in a closet by mistake.*

Sure, I say. *It's something special. It's good that you brought it to me.* I thank her and hug the quilt to my chest. It's heavier than it looks, layers upon layers of fabric stitched together. Calico, florals, and plaids mixed with squares of robin's egg blue. Stiff piping along the edges.

In my dream version of this, I steal the quilt. I smuggle it out of the church and into my car. It's my keepsake, my token, my reminder of Alan. It represents some tangible sense of peace, of knowing. I plan to sleep under it every night for the rest of my life.

In reality, I stand there for a long time holding the quilt, reckoning with what I know I need to do. In looking at the intricate stitching, the patchwork, I understand that this item is more a reflection of Sharon than it is of Alan. What is a quilt really except a decorative cover? Yet, it's also a source of warmth and comfort. I think of what the fabric conceals, the loose batting inside. Insulation held together by polyester threads. Tug on a few seams, and it might all spill out.

I look up and see her at the other end of the lobby, surrounded by a few of her friends. I take a deep breath and walk toward her, my heels echoing on the stone floor. I feel emboldened, like the quilt will protect me from any harm. It gives me something soft to hold against my chest as my heart beats louder and my eyes start to sting.

"This is for you, Sharon," I say, offering her the quilt. "Keep it somewhere safe."

Her eyes scan the quilt and then my face. We haven't really been alone this entire week, the two of us. It feels strange and uncomfortable. Though people are milling around, for a moment it seems like we're the only two people in the room.

Part of me wants her to give the quilt back to me, like a peace offering or an apology, something to help me remember her in all her complexity. But instead, she takes it and buries her face in the folds. "Thank you," she says. "It still smells like him."

"I'm so sad that he's gone," I say, letting the tears spill over. I don't try to stop them this time. "I wish there'd been more time. I wish there had been more..."

"I'm really glad you came, Gina," she interrupts. Her

mouth hangs open like she might have more to say, but nothing comes out. After a moment, she hugs me awkwardly, then turns and walks away.

I find my friends in the lobby along with Kris and the kids and they fold me into a safe circle and shelter me from the small talk and the crowds of people I barely know. I scoop up Miles and hold him against my chest until my arms are sore. I feel connected to my chosen family in a way I didn't two hours ago.

Someone suggests we all sneak away to my favorite coffee shop for a while. We can hide out there and pretend like it's any other summer day in Colorado. Kris holds open the large wooden door, and a rush of air flows in. We go and we sit and we sip our drinks. The kids order cake and frosted pumpkin bread and juice, more sugar than they're usually allowed in a day, but I'm happy to indulge them. We sit around a picnic table outside the coffee shop and watch the joy on their faces as they eat, the lightness they seem to feel at being free from the confines of church pews and dress clothes and weeping adults. A light breeze tousles their hair. They giggle. I wonder if this will be one of their shared memories – this day, the funeral, the Christmas music, the treats afterward. And, if so, will it be a sad one or a happy one?

Kris is squeezing my hand, running his fingers across my knuckles. He leans in and whispers in my ear, "The worst is over."

I nod, but think, *is it?* My head feels lighter. My shoulders have rolled back into a more open posture, and I'm able to breathe a little deeper. I'm no longer clutching my watch, willing time to move faster. But there's still a knot in my stomach, a burning lump, and I wonder what that means.

Chapter Twenty-Four

Atlanta, 1992.

Following my meeting with the county social worker, my mother receives a sealed envelope from my high school in the mail. Inside is a typed letter mandating that I attend counseling. They want a signed statement from a therapist verifying that I have completed five sessions. I don't know what explanation the letter gives or if anyone at my school has had a conversation with my mother or if she knows about the failed intervention during which Ms. Jones told me she couldn't help. I don't know what the school says the consequence will be if I don't go to therapy. I know what my mother tells me: that I have been labeled "at risk" for not graduating.

We're both standing in the kitchen, sorting through piles of coupons and magazines. "Well this is bullshit," she says, tossing the letter on the counter with a stack of unpaid bills.

It seems unlikely that anyone at my school believes I won't graduate. I have a high GPA and participate in honors classes, sports, and extracurricular activities. I do as much as I can to excel – in part because school is my refuge, in part because I've felt pressure over the years to do all the things Alan can't, to appreciate every opportunity I'm given; and lastly, because somewhere deep down I hope my achievements will win me more attention from my father.

Not to mention staying busy after school keeps me out of the house. It lightens the burden to cook dinner and take care of my brothers. But I'm not sure if my mother even knows this. She doesn't see my report cards. I don't show her my As on tests and term papers. She works late most nights and doesn't ask questions about what I do after school.

It strikes me that the school administrators might be giving me an excuse to get help without tipping my mother off to the fact someone reported our family for abuse. It could be that they're simply following protocol. Or they could be giving me a tiny window out. Either way, I'm intrigued.

My mother is muttering under her breath, shaking her head, having a pretend conversation with someone. "It's those kids she's been hanging out with," she says, unaware I'm still standing next to her. "I think they're doing drugs. She shouldn't be associating with them."

By *those* kids, she means the handful of my friends who wear army boots and plaid flannel shirts and listen to grunge music – the poets and writers. We all work together on the school literary magazine. A couple of times a week, we gather in a windowless classroom on the basement floor of our high school. We arrange the desks in a circle and pass around a stack of student submissions – short stories, essays, and poems. We jot down notes and discuss the merits and flaws of each piece and vote on which pieces should be included in the next issue. Some submissions are easy to reject – the sappy love poems that rhyme and lack any originality, the essays that rail against teachers and the establishment without any unifying theme or insightful takeaway. Others we debate at length, like the short story about a young girl whose parents are so busy with their own lives that they fail to see her anymore. They neglect to see how she's changing ever so slowly into a ferocious wolf. By the time they realize it, it's too late. She devours them all. I love the extended metaphor, how the wolf represents darker feelings, the resentment so many teenage girls feel but rarely can express. But some of the other editors think it's too melodramatic. "No one hates their parents *that* much," one girl says. We publish the piece, and it goes on to win a state award.

A few of the literary kids smoke Camel cigarettes in the student parking lot. One day my mother picked me up early for a doctor's appointment and saw me standing with them in a huddle, ribbons of smoke floating above our heads. "Those kids really have some nerve smoking on school property," she said.

My friends sometimes offer me a cigarette, but I decline. Though I like the earthy smell of Camels much better than the menthol of my mother's Salem Ultra Lights, my determination not to be like her is stronger than my desire to fit in with them. I've seen the way the cigarettes have turned her fingernails yellow. I can see the tiny wrinkles forming around her lips. I hate the way all my clothes carry the stale smell, no matter how many times I wash them. Most of all, I resent the way she spends our grocery money on her habit.

Aside from the smoking, the most rebellious thing my friends do is sneak out to see their favorite bands play at music halls in Midtown Atlanta. I go with them once to a place called The Masquerade, an old mill that's been converted to a concert venue with three stages called Heaven, Purgatory, and Hell. It's dark and grungy and full of smoke. But the music is transformative. We jump, dance, and rush the stage. Dancing under the pulsating lights, the bass vibrating in my chest, I am happier than I have been maybe ever. Years later I'll look back and wonder if this is what childhood is meant to be like – wild and free. Full of wonder and irrepressible joy.

My friends are passionate, I tell my mom. They push boundaries. But at the core, they are really good kids. None are doing drugs.

Mom makes an appointment with a therapist in the same group as the marriage counselor she and my dad had seen so many years ago. They accept patients on a sliding scale, and she says my dad will cover the balance.

I'm not sure she actually believes my problems can be traced to my father leaving, but nonetheless, she uses it to guilt him into paying. She tells him it was all his fault. "He said he didn't think therapy did any good for anyone—look what it solved in our marriage," she says. "But then I told him you're depressed and confused because he left us."

When Mom and I get to the therapist's office, we are greeted by Lorie, a stylish woman in her forties, though her shoulder-length blonde hair and trendy pants suit makes her appear younger.

Lorie leads us to her office and sits across from the two of us for a few minutes while my mom explains that she received this letter from my school and she suspects I am depressed and possibly on drugs and crying out for attention.

I barely say a word. I sit there, arms crossed, trying to avoid eye contact with either of them. I glance around Lorie's office. It is decorated like someone's living room—overstuffed couches framing a rustic wooden coffee table and various landscape photographs and paintings hanging on the walls. It reflects her personal style without revealing anything personal about her. There are no pictures of her or her family, although I notice she wears a wedding ring.

Lorie thanks my mom and then suggests that she and I chat alone for a while. "Kids find it easier to be honest without Mom or Dad in the room." She winks.

As soon as my mother leaves the room and closes the door, Lorie lets out a huge sigh and asks me outright, "What's going on at home?"

I am reluctant to say anything, not sure if this new person will believe me, not sure whose side she is on. How do I know she won't repeat everything I say to Sharon? Sensing my hesitation, Lorie shifts gears, asking me instead about school, friends, music I like, and books I've read. I don't believe her when she claims to like the same music as I do. REM, 10,000 Maniacs, Bauhaus, The Cure, and Morrissey don't fit with her generation or tidy appearance.

We spend nearly an hour talking about music and books and talking about nothing. But we are talking, and I think that is her goal.

Over the course of several weekly meetings, I open up a little and tell Lorie progressively larger pieces of my story, still holding back the most painful details. I tell her about my dog, Puff, who died. Puff was a white terrier, a little cotton ball of goofy energy. My parents had given her to me when she was a puppy, around the time Will was born. It was as if for a brief moment they knew that I would get lost, sandwiched between a new baby and Alan's intense needs. I'd need someone to love me in a way that they could not.

In the beginning, Puff slept in my room with me. I'd place her gently in the back of one of Alan's Tonka dump trucks and give her rides around the house. I'd tie bows in her hair and sneak her scraps from my dinner plate, cradle her like a baby and rub her pink belly until she fell asleep in my arms. But we never properly trained her, and she peed all over the house. She chewed the legs of furniture and yapped whenever I left her alone. Eventually, Mom said she had to sleep in the basement, where she howled and scratched at the doors. Then my Dad bought a wooden A-frame doghouse for the backyard, and for the rest of her life, Puff lived and slept outside. I still played with her every day, but over time she developed mange, and her fur began to fall out in fluffy clumps. She began to look less like a dog and more like a scaly rat. When she died, I felt sad but also relieved that she was no longer suffering. It's not her fault we couldn't give her the life she deserved, I tell Lorie.

Lorie listens to this story. She listens to other stories I tell her, like the one about the time Alan got mumps and my mother said he was going to die. How his fever spiked so high and his neck looked so swollen, I thought his head would explode. I tell her how terrified I was for him, and also how sad I was for Will and me because nothing ever happened to us that made our parents drop everything and give us their undivided care. I tell her how I'm jealous of Will because no one expects him to cook or clean or take care of Alan like I do. I tell her how I feel so guilty for wanting more, but I do. I want so much more. I want more freedom to hang out with my friends. I want to know how it feels to let go, to party, to make mistakes. I want to open the pantry and find that there's always food, maybe even my favorite snacks. I want to stop worrying all the time. I want to sleep soundly at night without keeping one ear open for Alan rummaging through the garbage. I want my mother to pay the bills so that the phone isn't turned off again. I want someone to tell me I'm doing a good job at school, to notice how hard I'm studying, to say that they are proud. I want my dad. I want him to kiss me on the forehead and tell me he's here now, he's staying, that everything will be okay.

I don't tell her about Alan's violence or Mom's long

absences or how she often says she wants to die. I don't tell her that what I really want more than anything is to feel safe.

Lorie also meets separately with my mom and a few times with us together, and then one day she asks my mom to drop me off and not come in.

I greet Lorie and sit down on the couch across from her. She and I just stare at each other for a moment. Her forehead is wrinkled. She looks as if she is searching for the right words. I pull the cuffs of my sweater sleeves over my hands and fidget in my seat. After what feels like an eternity, she says, "Your mom thinks you exaggerate about how difficult things are at home."

Here it is, I think. The moment Lorie will tell me my mother is right, that I'm making things up, that I'm crazy. I begin to wonder if it's true. Maybe I am the pathological liar my mother says I am. Maybe all I have to do to make this nightmare stop is to be quiet and deny it all. My mother is right. I've brought all this pain on myself. But then, what about Steph? And Lucy? What they saw? And what about my body, the bruises, the way I feel so anxious all the time? Is my body lying too? I wonder what Lorie would think if she knew, I mean *really* knew everything.

"I never asked for any of this," I say. "I never complained to anyone about Alan or my mother or anything."

"I know you didn't," Lorie replies. "In fact, I think there's more going on than you're telling me." She pauses again, searching for the words, then says, "I think your mom is in a lot of pain, and her sense of reality is clouded by that pain. I think Alan is confused about who is in charge at home, and he wants more attention from your mom, and when he can't get that attention, he takes it out on you. Does that sound about right?" She waits a beat, then continues, "I think your dad has been in and out of your life in a way that is painful and confusing for all of you."

I don't respond. Her words feel truer than anything I've ever heard from an adult. All these weeks, I thought she was going through the motions, listening to me talk about nothing. I thought we were simply fulfilling my school's request for counseling. I assumed we'd reach the end, and she'd sign a form and that would be it. But here, she'd been working out a puzzle week after week, reading between the lines, intuiting what I was unwilling to say.

"You're taking care of the household, and no one is taking care of you," she says, finally. "Don't you want someone to take care of you?" She clasps her hands and holds them against her chest like she's pleading with me...or pleading *for* me.

I am silent. Though I have grown more comfortable around Lorie than during our initial meeting, in the end I fully expected her to take my mom's side. The honesty of the moment scares me. I sit there for several minutes, staring down at the carpet. I can sense Lorie still looking at me. I can feel the empathy in her body language and the space she is giving me to absorb her words. At home, I am alone, unseen. Here, someone has really seen me. She sees right through me.

"Just breathe," she says, leaning forward, "you don't have to talk. Just breathe."

I let out a long, slow exhale. My chest moves in and out. In and out. And then out, out, out. An enormous weight is lifted as I realize she really does get it. She gets the complicated dynamic of Alan's disability, the love and resentment I feel toward him, the affection and the fear. No one has ever said to me that my mother's reality might not be real, that my unease might mean something, that I should listen to it. Lorie is right. I want to be cared for. Everything is not fine.

I close my eyes. All the emotions I have been holding so tightly unravel, and I start bawling. I give in to the tears, chest heaving, and cry for what feels like an hour.

Lorie inches her chair closer and leans in. Part of me wants to climb into her lap and let her hold me. I want to be four years old again. I want her to stroke my hair and rock me to sleep.

It's all I've ever wanted. Every time I sat alone watching my parents orbit Alan, tending to his needs. Every time I watched them cradle him and rush him to the hospital, unsure whether he would be okay. Every time I realized he would never really be okay, not ever. Every time I desperately wanted Alan to play with me and realized he couldn't do the things I could do. Every time I felt guilty and sad about my able, healthy body. Every time I tried to comfort Will when my parents weren't available. Every time my mother came undone, and I had no one to turn to for help. Every single time. I longed for a safe adult to swoop in and make it all okay.

I stare at my size ten tennis shoes, the laces untied, and reality sets in. I am practically an adult. This woman can't hold me. No one can. I am no one's child. I sit up straight and reach for a tissue.

"Look at me," Lorie says. "Look at my eyes for a minute."

Her face is soft, full of compassion. Her eyes are brimming.

"You deserve so much more than your parents gave you," she says. "So much more. I want you to know I am proud of you, and I'm confident you're going to find your way in the world despite their fuck-ups."

I am surprised to hear her say "fuck."

"I want you to start thinking about what life holds for you after you graduate and leave home," she says. "You can't change your family, but you can survive it. You can heal and make a better life for yourself."

I see Lorie a few more times after this. Our sessions are lighter as we move toward an ending. She asks me what I want to do, what I want to be. I admit to her that I've dreamed of being a lawyer or maybe a writer. I want to travel. Even as I tell her this, I feel a twinge of shame like I'm betraying my family. I also feel exposed by telling her what I long for, what I might need. But as I speak, Lorie's face lights up. She leans closer, as if to say, *Tell me more.* And so, I continue. I tell her I want to date. I want to feel cherished by someone. I want to find my soulmate, someone who really sees me and loves me for who I am, no matter what my childhood history is. I want to build a new life with this person and have my own family someday. I want kids – two, maybe three. I want to be the mother I wish I had and give them everything I wish I'd been given. But first, I tell her, I want to go away for college. I want to be successful, like my father. But unlike him, I want to share that success with my spouse and kids. I want to be present for all of it. To savor it.

Lorie has me make a list of colleges I want to attend, and we look at brochures and scholarship applications together. She helps me imagine myself living in different places. I don't realize it at the time, but she's planting seeds, sparking my imagination, helping me chart a path.

At our last session, I bring her my school yearbook and ask her to sign it. She flips through the pages carefully and stops somewhere in the middle. She stares at me, thinking, and then writes a few words, closes the book, and hands it back to me. I hold it against my chest, too self-conscious to read what she wrote in front of her.

Later, at home, I flip through and find her looping penmanship. She's written simply, "Trust Thyself. Have Courage. Go the Distance. – L."

Part Five

The Four Corners

Chapter Twenty-Five

August 19, 2016.

"When I die, I want my ashes spread here," I say to Kris as he drives.

"On the highway?"

"No. There." I point out my window toward the Sawatch Range, a parade of 14,000-foot peaks that tower above US-285 as it winds southwest from Denver. Against the backdrop of mountains, the cars along this route look like little ants marching in a line. What does that make the four of us, I wonder? We are smaller than ants.

Early this morning, we stuffed our clothes into whatever suitcases had space, tossed them in the trunk, and hit the road. We barely said goodbye to my family. It's more accurate to say we fled. We're needed back in Arizona, I told them. The kids have missed more than a week of school already, and I have deadlines to meet. Kris's boss is calling.

All of this is true, but it doesn't really explain my rush to leave.

I wanted to drive straight through. It's fourteen hours from

Boulder to Phoenix, not too bad when you consider that Kris and I could switch off driving. The kids could sleep and watch movies in the backseat. But Kris thought we should break it up over two days, stay overnight in Durango, ease our way back into the desert, the heat, back to normal life. "Let's take a night to catch our breath," he said. "We'll eat a good meal, walk along the river. You can go to bed early."

So that's what we're doing. We're etching our way. My forehead is pressed to the glass. I'm willing myself to memorize every beautiful scene, every crag.

We switchback up and over mountain passes. As we drive along each hairpin turn, I feel myself swallowing the questions and secrets of the past week further and further down. I'm winding up the loose threads, tucking them away for now. I tell myself I'll be back. I always come back.

If you were to sketch a topographic map of my life, mountains would occupy the middle space, the backbone. Everything leads to here and everything emanates from here. When I was a kid, my dad once took me hiking along the weathered granite hills of North Georgia. He planned for us to go just two miles, thinking that's all my young legs could handle, but I kept pushing farther until finally he said we had to turn around before dark. Not wanting to leave, not wanting my time with him to be over, I sat down in the middle of the trail and cried.

In my twenties, in between semesters at college and graduate school or on my days off from work, I did not go visit my family like other students did. Instead, I headed for the Appalachian Mountains, sometimes driving a couple of hours just to sleep out on a grassy saddle before waking at dawn, packing up, and driving home in time for work or school.

The peaks of central Colorado hold special meaning, though, because for the past several years they've been our refuge. The way to survive living in Phoenix, we've learned, is to leave every summer like the snowbirds do. For the past several years, we have made a pilgrimage every July, escaping Arizona's oppressive triple-digit heat and renting a house that's perched 10,000 feet high above the town of Breckenridge. We stick our hands out the car windows as we climb north out of the Monument Valley into Colorado, and up and over the Continental Divide, feeling the temperature drop every few miles. By the time we pull up to the house in Breckenridge, we're putting on fleece jackets. It takes us a couple of days to acclimate to the elevation. At first, every step leaves us breathless. We sip water to keep headaches at bay. Once we feel strong enough, we explore the miles of trail that radiate from the house's front doorstep.

The peaks are massive and also gentle with their soft green foothills skirting the base. I'm fascinated by these ridgelines, how they form the Great Divide, how the peaks got their names. I love mining-era history and how along some trails you can still see bottomless shafts or the remains of century-old log cabins. Within the Sawatch, you'll find a handful of mountains named for Ivy League schools: Mounts Harvard, Yale, Princeton, Columbia. There's also Mount Massive and Mount of the Holy Cross. And Mount Elbert, the highest peak in the Rockies.

As we drive by at fifty miles per hour, the mountains don't move. They fill my window like a slow-scrolling painting. For hours, I study it.

It's not just the scenery that gets me, though. It's the way quirky little towns tuck beneath and between the summits and somehow manage to thrive. It's the way you come around a curve in the road and discover a metal shack housing a Thai restaurant or an espresso bar sitting all alone along the dusty highway shoulder, and you stop, because *why not?* And you discover the food is so fresh and delicious that you think about that meal for years afterward. It's the old western storefronts and roadside fruit stands and the signs advertising parcels of land that make you wish you could stay here forever. It's the trailheads that beckon you to stop and explore closer, trails that are so plentiful and remote you can hike all day without seeing another human being.

It's always been this way. For as long as I can remember, mountains pull me in. They heal me. Something about their size or the improbability of the peaks scraping the sky or the millions of years of geologic history contained within. If mountains like these exist, then anything is possible. There are forces so much bigger than life or death. There is beauty and good in the world.

When I die, I want to be part of this beauty. I want to curl up in the crook of these mountains, lie down on the blanket of sagebrush at their feet, and go to sleep for a very, very long time.

Kris's relationship with mountains is a little different. He sees them as bursting with potential for adventure. He loves the way mountain ranges create their own weather systems, how it can be sunny one moment and snowing the next. He looks up at a sheer face of rock and wonders if it's climbable. He looks at maps and deciphers which routes haven't yet been traversed. Then, he traverses them. Over the years, he's mapped and published several uncharted routes.

We crest a high mountain pass, nearly 12,000 feet, where the road slices through solid rock, and begin the swirling descent down. Kris takes his foot off the brake and lets the car glide, slowing down only before the tightest turns. My heart starts to race. It's thrilling, feeling my body pressed against the passenger door with a force so hard I wonder if I could fall out. The kids are in the backseat giggling. They like the sensation of falling. It's like a rollercoaster, they say. They raise their hands above their heads and sway from side to side. I feel a lump catch in my throat. I grab Kris's arm and ask him to slow down. He's only going forty, maybe forty-five, but it feels like we're careening downhill, racing. Gravity could win control at any moment and yank us down the mountain. I fear we might plunge over the edge.

Kris slows down to twenty-five as we come around another hairpin curve. As if by providence, we see a row of red flares, a warning. At the end of the flares is an SUV that's driven off the road, skidded into a ditch and overturned. A young couple is standing next to a police car, arms around each other, their faces gray. They're shaking but appear unharmed. We slow to a crawl as we pass the scene and it becomes clear – had they slid fifteen feet more, they would have gone over the edge and plummeted to a riverbed 1,000 feet below.

The kids fall silent. Kris reaches over and grabs my hand. He maneuvers around the wreck and continues down the road, driving more cautiously. I don't say, "I told you so." There's no need. I don't feel vindicated. In fact, I feel calmer than I have in days.

This has happened before—this thing where I've been in a car and had a premonition of danger. When I was twenty years old, I was sitting in the passenger seat of my best friend's old Ford Bronco. We were on vacation at the beach, driving down a sandy four-lane highway, listening to mixtapes, and singing along. My long blonde hair was tangled with sea salt. My skin rosy and sticky with sunscreen. I had my bare feet up on the dashboard when I suddenly had a feeling that I wasn't safe. My seatbelt was off, so I twisted around, pulled it across me, and clicked it into place. I put my feet on the floor, sat upright, and waited. Moments later, I looked to the right out my window and saw the grill of a large flatbed truck a split second before it crashed into us. The Bronco rolled and tumbled several times. I saw pavement and sky, pavement and sky, and then pavement. We came to rest upside down, still buckled to our seats. My mouth, which I'd opened to scream, was full of windshield glass, like pebbles. My friend and I were cut and bruised but otherwise unhurt.

I don't need another reminder that life is fragile, that things can change in an instant. I need to know how to prevent these catastrophes in the first place. My instinct is to take the scene and press rewind in my head. I wonder: What series of decisions made in fractions of a second led to this couple careening off the road? What micro-adjustments did the driver make? How did he course-correct? What was it about the texture and slope of the road's shoulder that kept them from going over the edge?

Somehow, if I can understand the sequence of events, I believe I can inoculate myself from the same fate. It's like the mental gymnastics we go through when we hear that someone has cancer —we wonder what the early warning signs were. Did they engage in high-risk behavior? Were genetics at fault? We try to keep ourselves safe this way, by finding something or someone to blame for what went wrong and avoiding the same mistakes. We all want to feel some measure of control over our lives because chaos is too painful. We don't want to believe that we're all just hugging the curves, tracing the edge between life and death.

Of course, no amount of dissecting a tragedy will prevent more bad things from happening. It occurs to me that my unresolved questions about Alan's death might be serving the same charade. By investigating, analyzing, and overthinking the details leading up to his death, I might simply be trying to bypass my grief, control it, or avoid the pain of losing someone else that I love. I might be looking for a way to protect my future self.

Maybe the more important question is this: What voice told me that I should put on my seatbelt that day when I was twenty? What voice told me that Kris should slow down right now, right here, before this curve? What voice is telling me to seek answers for Alan?

Is it my own?

Chapter Twenty-Six

Once we get to Durango, we decide to walk around the historic downtown. Nestled at the base of the San Juan Mountains with the Animas River flowing through it, Durango is known for its narrow-gauge steam railroad that makes daily trips north to the town of Silverton and back, gripping the mountainsides along the way. While today Durango is more a hub for outdoor adventurers and tourists, in many ways, it still feels like an old railroad town. Much of the architecture along Main Street dates back to the late 1800s and early 1900s.

It feels good to stretch our legs after a long car ride. The kids want to see the railroad depot. Kris wants to grab a beer at a local microbrewery. After walking several blocks, we stop by a pizza place where we sit on a shaded patio and order slices. We fold them in half and take big bites, letting grease drip from our chins. Then, after dinner, we stroll along the sidewalk flanking the Animas, the rapids providing a sort of white noise that means I don't have to speak. Bronwynn and Miles take turns throwing rocks into the still pools behind the churning water. They compete to see who can make the biggest splash.

I take a step back and watch my children moving through space and time. They look happy and healthy, leaping along the shoreline. Their arms move like windmills as they try to throw the rocks farther and farther. They are simultaneously a part of me and separate from me. I've always had this visceral awe, marveled at how they formed in my womb and burst forth into the world their own unique people.

Right now, they look like a dream, like if I were to reach out and touch them, my hand would slip right through their bodies. I wonder if they are a conduit between this life and whatever comes next.

I wish they could tell me what Alan might have felt, what he knew at their ages. I wish they could tell me if their affection as siblings is typical and whether it will endure. I want to imagine them this connected as adults. I want to know that they will never question their love for one another.

That night in the hotel, I can't sleep. I listen to the rhythm of Kris's and the kids' breathing. I stare at the sliver of blue moonlight creeping in through a crack in the curtains.

There's only one way I know how to make sense of the unknown. I research. I list facts. I document. I create timelines.

I grab my laptop, sneak into the bathroom, and sit on the cool tile with my back to the door. I open my email in one browser tab and a blank document I title "Alan notes" in another tab. Maybe I can find a thread, a pattern, I think. Draw a map that will navigate me toward some answers. I search my inbox for every email containing Alan's name. I have messages going back to 2009 when Kris and I were still living in Colorado, about thirty minutes away from where Alan was living with Sharon and Mike. Our daughter Bronwynn was a toddler, and I was pregnant with Miles.

I remember Alan's excitement that year, his anticipation of a new baby. He obsessed over my growing belly, always wanting to touch it, asking me when the baby would come out. He didn't have a sense of how long nine months is to wait. He was confused, impatient. That impatience was heightened by the fact that we didn't find out the gender of the baby. *What is it?* He would ask repeatedly. *When can I play with it?* To him, I think a new baby held the same excitement as Christmas morning, a shiny new toy or puppy.

My relationship with my mother back then was rocky at best. During that time, she desperately wanted to be involved as a grandmother, and I wanted my kids to know her too. But she struggled with boundaries. She wanted to see Bronwynn several times a week and resented me if I told her we had other plans. When we did get together, she'd sneak Bronwynn sugary treats and let her watch scary television shows, telling B it was "their little secret." I remember wondering if Sharon could learn to respect my parenting style or me as a mother. I wondered if she understood that I was building a family separate from my family of origin, that I was consciously trying to mother differently than she had. To me, that meant fostering a healthy relationship with food. I didn't want my daughter to feel like she needed to hide what she eats. It also meant that we wouldn't keep secrets.

Once, I left Bronwynn at Sharon's house while I went to a nearby coffee shop to write. This was something I was reluctant to do because I worried about Alan's behavior around the baby. I worried he'd have a fit in her presence and that she'd get hurt somehow. Or that he'd squeeze her too hard, unaware of his own strength. But this day my mother arranged for Alan to be with a respite caregiver for a few hours so that she could have time one-on-one with Bronwynn. I agreed and relished the couple hours I spent sitting on a sofa with my laptop, sipping a cappuccino.

However, when I came back to my mother's house, I walked into a strange scene. Bronwynn was crying hysterically as my mother tried to wrestle her into a neon pink cowgirl costume, complete with a hat and fringe. The sight stopped me in my tracks. I asked Sharon what she was doing. She said she wanted to take silly photos of the baby, but she knew I wouldn't approve, so she was trying to do it quickly while I was out. "It's harmless!" she exclaimed as B wailed.

Of course, I didn't approve. I bristled at all the times she dressed me up as a kid just to show me off to strangers. I didn't want her to force my daughter into the same uncomfortable situations. It felt like pageantry. More than that, though, the scene triggered something deep inside me, the felt sense of my needs being dismissed. Though it wasn't just my needs this time. My daughter was crying, and my mother was ignoring those cries.

I took a deep breath and tried to stay composed. I told her it looked like Bronwynn didn't approve of this activity either. "You can't force her to play dress-up with you," I said. "Do you hear her? She hates it!"

I looked at Sharon's face and saw a blankness that harkened to my childhood. It was as if she couldn't register what I was saying. She was not fully present. It reminded me of the days she was depressed, desperate for something to distract her from that depression. That something would *not* be my baby, I thought.

I felt a fire ignite in my chest, a fierce protectiveness, the intensity of which I hadn't yet experienced as a mother. This is what it is like to see your child in pain, I thought. Had my mother ever felt this way toward me? Had she wanted to protect me?

The difference between me and my mother, I realized, is that I knew better. I was clear-headed. I understood at this moment that I had more power to protect my family than my mother did. I scooped up my precious daughter, walked out, and never let my mother babysit again.

None of this is documented in my emails, which are all polite and short. Most are group messages Sharon sent to inform my dad, Will, and me about Alan's ongoing needs. I open the emails one by one and start typing notes and creating a timeline:

August 2009:

Alan is accepted to a group home in rural Colorado that specializes in adults with Prader-Willi Syndrome and other developmental disabilities. He's been in other group homes before and been kicked out, but we're hopeful this time because this home is on a ranch with animals Alan will love. Plus, it's a food-controlled home whose staff has experience with managing violent outbursts. If Alan successfully completes a trial stay, he'll be admitted as a permanent resident.

Miles was born in October of 2009, and the next couple of months are a sleep-deprived blur. I don't remember this, but I see it documented in my emails that Sharon sent everyone photos of Alan at the group home. She reports that he's doing very well. He's lost some weight, which she attributes to all the chores he's doing with the animals around the ranch. My father goes to visit Alan at the home and later replies to the group thread saying that Alan is doing really well there, that he seems happier than ever.

Then, in November, Sharon writes again to say that Alan

did not successfully complete his trial stay at the home. The message is abrupt, confusing. My dad replies to ask for more details. *What happened?*

My mother explained that there was an inadvertent error in Alan's medication. A miscalculation in dosage led to Alan acting more combative, and while the caregivers corrected the mistake within a day, Sharon said they were "very negative" with Alan and couldn't be trusted. After that, Sharon brought him home.

I remember this email thread. I remember feeling confused and disappointed. I remember and can see that I emailed my dad and asked him to intervene. I asked if he'd call Sharon and work out a plan for Alan. I suspected that the email explanation for Alan's dismissal didn't tell the whole story. If my parents couldn't find a way for this group home to work for Alan, I worried that there wouldn't be other options for him long-term. My dad replied and said he agreed, that something didn't add up with what he'd seen when he visited the home. He explained how he felt he'd been shut out of any decision-making process when it comes to Alan. His hands were tied, he said, but he agreed to talk with Sharon. Looking back, I can't be sure if he ever made that phone call. There are no further replies in the email chain.

Sometime around Thanksgiving that year, Will and I took Sharon out to lunch and asked her pointedly what long-term plans she'd made for Alan. We told her that we didn't feel equipped to manage his intense needs or his food restrictions, and we hoped she would reconsider the group home and send him back there.

"I don't have a long-term plan," she replied matter-of-factly. "If I die, either you or your dad will have to take him, or he'll become a ward of the state."

Her reply felt loaded, like she wanted one of us to relent

and say we'd take guardianship of Alan. I remember at the time I was thinking about my kids, how I refused to put them in the path of Alan's violence. I knew Alan was not able to control his body, that a surge of hormones or hunger could lead him to lash out at the nearest person. I loved Alan deeply and wanted what was best for him. I didn't want him ever to be institutionalized. But what came first for me was the safety of my children. I was ready to walk away from Sharon and Alan if necessary in order to protect the kids.

Historically, I've been the one to stand up to Sharon. Will tends to placate her, protect her. He doesn't like to rock the boat. But as her words settled over us, I watched Will's face flush with anger. His hands balled into fists under the table. I could tell he was trying to stay calm. His response was direct, measured.

"I hope you'll consider meeting with a social worker or a lawyer," he said. "Figure out what your options are and put some long-term care plans in writing. You owe that to Alan. And to us."

In the spring of 2010, Kris and I prepared to move with the kids to Phoenix. Kris had been offered a job there, and we both were up for a change of scenery. By then, our interactions with my mother had grown increasingly volatile. She would call us begging for help caretaking Alan and then scream that we didn't love her if we refused. We attended awkward family dinners during which she sedated Alan so that he'd behave and not eat too much. More than once, Alan fell asleep at the table. Mike was away traveling for work, which increased my concerns about Sharon and Alan. I dropped by a few times to check on them and discovered her still in her bathrobe late in the afternoon. Yet, when Kris and I expressed concern or offered to call a social worker or therapist on her behalf, she insisted we were overreacting. Everything was fine.

I didn't know how to make sense of it, but one thing was clear to me: I didn't like how I felt or who I was in proximity to my mother. I was regressing into a younger version of myself. Hypervigilant, sad, confused. The more time I spent in Sharon's world, the more my sense of self, my independence, slipped away.

I saw the move to Phoenix as an opportunity to make a clean break, but I was afraid to say this out loud. Afraid of how she'd react, or maybe afraid that my empathy for her would prevail, and I wouldn't follow through with expressing my needs. So I carefully composed an email of my own. I said that I did not want to have contact with her anymore. I said that our relationship wasn't healthy for either of us. I could no longer caretake her and also mother my children. I emphasized that I welcomed hearing from Alan. But in order for me to be a healthy parent to my kids, I needed distance from her and from the painful memories of our shared past. I told her I hoped she understood.

Her reply came within a few hours and was brief. She thanked me for my honesty, said that she loved me and that she really hoped I could "work through all of this."

I initially felt relief. *She's not arguing. She's letting me go.* Then anger. *What does she mean she hopes I can work through this?* Once again, she was placing the responsibility on me.

Mid- Late 2010:

Sharon's emails consist solely of medical updates on herself and Alan. One note says that her surgery went well, though I have no idea what surgery she's referring to. I didn't reply to ask. A few months later, she writes to say Alan has fallen down and broken his foot. A few months later, Alan has surgery on the broken foot because it didn't heal properly. A few months after that, she thinks she sees blood in his urine, fears he has cancer, and takes him to the emergency room for tests, all of which are normal. Two weeks later, she worries about his breathing and takes him to a pulmonologist who declares his lungs are normal.

As I sit now in the hotel room reading these emails, I'm reminded of the time before my parents divorced, when my mother used Alan's disability as her siren. Her code red. *Something is wrong. It's Alan. Come quick.*

I remember a therapist trying to explain to me the way my mother's mind works, how it takes in information from her environment and distorts it. It's like looking at the world through a smudged camera lens, the therapist said. A minor threat becomes a catastrophe. A slight rejection or disagreement equals abandonment. A momentary sadness means she'll never experience joy again. Or, in this case, a urinary tract infection in Alan means he has bladder cancer and will surely die.

Reading Sharon's words leaves my stomach in knots, my thoughts racing. I toggle between concern for Alan, compassion for Sharon, and confusion. Is all the noise really about Alan? Is it about Sharon? Or is it about me?

At some point, I see that I stopped replying to her messages. I relied instead on Will to keep me posted on Alan's well-being. I also sent Alan cards in the mail and let him know he could call me directly anytime he wanted. Kris continued to act as a mediator, setting up visits and calls with Alan on my behalf. I was here for Alan, I said. My loyalty was to my brother.

By the end of 2010, Sharon stopped including me in the

group emails. In February 2011, my stepmother forwarded me a message that said Alan had been hospitalized and was in the intensive care unit with breathing problems. He suffered cardiac arrest, she said, and no one knows exactly why. This, I realized, was not a false alarm.

The next day I flew from Phoenix to Boulder to visit Alan. I took Miles with me. He was fifteen months old at the time and a joyful distraction during the visit, giggling and babbling and toddling around. By the time Miles and I got there, Alan was improving. He was on supplemental oxygen and was sitting upright watching movies and chatting about cars and dogs. The doctors didn't figure out exactly what caused him to go into cardiac arrest, but they thought it could have been a respiratory virus or an allergic reaction of some kind. It's possible, they said, that he had eaten too fast and aspirated some food.

I wish I'd asked more questions back then. What was Alan's long-term prognosis? Did they think this could happen again? What could prevent it?

I continue to read the emails and type notes in the document. I click over to medical journals and read about the symptomology of Prader-Willi Syndrome but don't see anything about heart or lung problems. I see papers and studies that try to map all the complexities of the syndrome, from the psychological symptoms to the cognitive delays to the endocrinology. I see journals that discuss the need for appetite control to prevent obesity among children with Prader-Willi. I see where some doctors list possible treatments and medications but question whether the potential benefits outweigh the side effects.

I'm not sure how long I've been at it. An hour? Maybe two? My eyes are heavy, and the words start to blur on the screen. I don't know what I'm looking for. Patterns? Medical jargon? Something my mother might have said or done? I'm jotting down the dates. August 2010. February 2011. July 2011. November 2011. Then, there's no news for two years.

In March 2014, there's an email from Will. Alan was in the hospital again with breathing problems, but just for one night and only for observation. He recovered quickly and was available by phone the next day. I remember this email. I remember feeling a punch in the gut as I read the first lines and relief by the end of it. Alan was not okay. Alan was okay.

Scrolling up and down my inbox is like moving backward and forward in time. 2010. 2011. 2014. Suddenly, I notice a message from July 2015, and I freeze. The subject line says, "Colorado visit." I know instantly what this is. Kris, the kids, and I were spending the month in Breckenridge to escape the Phoenix heat, and I was arranging a visit with Alan. As I open the message, my hands start shaking, and I'm unable to type or even scroll further down the screen. This wasn't what I was looking for as I began researching. But here it is staring at me like a neon light on my computer screen: A record of the last time I saw Alan alive.

There's no way I could have known that this would be the last time I'd see my brother. Did I have any sense of the impending tragedy? When I say goodbye to some people, I pause and reflect. My father, for instance, who is in his 70s – when we get together, there's a tiny voice telling me to savor it. Even though Dad is strong and healthy, he is getting older, less resilient. You never know what could happen.

But not my brother. Even with a list of maladies and hospitalizations trailing behind him, I didn't for a moment consider that this overcast day in July would be the last time I'd see him breathing. That the grilled cheese sandwiches we consumed for lunch would be our last shared meal, that the brief visit during our annual Colorado vacation would be so significant. As much as my mother tried to convince everyone over the years that Alan is delicate, my predominant memory of this day is Alan being imposing, invincible. I felt it as he hugged me so hard that my shoulders cramped and throbbed. I felt it as he refused to let go and Kris had to peel him off of me. He was, in my mind, like a sturdy oak tree rooted deep on this earth. Nothing except a bolt of lightning could bring him down.

I close my laptop. I'm exhausted and aware now that what I am looking for is probably not on my computer after all. I climb back into bed next to Kris, pull the crisp cotton sheets around my chin, and lay there awake, listening to him snore. The noise would have annoyed me before, but I find the rhythm soothing now. I roll on my side facing Kris, place my hand gingerly on his chest, and feel it rise and fall, proof that he's breathing, that his heart still beats inside his body. I've lost something with my brother's death. There's a hole in my universe. Its edges are undefined. But I'm also aware of what I've gained over the years. I still have so much in Kris, in my kids, in myself. My heart is still beating too.

Chapter Twenty-Seven

The next morning we drive southwest from Durango toward Arizona. The landscape around us fades from green to yellow to tan. Mountains shrink to rolling hills then dissolve to plains. The two-lane highway stretches out like a long gray ribbon across an ocean of brown. The only green we see now is sagebrush along the road.

Bronwynn and Miles are fighting for space in the backseat. Miles complains that Bronwynn's leg is on his side. Bronwynn whines that she's uncomfortable and needs to stretch out. Miles retaliates by draping his arm across her headrest. She grabs his wrist and shoves it away.

"I'm older and bigger," she cries. "I need more room."

"That's not fair, B!"

"Is so!"

"Stop touching me!"

I exhale with a sort of groan that says I've had enough. I reach back and place a sweatshirt across the center seat, a no-fly zone. "There. See this boundary? You each stay on your side," I tell them. They quiet down, but I sense it's only a temporary reprieve.

They've exhausted all the movie options on their tablets. They don't want to draw or read. As the sun beats down on our car, Kris cranks up the air conditioning. The whir of the fan makes it hard to hear music or audiobooks, but it also muffles the kids' voices.

It's late morning, and I'm already tired. Without the mountains as a reference point, the endless desert view gives me the sense that we are suspended in between Colorado and Arizona, like our wheels are spinning, but we're not moving any closer to home or farther away from my family.

A couple hours south of Durango we begin to see signs along the highway indicating that we've entered the Navajo Nation. Our phones are confused, switching back and forth between Mountain Time and Arizona Standard. The Navajo Nation is largely within northeastern Arizona, but it observes daylight saving time like New Mexico, Utah, and Colorado. Arizona does not. So, as we drive within range of different cell phone towers, our clocks toggle back and forth an hour.

We round a bend and see another large sign, this one alerting us that the Four Corners Monument is ahead, a right turn off US 160 onto a spur road.

"Hey! Did you see that?" Bronwynn points excitedly out the window. "Four Corners! Can we go?"

Kris and I look at each other. He shrugs. I look at my watch.

"We're in kind of a hurry to get home," I say.

"But we've never been!" Miles says. "You said you'd take us sometime, Mama."

"Yeah, Mom. You promised."

"It won't take that long," Kris says, grabbing my hand. "It might be fun."

I turn around to look at the kids in the backseat. They're

both sitting up perfectly straight, grinning at me as if to say, *Look at what great kids we are.*

"Alright. But it's just a quick stop, okay?"

"Yes!" they shout in unison.

At the four-way stop, we turn right toward the monument. The road continues half a mile or so to an entry gate where an attendant asks for fifteen dollars. Five dollars each for every visitor over age six. Kris hands him the money, and we drive into a heavily pitted dirt parking lot. Ahead to the left are bathrooms. To the right are wooden stands with vendors selling turquoise jewelry, Kachina dolls, and fry bread. Beyond that is what looks like a concrete amphitheater.

The kids jump out of the car and run toward the amphitheater. Kris walks with them. I lag behind. The sun is blaring. I wish I'd brought a hat. I shuffle over toward the kids who run circles around me. The concrete amphitheater frames a giant patio where the name of each state is carved alongside its state seal, and lines point inward toward a metal USGS marker. Tourists are lining up to take photos on the quadripoint.

"You know, there's controversy about whether this is actually the real Four Corners," Kris says. For the past ten years, Kris has studied maps and GPS. He works for a company that makes GPS apps for hikers and mountain bikers. It's the perfect marriage of his passions – the outdoors, history, and technology. He never misses an opportunity to share his knowledge with the kids.

He goes on to explain how the boundary was surveyed sometime after the Civil War and then again around 1912, when Arizona became a state. The monument was established in 1931 when the Navajo placed a bronze plate on the spot. Later, the advent of satellite technology and modern mapping showed that the actual quadripoint is as much as a mile away. But the US Geological Survey agreed to honor the Navajo Nation's monument instead.

The kids are jumping with pent-up energy and excitement. They're looking at Kris but not really listening to his geography lesson.

"Come on, Mom!" they yell as they join the queue waiting to take photos.

The line's too long. "We don't need a photo," I reason.

Kris looks at me as if to say, *What's the harm?*

The line moves quickly, and in less than ten minutes we find ourselves at the bronze plate, looking down at the quadripoint. The kids jump back and forth across the lines. They crouch down on all fours, placing their hands and feet in separate states. They're small enough that they have to stretch a bit, like they're playing a game of Twister.

Kris snaps a few photos of the kids, then suggests we all stand up and position ourselves in separate states. I stand in New Mexico while Kris is in Colorado, Miles in Arizona, and Bronwynn in Utah. We touch hands, and the kids laugh at the improbability of being in separate states yet so close together.

I'm trying to be present with them, trying to enjoy the moment. But the whole time we're there, I'm thinking about Alan, how he would have enjoyed this too. I realize had Alan been here, I would have felt the same internal conflict I feel now – the impatience of wanting to keep the trip moving alongside my desire to accommodate the kids' thirst for adventure. I'm experienced when it comes to putting others' needs ahead of my own. But with my kids, it feels different. For the most part, I'm happy to follow their lead. It's the natural order of things for parents to prioritize their children. There's no resentment born in that. Plus, as an adult, I've learned to meet my own needs in other ways – through writing and exercise, self-care and adult friendships. Indulging my children doesn't necessarily mean neglecting myself.

"Here, everyone put your toes in the middle," I say, grabbing my phone to take a photo. I hold it overhead and point it downward so that the frame is filled with just our four feet, each in a different state, pointed perfectly at the quadripoint.

"Let me see," Kris says, and I hand him my phone. As I do, the kids shuffle over toward him to look at the screen. He squats down to their eye level, and they all hunch over looking at the photos of themselves.

I look at the ground and realize I'm standing alone on the Colorado/Utah side now while Kris and the kids are in Arizona and New Mexico. I gaze over at them, my chosen family, and I start to cry. They're only inches away from me, but it feels like there's a crevasse between us. A divide of my own making.

My body starts vibrating. I can sense the line of tourists beside us, waiting. In my periphery, a tall bearded man clears his throat, shifts his weight from one leg to the other, adjusts something around his neck. Just one more minute, I want to say. I need another minute. But my mouth won't form words. I close my eyes and open them slowly, thinking maybe the scene will shift. The sun is intense, and I feel a drop of sweat form at my temple and trickle down my cheek. I try to lift my foot and step toward Kris, but it doesn't want to move. It's like the ground is holding me in place, the bronze plate a giant magnet. I feel a buzz through my legs. I'm stuck here, I think. I have become the quadripoint. Sister, daughter, wife, and mother. People have lined up to watch me. The sun is overhead now, so even my shadow is directionless.

The bearded tourist clears his throat again. "You done over there?" he asks. His voice echoes off the concrete. I turn my head toward him – middle-aged and potbellied, wearing cargo shorts and a polo shirt, clutching a large black camera with a thick woven strap. Who is he, I wonder. Where does he come from? Where is he going? Does he even know? I stare at the man and feel myself slowly come back to my body. Maybe none of us really know.

"Yes, sorry, we're done," Kris replies with a polite wave. He looks at me tenderly, as if to say, *Don't worry about that creep.* I take a deep breath and wipe my eyes. I'm not sure if it's a conscious decision or a reflex, but looking at my family across from me, something shifts. The thoughts about Alan that had been lingering seem to dissipate. Or maybe I swallow them further down. What I notice is this: My chest opens a little bit. My shoulders slide down my back. I unclench my hands. I wiggle my toes. My mind settles just enough so that Kris's face comes into focus. I'm seeing his eyes more than I have the past week that I've been in a fog.

Bronwynn looks up and notices my tears. She grabs my hand, "Come here, Mommy." And pulls me over the crevasse. I step over the state lines and stand next to them. I kiss Bronwynn's hand and pull her and Miles into a huge hug and bury my face in the tops of their heads. They smell like dust and sweat and apples.

I breathe them in.

Part Six

The Way Out

Chapter Twenty-Eight

Phoenix, October 2016.

I can put the questions about Alan out of my mind, but they don't leave my body. Weeks after the funeral, my mind is numb. The intense feelings, the intrusive thoughts that arrested me before have evaporated.

I am at the grocery store, and I'm not thinking about Alan. I'm dropping the kids off at school, and I'm not thinking about Alan. I'm watching their swim practice, and I'm not thinking about Alan. I'm stuck in Phoenix traffic, inching along the I-10, and I'm not thinking about Alan. I'm drinking sangria on the patio of my favorite restaurant. I'm on the phone. I'm watching television. I'm folding laundry. I'm paying a bill. I'm not thinking about my brother.

I begin a sort of mental contortionism, wherein I convince myself Alan is not dead at all. Or he died many years ago, when we were kids. Or he is recently dead, but I must not care because I don't feel anything. I start to believe that if the weight of our grief is proportionate to the amount of love we felt for someone, maybe I didn't love Alan as much as I thought I did.

Except, there's this: At night, I find myself waking up, my face and pillow wet with tears. I'm unaware of feeling any pain, but it's leaking out of me. It's bubbling up from nothing, like the Salt River. It's forming a trickle, stretching, collecting into pools, and pouring out of my eyes.

I try to read books, to lose myself in a good novel, but the words fall apart. I read sentences three, four times. Words like "said" and "their" and "more" and "where" look odd to me. Why are they spelled that way? They don't make sense. How can I read a story when half the words are misspelled?

Also, my entire body aches. My leg muscles are sore, like I've run a marathon day after day after day. I'm wincing whenever I stand up or sit down. My hamstrings are so tight that I've started to walk hunched over. My neck is stiff.

For the fifth night in a row, or maybe the fifteenth, I fall asleep with the kids at 8 p.m. and wake up at 3 a.m. When I'm making the morning coffee, Kris approaches me from behind, wraps his arms around my waist, and kisses the top of my head.

"I think you should see a doctor," he says.

"For what?"

"I'm worried about you. The fatigue. Your legs. Look at how you're standing."

"I'm just exhausted," I tell him. "It'll get better."

I don't really believe it will get better. But I say this to Kris because I think it will get better for him. He'll get used to the new version of me, numb and decrepit.

Kris lets go of my waist and reaches into a cabinet, grabs two coffee mugs, and hands them to me. "It could be a virus," he says. "or, I don't know –" He sighs.

"What?"

"Something more serious. Your heart or lungs?"

"My body's always been healthy. It's a lack of sleep. Really."

Even as I say it, I don't really believe it.

It occurs to me that while I've actively avoided thinking about Alan's death, Kris hasn't. Whereas I've accepted the random aches and limping as my new normal, Kris hasn't. He sees the sister of a man who died suddenly at age forty-three of unknown causes. If Alan had warning signs like fatigue and muscle pain, he wasn't able to communicate them. Kris is watching me, and he's worried that my heart will be the next one to stop beating.

Those thoughts that plagued me in the days after Alan died are churning in my stomach. They're changing shape. As Kris suggests doctors to me, I realize I'm not at all worried about dying. But I am worried about something.

That thought, *It's my mother's fault. She did this,* has morphed over time. Now it's *They.* They did this. They, meaning the doctors. Or maybe they, meaning something broader, like the medical establishment, the systems meant to protect disabled people. I realize I feel anxious at the idea of seeing a medical professional. My brother's body failed. Or, was it the doctors who failed him?

I wonder how much Alan's doctors knew about Prader-Willi Syndrome and the associated complications. Medical research is limited, but most experts agree that the life expectancy of a person with Prader-Willi is not all that different from the average life expectancy, provided they are closely monitored by professionals who understand the condition. Alan's doctors didn't directly cause his death, but I can't shake the idea that they missed something, that they should have known more or done more. Maybe they missed an interaction with his medication. Maybe he had a hidden heart defect that they should have uncovered. Maybe they falsely viewed my mother as the martyr and gave her attention that should have been given to Alan. Maybe they assumed that she knew what was best for him. Maybe she knew what was best. Maybe she didn't. Maybe the doctors should have known the difference.

Putting these concerns aside, I'm still not inclined to go to the doctor. Even before Alan died, I'd let years pass between check-ups. Because I've always been relatively healthy and also because I like to avoid tests and medications unless they're truly necessary. Call it denial. Call it a carryover from when I was a young girl and watched my mother take Alan to so many specialists who had so few answers. Or call it another bypass of my own pain, another way to remain unseen. If I were face-to-face with someone who could help me, I'm not even sure I could articulate my needs. I'm fine. I've always been fine.

Still, over the next couple weeks, Kris gently asks me whether I've considered his suggestion. Will I go to a doctor? Some sort of professional? For him? Please?

"I just don't know what they can do for me," I tell him. But I agree to look into it.

When I'm lying awake at 3 a.m., I begin to research alternatives to traditional doctors. Acupuncturists. Naturopaths. Sleep specialists. Something called Reiki. I read reviews and medical journal studies that document the benefits and drawbacks of holistic medicine. I make lists. Names. Specialties. Outcomes. Pros. Cons.

Fact: Naturopathic medicine is less invasive. It favors natural remedies instead of pharmaceuticals. The practice treats the whole person – mind and body – not just physical symptoms.

Fact: Not all alternative treatments are evidence-based or safe. Most are expensive and not covered by insurance. I could end up seeing a snake oil salesman disguised as a doctor.

Unknown: Whether any medical professional of any kind,

alternative or Western, can cure what is most likely an exhausted body, a confused mind, and a broken heart.

From 3 a.m. until dawn, I read anecdote after anecdote by people who have used alternative treatments and successfully cured their migraines, diabetes, endometriosis, anxiety, thyroid problems, insomnia, ulcers. I read cautionary tales about dead people who thought alternative medicine could cure cancer or appendicitis or a blocked artery.

As I dig deeper, there's one name that keeps coming up in my searches. A professor at the Southwest School for Naturopathic Medicine who also has her own practice in Phoenix. She's a medical doctor who went back to school to earn a doctorate in naturopathic medicine. She's won awards and published papers. Her practice is described as a blend of Western and alternative medicine tailored to the individual's needs – the best of both worlds. She takes insurance. Beyond that, she appears smart and kind in her photo.

When I call to book an appointment, the receptionist tells me to expect it to take two hours, possibly more. "Dr. Taylor likes to gather a complete medical history, dating back to your childhood," she says.

"Okay," I reply nervously and block out the morning of the appointment in my calendar.

The waiting room smells like lavender. A stone waterfall babbles in one corner. The receptionist offers me tea and invites me to wait on a leather sofa. Ten minutes pass peacefully. This is new to me – waiting to see a doctor and not feeling nervous.

Dr. Taylor comes out to greet me. She's about my age and

taller than I'd imagined. I'm used to being the tallest woman in the room, but I have to look up to greet her. She smiles warmly and extends her right hand. As we shake, she places her left hand on top, a gesture that might make me bristle in other settings, but here it feels warm and safe. Her green eyes are compassionate. Her hair is wildly curly but contained in a low ponytail. She's wearing blue scrubs accessorized with a delicate crystal necklace and dangling silver earrings. Call it curiosity or the promise of healing, but I'm drawn to her.

Before she examines me, she leads me to an armchair in her office and invites me to sit down. She pulls out a legal pad and asks me about my current symptoms, somehow managing to maintain eye contact while she writes notes. I tell her about the insomnia, the muscle aches, the fatigue.

"My arms and legs feel heavy and sore all the time," I tell her. "Curbs and stairways are too tall. Typing on my computer is exhausting."

She writes this down, then asks me to go back and try to remember any medical issues I had as a child. My mind goes blank, like a light switch turned off. I don't think I had any issues, I tell her.

She asks me about my first period, how old I was, whether I had painful cramps. I tell her I can vaguely remember how old I was, thirteen or fourteen. I was one of the last of my friends to start their period. I recall buying my own tampons and taking handouts from friends because I didn't want to bother my mother with anything that was happening in my body. But everything else is fuzzy – did I have cramps? Was my bleeding heavy or light? Was my cycle consistent from month to month? Who knows. I can't say whether the details are unclear because of my current brain fog or because I learned at a young age to ignore and deny any discomfort. Alan's physical and medical needs eclipsed mine. I don't remember going through puberty, though obviously, I transformed at some point from girl to woman. I was invisible – not just to my family, but to myself.

Dr. Taylor asks me what prescriptions I've taken over the years. Just birth control, I tell her. Antibiotics once or twice in college for those winter colds that turn into bronchitis when you're stressed and studying for final exams. She asks me about my current sleep patterns as well as my historic sleep habits. I've never been a good sleeper, I tell her.

"Is it that you have trouble falling asleep or staying asleep?" she asks.

"Staying asleep."

"What time do you wake each night?"

"Just after 3 a.m.," I tell her. "Like 3:11 or 3:12 every night. It's bizarre."

"That makes sense to me, actually." She scribbles more notes. Her pen moves quickly across the tablet and makes a scratching sound that I find soothing.

She tells me about something called the Chinese Medicine clock. She draws a circle on a blank sheet of paper and labels the clock hours and then draws a line to 3 a.m.

"Three in the morning is when the lungs are at their highest energy," she tells me. "Something is catching your breath and waking you up," she says. "Chinese medicine would say that this is the time of peak emotion, especially sadness. Is there anything going on for you personally that you're grieving?"

I tell her that my brother died six weeks ago but that I haven't felt much of anything since the week or two after. I don't tell her about the toxic thoughts I've swallowed, that I suspect they might be infecting my blood, my bones, my muscles.

She puts down her pen and looks at me. "I'm so sorry to hear about your brother. Was it sudden?"

I tell her the story, what I know and what I don't know. I tell her about Alan's Prader-Willi Syndrome, and how it's unlikely that my symptoms would in any way be related to how he died. She listens, curious and empathetic, but not pitying. I appreciate that she seems strong and compassionate. Often, when I tell people about Alan and how suddenly he died, they are more emotional than I am. I end up feeling like I have to comfort them, rather than them comforting me.

"Well," Dr. Taylor stands up. "Let's do an exam and some bloodwork to see if we can get a clearer picture of what's happening with you," she says.

Over the course of several visits, Dr. Taylor inventories what I need. She listens to my heart and lungs. She draws vials of blood. She takes a sample of my saliva. She looks into my eyes and ears. She runs her fingers across my chin and neck, checking my lymph nodes and thyroid. She presses her hands into my abdomen, kneads my stomach like dough, asks me if there's any pain. She has me lie down and breathe into different parts of my chest, invites me to bring awareness to parts of my body that have been sore and those that have been numb.

Every visit, as she places her hands on different parts of my body, I sense something – a tingling, a jolt, like frayed electrical circuits are firing in my legs, in my chest, in my belly. Like the parts of my body that were hibernating are waking up. Or maybe it's my mind that's slowly waking up to the sensations in my body.

My bloodwork shows a deficit in iron, vitamin D, and vitamin B. She also notes that my cortisol levels are abnormal.

"Cortisol is your stress hormone," she says. "Your cortisol levels are spiking early in the morning and then plummeting. This tells me that you've been under extreme stress for quite a while, maybe years. Your adrenal glands are slowly failing."

None of this is life-threatening. "It is a quality of life issue," she says. "You're far too young to be wasting away. If this gets worse, your blood pressure will drop, and you might have fainting spells and debilitating fatigue. If your adrenals fail, you'll have to start taking synthetic hormones. You're too young for that."

She injects me with a cocktail of vitamins and prescribes supplements to jump-start my adrenal glands. She also tells me I need to grieve. "Whatever emotions you suppress will show up in your body," she says. "I can treat the symptoms and help to bring your system back in balance, but it's up to you to create the time and space to release the feelings."

Time and space are foreign concepts to me. What does it mean to take time? To create space?

I start with filling in tiny spaces on my calendar. I go back to Dr. Taylor every two weeks for vitamin injections. The shots cost twenty-five dollars and take just a few minutes to administer. At the end of each appointment, she wraps me in a warm embrace, pulls back, squeezes my shoulders, and tells me, "Take care of yourself."

The B vitamins leave me feeling a little jittery for a few hours, like I've had too much coffee, but as my body absorbs them, I feel calm and clear-headed and more energetic. The effect lasts for several days. The vitamin D and supplements seem to be helping too. My arms and legs feel lighter. I'm able to stand up straight. I catch myself laughing more.

Yet I begin to wonder if the hugs aren't the most healing part of my treatment. Because each visit, after Dr. Taylor embraces me and says, "See you in two weeks," I walk out to my car, sit in the driver's seat, rest my head on the steering wheel, and cry. Her words and touch feel like an invitation. I am invited back into my own body. I am listening to what it needs.

I'm still waking up at 3:12 a.m. Something is still catching my breath. The tears are still springing forth unbidden. But instead of wiping my cheeks and staring at the clock until sunrise, I'm burying my face in my pillow and allowing more tears to come, to rise up from my legs through my stomach, to seep through my chest and neck and pour out my eyes. With the tears, I feel something else washing away. It's not just pain. The questions and thoughts I swallowed are wresting loose. Bit by bit, they're coming out of my mouth and eyes, metabolizing as grief, evaporating into the universe.

Chapter Twenty-Nine

Atlanta, 1993.

I am seventeen. What I remember most vividly about the night I finally move out is not the look on my mother's face – a sort of crazed fury and panic. It's not her booming voice as she screams at me from the front door. It's not even the words she uses: *Coward. Bitch. Selfish. You're just like your father.* The words echo off the neighboring brick houses. It's not the dogs barking or the neighbors peeking from behind their curtains.

No. What's indelible is this: The looks on my brothers' faces. Will especially. His eyes are accusing and pleading. *How could you? How could you abandon us like this?* I see the wrinkles in his forehead, the red in his cheeks, the tears welling up. My chest tightens. *How could I?* There isn't enough time to sort this out. He is fifteen. He is strong, if sensitive. It hurts to leave him here, but I know he can survive without me.

"Everything is going to be okay," I tell him.

Everything is not okay.

Alan is sobbing. Not because I'm leaving but because Mom is yelling. "I didn't do anything!" he yells. "It wasn't me!" He pounds his fist against the wall. He assumes with all of us screaming that he must be in trouble. It's a conditioned response.

"Shhhh, Alan. We know. We know," Will is saying.

I'm halfway to my car, a little Mazda sedan my father bought me last summer against my mother's wishes. I'm carrying a plastic milk crate full of books, clothing, and toiletries, a duffle bag slung over my shoulder. In my purse is the envelope of cash I've been saving for months.

I want to turn around and comfort Alan. I want to tell Will again that everything is going to be okay, but I have to keep walking. If I turn around now, I worry I'll lose my nerve and stay. *It's not your fault,* I want to yell. *I was never meant to take care of you. This is Mom's job, and I'm leaving now so that she can do it.*

But will she do it? Can she keep them fed? Can she keep herself alive?

I've tried to run away before, false starts that left me wandering dark Atlanta streets alone, panic gripping me, hurrying home by daybreak and sneaking back into the house through a basement window. Each time, I was showered and dressed and ready for school the next day, as if nothing had ever happened. No one noticed I was gone.

When I was able to drive, I cast my net a little wider. I began to look at the streets and buildings of Atlanta differently. Driving along, I'd see a sheet of cardboard under a bridge – something I once assumed was trash, now I saw as a bed. "Somebody slept there last night," I said to Will. "See the indentation and the pine needles piled up there?"

Abandoned buildings suddenly had potential. I could sleep

there in a pinch. I wondered about homeless shelters or safe houses for teens. Would they take me?

A few weeks ago, I applied for a lease at an apartment complex a few miles away. The red banner over the office door said FALL SPECIAL. 1 MONTH FREE. STUDIOS $275/MO. I figured I'd only need the place for a year, until I left for college. Despite everything, I plan to go to college. I ran the numbers in my head as I scrawled out the application form. *Dad could send my child support payment to me instead of my mom. I have money saved from babysitting. Are utilities included? Is there furniture? Do I need furniture? Will I need a phone? I don't need a phone. I can make calls at school. What happens if you can't pay rent on time? Should I ask? I shouldn't ask.*

When I handed my application to the woman at the front desk, she asked to see my driver's license. Just like that, it was over. They wouldn't rent to anyone under age twenty-one.

What I have not at any point considered: Asking my father to take me in. Not necessarily because I don't want to live with him, but because it's never felt like an option. My obligations are here, in Atlanta. My brothers are here. My school and friends are here. If living with him had been an option, wouldn't he have offered to take us when he and my mom divorced? Or when Alan threatened me with a knife and I called him for help?

Ever since that day in the therapist's office when she told me I'm not the crazy one, when she instilled in me this belief that I can chart a path out, I've pictured being on my own. It's terrifying, but it also feels right, like this was the solution all along. Since those early days when I abdicated my needs for

Alan, I've mastered not needing anything from my family. The challenge now is convincing them that they no longer need me.

Tonight felt like the time. I have been planning what to do, how I might successfully leave. I've just been waiting for the day to reveal itself to me.

I felt it percolating as I cooked dinner. My mother screamed at me about something mundane – laundry I forgot to fold, dirty dishes in the sink, someone's muddy shoes in the middle of the floor. *Why hadn't I noticed these things? Why hadn't I taken care of it?*

"I don't know. Why didn't *you* take care of it?" I snapped.

This angered her more.

I drained the pasta, stirred in powdered cheese and water. We're out of milk. We're always out of milk. I served heaping spoonfuls of watery mac and cheese to my brothers and mother. I served the rest to myself. I set my plate down hard on the kitchen table, yanked the chair back, and plopped down next to my brothers to eat while my mother sat with her food on the sofa ten feet away. I wanted her to hear me, to see me, to know that I was angry too.

I looked up from a bite of food in time to see her fling her dinner plate at my head like a frisbee. I ducked as it landed on the linoleum floor. It spun a few times like a tilt-a-whirl before it came to rest, the dregs of macaroni and canned green beans strewn across the floor. The absurdity of it stopped me from responding immediately. *This is what it's come to*, I thought.

I felt sorry for her.

For too long she's battled with money, with my father, with Alan, with the demons inhabiting the corners of her mind. She's broke. She's broken. And as much as I've wanted to save her, I finally see it. She doesn't want to be saved.

This was it. This was the opportunity. Before this moment, I had been imprisoned by the belief that I had no control, no options. I felt trapped because for so long, I had been trapped – trapped by my mother's depression, trapped by my responsibility to my brothers, trapped by Alan's violence, trapped by my father's inaction, trapped by the belief that if I told anyone the whole truth of the situation, my mother would die.

Now I understood: I can walk away. She won't call the police. She won't come after me. I can see how scared she is. Every way she's threatened me, punished me, sucked the air from around me – it's all her attempt to keep me from abandoning her.

It's time to go.

I drive a couple miles to my friend Angela's house – a brick, three-bedroom ranch, smaller than my mother's house but infinitely more inviting. It's the house where our friends often congregate after school. The galley kitchen is typically stocked with snacks like carrot sticks, apples, cheese slices, and pretzels, and we all know we can grab a Coke from the fridge without asking. Angela's house has a finished walk-out basement that no one uses except her older brothers who are away at college. She asked me a few weeks ago if I wanted to crash there after she noticed fresh bruises on my arms. I thanked her and said I'd think about it.

As I walk up to the door, Angela looks as if she's been expecting me. She and her mother welcome me inside. They grab my stuff and carry it to the basement. They don't ask questions. This space feels like an unexpected kindness.

Angela's mother agrees to the idea of my moving in on three conditions: I have to finish high school. I have to submit my college applications on time. And, I have to have at least one of my parent's permission. She doesn't want the authorities coming after her accusing her of kidnapping.

This means that, with Angela's mom watching me, I have to make a long-distance call to my father. My fingers shake as I turn the rotary dial. *What if he tells me I have to go home? What if after all this time, he wants me to live with him instead?* I want his approval, but I also want to stay in Atlanta and finish high school with my friends. I want to know that somewhere, someone who matters can tell me I'm not an awful person for leaving. But mostly, I just want him to tell me that everything will be okay.

The room starts to sway the moment I hear my father's voice. Years from now, I won't remember the entirety of this conversation. I'll remember trembling and weeping and wiping my snot off the phone's receiver. I'll remember the crackling, static-like noise it makes when I wipe it off. I'll remember my dad saying, "What happened? Take a deep breath and tell me what happened." I'll remember that his voice sounds generous and patient. I'll remember thinking, *Where do I even begin? You've been gone too long.* There is so much he doesn't know about me, my brothers, our life. I'll remember stuttering and repeating to him the words I heard him say when I was five, just before he moved out: "I just can't do it. I can't live with her anymore."

"Ok," he says. Without further explanation, my dad understands. He concedes. It's enough.

That night, when I'm in an unfamiliar bed in the quiet, cool basement, I let the darkness wash over me. The house is so quiet. I'm not used to this stillness. I bury my face in a pillow and howl. My chest convulses as I gasp for air and sob. I kick my heels into the mattress. I roll over on my stomach and pound my fists until my forearms are sore. This is what I imagine an exorcism feels like. An act of depossession.

I'm seventeen.

I'm severed from my family.

I'm detached.

I'm free.

I'm alone.

I've always been alone.

Let the morning come, I think. Whatever is next, let it come.

. . .

The morning after I move out, I go to school like it is any other weekday. Everything looks dull and slightly out of focus. Will ignores me in the hallways. I try to chase him down, to tell him I'm sorry, but he brushes me off, disappears into the crowd.

Conversations feel distant, like I am underwater. I'm amazed that people can talk about trivial things like calculus or music or the homecoming football game. Can people not see that I've changed, that I have done this crazy thing, this really awful, really wonderful, really scary thing? Is it even real? Did I really leave home?

I startle easily. Navigating the crowded, noisy hallways in between classes, I am alert. I expect my mother to jump from behind a corner. Some jock closes his metal locker door and BAM! She's there. Standing behind it, arms outstretched, ready to strangle me.

I need to pee. I wonder if she is hiding in the girl's bathroom. I peek under the doorways of every stall. For hours, for days, I worry that I am in trouble – with my teachers, the police, my father. I feel like there has to be consequences for abandoning my responsibility to my brothers.

Every evening as I lie in bed, waves of panic wash over me. *What is she doing with Alan after school? Is Will the one cooking dinner now? Is there food in the house? Should I give Will my lunch?*

Every morning, my alarm goes off, and I climb out of bed. I eat breakfast with Angela and her mother. I begin to register that there's always enough food, that I don't have to guard it from anyone. I eat slower. I drive to school. At school, bells ring, and I shuffle from one class to the next. Day after day, week after week, I get up. I show up. I move through.

Slowly, I stop wondering who is taking care of things at home. Those thoughts don't disappear, but they fade from my consciousness. Also, I stop fearing the phone call that tells me my mother has finally killed herself. It never comes.

The hyper-vigilance wanes, and what takes its place is a taste of lightness and freedom I've never experienced before. One night, Angela and I sneak out and smoke a joint. I get high not just from the marijuana, but from the realization that I'm doing something reckless and irresponsible for the first time.

I begin to think about my life, my future, college, dating, hanging out with friends, and traveling. I gather college applications and fill them out. I write essays. I apply for financial aid and scholarships. I go to the movies with my friends. I get a part-time job after school. I buy myself groceries and new jeans. I put the rest of my money in a checking account. Angela and her mom have given me more than a place to sleep. They've given me a taste of normalcy. For once, I'm a typical teenage girl.

My mother does eventually call, weeks later, to tell me she is sorry, to tell me she is making changes, that she has started psychotherapy and is taking medication.

"Come home," she says, her voice pleading.

"I don't know, I –"

"Don't you think this has gone on long enough?" she adds.

At those words, my heart starts to race. *Has it gone on long enough? What is enough?*

I'm tempted to go home. I miss my brothers. And despite

her limitations, my mother too. I care about her and want to see for myself that she is okay.

I tell her I'll think about it and hang up the phone.

As the adrenaline begins to ebb, what I feel is equal parts sadness and liberation. Plus awe and deep gratitude for the choice that I made. Because here's the truth: If I were to rewind the tape, I don't know if I'd have the courage to leave again. There was a tiny window, a moment when the clouds parted in my mind – *the* moment of clarity required to act, to be selfish, to listen to a tiny voice deep inside me telling me what I needed. I pursued that tiny voice and now I'm here, alone in a basement, feeling sad but safe with the support of my friends. What I don't realize is that from this day forward, it will be a battle to remember why leaving my family was the best decision I could have ever made. Because as the tiny voice inside me grows, my family's voices will grow louder. They'll demand more and more from me. It will be a tug-of-war between honoring my own needs and theirs.

I call my mother back and tell her that I will stop by the house to visit, to check on my brothers, but I won't stay.

. . .

In the coming year, I'll graduate high school with honors. I'll go to the University of Georgia with two scholarships, one to cover tuition and the other to cover room and board. My dad will fly to Atlanta and help me move my stuff into the dormitory in Athens, ninety miles away. He'll buy me new clothes and books and a miniature refrigerator that I'll stock with snacks and Coca-Cola.

I'll relax as I realize that Alan isn't around to punch me or drag me by my hair. He's not around to eat all my food. I'll stand in awe of the buffet in the university dining hall, the easy access I have to all kinds of food. Day in and day out, I'll eat until I'm full.

I'll enjoy studying at night without worrying about where my mother is and whether she is safe. I'll feel light and happy as I walk to and from my classes. As I ride the bus. As I go out at night with friends. As I lose track of time. I'll have money in my checking account and all that I ever need, which isn't much but is more than I had before.

I'll also answer the phone when my mother calls and begs me to come home, to take time off from school and help her care for Alan. "Skip a semester, a few months," she'll say. I'll listen to her tell me, "I'm at the end of my rope. I don't know what else I can do. I'm all alone. I'm drowning."

My chest will ache. I'll consider dropping out because I'll hear how depressed she sounds. But I'll also hear that tiny voice inside me protesting. I'll call Lorie, the therapist I saw a few years ago, and ask her for advice. She'll tell me I have to say no. She'll tell me my future depends on me saying no to Sharon. *This is non-negotiable*, she'll say in a parental tone. *You will absolutely not go back home.* She'll tell me she's proud of me. I'll weep at her words. I'll exhale. She'll give me permission to go and enjoy college, to live my life. She'll offer to check on my brothers for me, to send my mother a list of crisis resources and respite caregivers.

I'll write Alan letters and sneak home to visit him when I know Sharon is working long hours. On school breaks and holidays, I'll sleep over at the house for a day or two, long enough to see that Will and Alan are really doing okay, that there's food in the refrigerator. Almost as soon as I arrive, I'll hear the voice telling me it's time to leave. Then I'll go to other places – to the mountains, to the beach. I'll crash on friends' couches. I'll work summer jobs that provide free housing. I'll continue to write to

Alan, send him photos and cards, send him cash to spend on his birthday.

When Will decides to attend the same university as me and earns the same scholarship, I'll look out for him in a sisterly way. I'll show him around campus. I'll buy him dinner and help him with his laundry. I'll listen to him tell me that things were bad after I moved out. I'll listen as he tells me how angry he was, how he felt like I abandoned him. I'll apologize and explain to him why I had to go, that it wasn't really a choice; it was survival. He'll tell me he forgave me a while ago. He'll explain that once I was gone, he saw more clearly how depressed Sharon was, how violent Alan could be. He'll thank me for protecting him all those years, for being a buffer between him and them. He'll tell me he always considered me his second mother.

I won't move home after college. I'll go on to graduate school to study journalism. I'll rent an apartment. I'll work as a reporter at the local newspaper. I'll buy myself a laptop and work clothes. I'll hear that Alan was accepted into a group home. I'll go to my mother's house and help him pack. I'll write essays in my free time. I'll hear weeks later that Alan was kicked out of the group home for bad behavior. I'll visit him at my mother's house. I'll return to my life.

I'll learn how to drink wine, not because I think it tastes good but because it feels like a grown-up thing to do. I'll date a few men. I'll break up with them. I'll make friends who become my family.

· · ·

Kris and I meet after I complete graduate school when I am twenty-five. He is the web geek at the first magazine I ever work for, an outdoor travel publication based near Allentown, Pennsylvania.

From the get-go, I find him attractive. At the office, he fastens his long, wild, curly hair into a ponytail. He wears short-sleeve button-down shirts that complement his broad shoulders and climber's biceps. Behind his glasses are sharp eyes, the bluest I've ever seen.

In his free time, I learn, he's a bit of an adrenaline junkie. He climbs 14,000-foot-tall mountains, skateboards in empty swimming pools, and careens down rocky hillsides on a fat-tired bicycle. Each Monday, he shows up to work with a new bruise or scrape, souvenirs from the weekend's adventure.

This will be the story we tell our kids one day about how we fell in love: One winter evening, Kris hosts a happy hour at his apartment. Fresh snow is falling. We all pack up and leave work early and head to his place before the roads get too bad. Kris is used to the cold, he tells me. He grew up in Wisconsin. We should go snowboarding, he suggests. When I tell him I'm from Atlanta and that I've never been on a snowboard, he insists that we must go outside and try it immediately. With our co-workers watching, he sets me up with boots that are two sizes too big, straps me to a waxed fiberglass board, gives me a few pointers, then nudges me down a hill behind his apartment building. I decide snowboarding is easy and fun until he takes me to a *real* slope at a ski resort a few weeks later. During my inaugural run on the bunny hill, I fall and break my arm.

This is our first date.

With my arm in a sling, he takes me on other, gentler adventures. Snowshoeing across a frozen lake. A pub crawl in Philadelphia. Long walks during our lunch breaks at work. I can't get enough of him. His voice is infused with passion and kindness and a yearning for life. I just want to be around him and hear him speak more.

In the beginning, this is all we do. We talk, sometimes until three in the morning, me sitting in the passenger seat of his Jeep with the heat cranked up and my legs sweating. Or sprawled across the futon in my apartment after cooking elaborate meals together, me with my one good arm. We discuss books and travel and movies and all that we dream of doing, of being.

For all his risk-taking, it's weeks before Kris ventures to kiss me. He waits until my arm is healed and we can properly embrace. The moment is like throwing gasoline on a smoldering coal.

In time I start joining him on bigger adventures. We fly to London on a whim one weekend because an airline is selling last-minute tickets for $199. We go camping in the Catskills and stay up all night, cocooned in our down sleeping bags. The stars are so thick against the black sky, like nothing I've ever seen before. I gaze up and see for the first time a future that doesn't have to be defined by my past.

He proposes to me on a mountain bike trail next to a roaring creek. We're both sweaty and covered in mud and bicycle grease. "You're my adventure partner," he says. "My love. My best friend. Now, I want you to be my wife."

It will sound like a fairy tale. Our kids will beg us to tell it again and again. It will be easy to assume in the retelling that I am pining for an ideal, trying to shape the future like my parents did. But I know deep down that what I have with Kris is different. Deeper. More authentic. Built on a foundation of vulnerability and courage and truth.

I know this is real because, unlike my mother, I am not looking to be rescued. I have already rescued myself.

The distancing from my mother and brothers will be a process, an evolution. It will be a corkscrew path that at times makes you feel like you're traveling toward the things you're most afraid of. It will forever be a push and pull. All the while, I'll be trying to create something healthy to hold onto, something that will hold onto me and keep me from losing my grip and plummeting inward, back to where I started. Over time, I'll gain a deep understanding that I am not like my father. I never turned a blind eye to my mother's pain or to my brothers' needs. I didn't prioritize my own comfort or success over my family's safety. I did the best I could to hold us all together at my own expense.

The day I moved out I was not abandoning my family. I was starting off on a journey back home to myself.

Maybe the raindrop can choose the path it will take.

Chapter Thirty

Phoenix, December 2016.

Fact: The voice I'm hearing now is not my own. And it's not my mother's.

It's Alan's.

I hear his slurred words: *What about me?* he says. *You don't forget about me, Gina.* I hear him say, *I miss you.* I hear him say, *I hate you.* I hear him say *I'm hungry.* I hear him say, *I sorry. I so sorry.*

I don't know whether I believe in the paranormal, but as the holidays approach I feel haunted by Alan. In addition to hearing his voice, I see his unmistakable handwriting inside greeting cards I've saved from previous Christmases. I find his handmade clay ornaments on our tree.

Maybe I'm being histrionic, trying to avoid grieving Alan by pretending he's still here.

But he *is* still here.

Bronwynn comes running to me one day holding a piece of blue construction paper in her hand. "Mommy, what's this?" she asks, waving it like a flag. I take it from her, examine it, and recognize it immediately. It's an abstract watercolor painting that Alan made years ago, that he folded in thirds and stuffed in an envelope and mailed to me. On the back, it says "I love you" in his scratchy handwriting.

"Where did you find this?" I ask.

"It was under my bed," she said. "I saw it when I climbed under to reach my Legos."

I'd call it a coincidence, except the kids are finding artifacts stashed in other places too – in the cracks of armchairs, between books on their shelves, at the bottom of their school backpacks, under the bathroom sink. The worn papers, old notes, photographs of Alan are surfacing all over the house like an archaeological site. Except, no one is digging. They just appear.

There are other signs too. All over town, I see Alan's dog Clyde, the distinctive gray standard poodle who Alan loved more than any of us. Though it's not his dog I'm seeing. It's dogs that look just like Clyde. At the park. On the sidewalks. On the desert trails near our house. I bend down to pet all the Clydes. I look in their eyes, expecting to see Alan gazing back at me, but he's not there.

At home, I gather all the artifacts in a folder, along with some childhood photographs, plus the paper program, obituary, and CD recording from Alan's funeral. I put them in a locked cabinet with our family photo albums and other keepsakes. I try to put them out of my mind.

But they keep coming. The bits of paper, the Hallmark cards, finger paintings. In my car's glove box. In the back pocket of jeans I haven't worn in years. Had they always been here, and I'd just not noticed? Has Alan always been so alive in our home?

Call it metaphysical. Call it wishful thinking. I begin to wonder if Alan is trying to communicate with me somehow.

Maybe there's something he wants to tell me. I buy some sage and light it on fire, letting the white smoke and aroma fill the house. When I'm alone, I try talking with Alan, asking him my questions. When I see his preschool-like handwriting on a piece of paper, the words he wrote, the "I love you"s, I flip the paper over and write back, "I love you too."

I look for answers everywhere. For cosmic signs. In the swaying trees. In the sunsets. Sometimes, during those twilight moments between awake and asleep, I am sure I can hear his voice whispering to me. But I can't make out what he's saying. Is he happy? Is he at peace? Is he wondering what went wrong, like I still am?

People tell me I am shouldering the loss well, that I am strong. I hear this less as praise and more coercion, to keep my chin up, to hold it together and not tarnish them with my sudden, unexplainable loss. I hear their compliments as lies. I am not bearing anything well. I'm guarding my pain like a secret. I am doing what I have always done. I am fine.

I don't tell anyone that Alan is communicating with me. I don't say that I see his shadow in my periphery or that I hear his voice at night. I don't admit to anyone that I answer this voice, that I talk to him in the hazy hours between wakefulness and sleep. I show Kris the drawings and other keepsakes as they surface. He smiles and nods. He thinks I've looked for them and gathered them up intentionally, like I'm building a scrapbook, a memorial. He doesn't know that it's the other way around, that the artifacts looked for me.

Christmas comes and goes. Even after I pack up the photos and ornaments and macaroni art bearing his name. He's here. I feel close to him, but not any closer to answering the question of what happened to him. For as much as the intrusive thoughts have loosened their grip, I still wonder. Maybe I'll always wonder.

In lucid moments, when I'm lying in bed watching the sun come up, I can see what I'm doing to myself. I see how my fixation on what happened to Alan is an escape hatch from my own sorrow. When the pain becomes too much to bear, I flip open a door in the back of my mind and step into my questions, my research. I see myself bound by a puzzle with no solution, pursuing questions that have no answers. I see it, but I don't yet know how to stop myself from ruminating.

I'm on my back, under the bed cover, staring at the sun. I close my eyes and the bed starts to sway. I see myself caught in a river, swept away by a force larger than myself. I'm in a churning rapid, unable to find an eddy, a boulder, or a branch to cling to. I'm too weak to swim to shore.

Chapter Thirty-One

If there is a turning point in my grief, it is this: One day I find myself standing in the middle of the Arizona desert at the entrance to a large, circular Native American labyrinth. You've probably seen these labyrinths before. They're often depicted in art or carved into jewelry, perfectly round and symmetrical. Sometimes there is a stick figure "man in the maze" sketched in the middle.

Arizona is full of mystery. That there is a spiritual labyrinth in the middle of the Sonoran Desert is not unusual. Native American beliefs hold natural landscapes as sacred. From Mexico north to the Four Corners, the desert is peppered with archaeological sites, pueblos, medicine wheels, burial grounds, energetic vortexes. The brown, hot, dry, scorpion-and-cactus-filled landscape – a place that on the surface seems incompatible with life—houses the secrets and history of life that came before. The fact that native cultural sites have been appropriated for the wellness industry, becoming a lure for visionaries, shamans, self-healers, and spa-goers is sad but not surprising.

The magnetism of this landscape is well-documented and centuries-old.

What *is* unusual is that I am here, peering into the mouth of this particular labyrinth at this particular time. It's fall. The day is oppressively hot, maybe ninety degrees at eleven in the morning. There's no shade. I'm wearing a bathing suit, bathrobe, and flip-flops, having just wandered over from a luxury hotel pool. I gaze down the narrow dirt path and its low stone dividers. I contemplate walking forward with my bare toes, worried I'll encounter a rattlesnake or step on a prickly pear cactus. I hear the distant laughter of women lounging at the pool with their mimosas and bloody marys.

Yesterday, I drove more than an hour north from my home in Phoenix to spend the weekend here with a friend who is celebrating her fortieth birthday. She's rented a house on the edge of Yavapai tribal lands, near amenities like this resort and hiking trails. Her celebration includes fancy dinners, hiking, lounging in the rental's hot tub. It also includes a day at the Native American-owned spa, enjoying sage-infused aromatherapy treatments, getting stone massages, and sipping fruity drinks by the pool.

My friend's invitation came during a moment when I felt ready to escape, to leave my house for a few days and all the memories contained there. I couldn't say I felt much like celebrating. But I felt like relaxing and soaking up sunshine with friends. I wanted to drink a few cocktails and watch a sunset and sleep late. This remote retreat seemed like the perfect opportunity and perfect setting.

It was from my perch on the pool's expansive deck that I noticed a gravel pathway leading out into the sea of brown beyond. I stared at it for a while, letting the women's voices wash over me.

The things the women are discussing are important, and

they're unimportant. Books they recently read and loved. Their desire to go back to graduate school. Recent fights with their teenagers. Reality television. A promotion they want at work. Political activism. Volunteer work. Stuff their husbands do that they find annoying.

I am a part of the group and separate from the group. Happy to get buzzed and laugh with my friend, but also unable to integrate. I am holding back. An unspoken weight is holding me back. I want to be here. I want to feel normal, whatever that means. But I'm stuck. It's like I'm in a bubble or behind a layer of glass.

The longer I stared at the pathway, the more I wondered where it led. The more I tried to stay present with these women, the more the pathway started to look like a welcome diversion. When the women got up to refill their drinks, I couldn't resist any longer. I slipped on my sandals, walked down the trail, and ended up here.

The labyrinth spans 150 feet, half of a football field. It's perched on a plateau framed by desert sage and saguaros. A single, nonbranching path leads inward. There's an engraved metal sign that says *The Way Out is the Way In.* Smaller text explains the significance of the labyrinth and gives instructions on how to use it. At the base of the sign is a pile of smooth rocks the size of grapefruits.

Pause and take a deep breath at the entrance. Choose a stone from the pile. Holding it may help you focus on an intention. The labyrinth has only one path. Walk purposefully. The center is a place of meditation, clarity, and illumination.

A single, nonbranching track leads inward. There are no choices to make except to move forward or not.

The certainty of the route frees your mind to focus on your inner-most thoughts instead of navigation.

At the center, you leave the rock behind, like an offering or unweighting a burden.

You may choose to place your stone on the center pile.

Then, you walk forward and wind back out.

I'm not one for ritual or meditation, but as I stare at the sign and the pile of rocks, my senses are sharpened. Maybe it's the heat. Maybe having a sign tell me what to do feels refreshing, clarifying. But I am compelled to walk forward. My chaotic mind and body are suddenly focused on a task: Choose a stone. Walk the path.

The way out is the way in.

I tighten the bathrobe around my waist, bend forward, and pick up a stone. It's hot from the sun and heavier than I antici-pated. I step forward, gravel crunching beneath my flip-flops. I walk slowly, deliberately, holding the stone at my chest, protecting it like a baby. I whisper, "Tell me what I need to know. Tell me where to go."

If grief had a map, I imagine it would look like this, a serpentine trail that doubles back on itself so many times that even as you walk it, you have no idea where you're going. Yet, when you pull back and gaze at it from a distance, you see the symmetry, the concentric circles, how every meandering step makes sense. When you're inside, you feel utterly lost and alone. Only from above could you possibly see that wherever you stand is where you are meant to be.

I walk the path toward and away from Alan. The path away from my family of origin and back to myself. I trust the path, and I don't trust the path. It tangles and untangles simultaneously. It winds deeper and deeper. It tricks you into thinking you're too far in, that you'll never find your way out. It's nonsensical, yet compelling. You keep walking, even as you wonder why you're walking. It's then, at the precise moment when you think you must be doing it wrong, that you must have made a wrong turn, that you reach the center where a pile of rocks waits like an altar.

I can't say how long I've been walking. Ten minutes? Maybe fifteen? What I feel is relief and reluctance. I want to leave the stone behind, to put down this hot, heavy thing. I've been cradling it so tightly that my forearms are sore. I also don't want to let go. Sweat trickles down my back under my robe. My cheeks are burning. I look at the giant pile of rocks. I want to comply with the labyrinth's instructions, and I also want to run away. I wonder if all the people before me found what they're looking for, if they felt unburdened, if their questions were answered. Did they find peace?

In the distance, I hear my friend's laughter again. It's a cackling that tells me I'm missing a hilarious story, some opportunity for lightness, for fun. My chest aches. How long will I stay here trapped inside my grief while the world carries on around me? I wonder if the women have noticed my absence. I wonder what I'll say to them when I return.

I hold the hot rock to my lips for a moment, feel it burn. Then I squat down, find a flat place on the pile, and put it down. There it rests – my stone, my burden, perched atop a dozen other burdens. I give it a little wiggle to make sure it's secure, that it won't tumble to the ground. Then I say goodbye. I step around the altar and keep walking, winding outward. I once again hear the crunch of gravel beneath my feet, but my steps are lighter and faster as I go.

I can't yet see the exit, but I sense it's there. My chest is opening. I unfasten my robe and let the dry air touch my bathing suit, brushing over my bare legs. I breathe deeper. I make one last sweeping turn, double back over the path I walked inward, and then I am out.

My hands are still warm from carrying the stone. Even as I am back at the pool, lounging, clutching a cold drink. Even as we are eating dinner that night. I catch myself lost in stories, in friendship, in laughter. Even as I connect with the women and sense myself unwind, I notice my hands are hot. They stay that way for hours, for days, like a distant, throbbing memory.

• • •

Fact: Much like the labyrinth, a serpentine trail will lead me to details about Alan's death. This is the last bend in my journey, I tell myself. My last push for answers before I step off the trail and move on with my life.

With grief, we tend to think acceptance is the final stage, a finish line, or exit point from our pain. But what if it's a landmark? A place to catch your breath? A quiet spot you visit over and over again throughout your lifetime?

I navigate government offices and hospital administration in pursuit of facts, information, conclusions. I search for medical records online. I read HIPAA privacy notices to see what rights I have as a sibling to access those records. I make phone calls. I'm turned away. I double back and find a path through.

One day I call the county coroner's office to confirm that no autopsy was performed on Alan's body. A woman on the other end of the phone types his name and date of birth into a computer and tells me plainly, "There wasn't an autopsy, ma'am. I'm looking at the death record, and it says natural causes."

Another day, I dig my birth certificate out of storage and go to the public health department. I read online that immediate family members can request a certified copy of a death certificate, which is required by most hospitals if you want to obtain records. But not all health departments will release the death certificate unless you can prove you're a close living relative.

My friend Erica, who is studying to be a social worker, meets me there. She has worked as a victim's advocate with the Sheriff's department, offering support and resources to people who have experienced tragedy or been victims of crimes. She's exactly the kind of person you want by your side during a crisis – coolheaded, unemotional, yet compassionate and knowledgeable. When I tell her what I'm doing, how I expect it might be hard to gain access to these records, she says she is available to advocate for me.

"But I'm not a victim," I tell her.

"You're a survivor," she says. "You have rights as a survivor."

I turn that word – survivor – over in my mind. I've never thought of myself in this way. People who live through cancer, natural disasters, or car crashes are survivors. It will be years before I can look upon the trauma of my childhood or the trauma of Alan's sudden death and give myself credit for having survived.

Erica stands with me in line at the health department, a low-slung brick building that looks like it belongs in a 1960s true crime show. Her presence is soothing. For the first time in several months, I don't feel alone in my quest for answers. And maybe that's the point of her being here, not advocacy. Because in the end, it turns out there's nothing for her to advocate. The transaction is easy. I show a clerk my birth certificate and fill out a one-page form. I pay thirty dollars, and the clerk hands me an embossed copy of Alan's death certificate.

We walk out of the front door of the municipal building, sit on a bench under a maple tree, and stare at the crisp blue sheet of paper. Its edges are sharp, and it smells like fresh ink. I run my fingertips over the raised Colorado state seal. Erica sits beside me quietly as I begin to weep. I can't explain why I'm suddenly so sad. I got what I wanted, right?

Maybe it's because this is proof that he's really dead, Erica suggests. Maybe it's a release of pent-up anxiety I had wondering if they'd give the certificate to me. Maybe it's exhaustion from the whole process, not knowing if any of my efforts will actually lead to concrete answers. Maybe it's the frustration of not knowing exactly what answers I'm looking for. Maybe it's the pain of understanding, finally, the deeper truth: Grief has no right answers. There are things about Alan, his death, our relationship, that I'll never fully comprehend.

Maybe it's because a piece of embossed paper is a poor substitute for my brother.

· · ·

In the coming weeks, the death certificate unlocks more information from hospitals, insurance companies, pharmacies. The circuitous path leads me to a stack of doctor notes spanning years of hospital admissions and emergency room treatments from 2011 to 2016. There are more than a dozen hospital records, radiology reports, lab reports, emergency department notes, medication lists, discharge papers. Each has a different doctor's signature.

I am surprised at how easily I came to possess these papers.

I called the medical records office of the hospital where Alan died. I was told if I had the death certificate and a completed form, they could print out the information I need. A man told me I should write "closest living relative" on the form. I did, not knowing what "closest living relative" means or if I would qualify. I turned the form in, along with the copy of the death certificate. I got Alan's complete medical record in return.

I am flipping through the stack of papers and noticing patterns and themes. Certain words and phrases begin to jump out at me. I see the word "asthma." I see "sudden onset." I see "unknown reasons." I see "unknown etiology." I see "chest x-ray: normal." I see "history of asthma and seizure disorder." I see "history obtained through patient's mother." I see "patient's mother says." I see "mother reports." I see "patient himself can provide no information given his developmental delay." I see "patient denies having chest pain." I see "suspected pneumonia." I see "chest x-ray personally reviewed and not consistent with pneumonia." I see "asthma exacerbation." I see "patient given inhaler and steroids." I see "patient is not ill-appearing." I see "patient is hypoxic." I see "he does not have any known cardiac disease." I see "he is not currently on any type of daily inhaler or steroids." I see "his symptoms have improved." I see "he responded very well." I see "we will observe."

Taken together, these records are a lesson in contradiction and circular reasoning. No one had clarity. I close my eyes, and I imagine a group of doctors in long white coats, like ghosts. Each of them is holding one or two pieces of a complex jigsaw puzzle. None can solve it. I see them pacing the room, brushing shoulders with one another, scratching their heads, wondering how to put it all together, never once realizing that the others in the room might hold the crucial pieces. I wonder what they each were overlooking, how close they were to discovering some truth about Alan's condition. I wonder what my mother might have told them but didn't. I wonder if they felt a sense of urgency. I wonder if any of them knew, if they could have foreseen what was to come. How on one fateful night, they'd have to fight to try to save a life without knowing exactly how or when or why it slipped away.

Boulder, August 11, 2016:

Patient is a 43-year-old male with a history of asthma who presents to the emergency department by private vehicle accompanied by his mother. History is obtained through his mother. She states that his asthma has been aggravated by allergies recently and both she and he have had a cough lately. She went out to the store this evening and upon her return home, he was complaining of difficulty breathing. She gave him an albuterol breathing treatment as well as oral prednisone. His difficulty breathing got worse, and he told his mother he needed to go to the hospital. He became unresponsive upon arrival. He was pulled from the car and immediately brought to Room 2 on a stretcher.

Course of action:

2225: Patient arrives via private vehicle accompanied by mother. Unresponsive, apneic. Respiratory paged. OPA placed and ventilation by BVM started

2226: Patient is vomiting. No pulse. CPR started

2228: 1 mg epi, 1 mg bicarb. 1 g magnesium sulfate

2230: 1 mg atropine given. No pulse. Vtach on monitor. Defib pads placed.

2231: 1 mg epi

2233: intubation

2234: recheck pulses, asystole. 1 mg epi

2236: vented both sides of the chest with angio catheter. No rush of air. R side chest no air.

2237: 1 mg epi, 1 mg bicarb

2239: CPR *paused. No pulse.* CPR *continued.*

2242: 1mg *epi*

2244: OG *tube placed*

2245: CPR *paused. No pulses*

Time of death: 2246

Chapter Thirty-Two

No one talks about what grief looks like when the relationship you lost was fraught, when in a sense you already lost the person repeatedly while they were still alive, when you never really had them. You've lost someone, but they never belonged to you. Not fully. No one admits that a relationship with someone who is dead can be just as complicated as the relationship was when they were alive. There was suffering then, and there is suffering now. There was ambivalence then. There is ambivalence now. There was jealousy and fear. But there was also love. Then and now, the love is real.

It takes months before I come to this conclusion, before I recognize that my inner chaos is grief. The perplexity, the mental gymnastics. I never knew that the mind can be so overwhelmed with pain that it will flip through memories like a Rolodex, looking for templates, for context, some familiar thought or experience to categorize this new tragedy.

I've read the minute-by-minute account of Alan's death twenty times, maybe thirty. Each reading, I expect something to jump out at me, some answer or solution veiled by medical jargon, a smoking gun peeking from between the lines. *This is the remedy to your suffering,* I hope it will say. *This is why his death makes sense. This is how you can release yourself from wondering what went wrong.* Of course, I never see that. I strain my eyes. I contort my imagination. I want there to be more to the story, but all I see is an ending. I see an account of a man who was actively dying from the moment he arrived at the hospital. I don't see how anyone could have saved him. He was already gone.

Thoughts are thoughts, not facts. I know now that thoughts intertwine with memories, facts, and experiences. The sum of this equation equals the truth of one's existence.

Upon examination, I realize the thought, *She did this,* mirrors a thought I had as a child: *He's going to do it. He's finally going to kill me.* I had this thought as Alan dragged me by the hair and slammed my face into a wall. I had this thought the night he held a steak knife to my chest, his cheeks hot with rage, his eyes vacant. I had the thought when he threw a chair through the plate glass window. I had the thought when I cowered on the other side of my bedroom door as he beat it down.

It also mirrors the thought, *She's going to do it.* It, meaning take her own life. My mother for so many years was on the edge of survival, ready to tumble (or jump) into the abyss. My anticipation of her dying became woven into my psyche. This thought was almost comforting, an acceptance of the inevitable. If I knew she was going to die, I could detach myself emotionally from her. I could grieve the loss in advance.

The sum is this: I grew up with the belief that one or all of us might not make it out of my family alive. It was a core truth of my existence. In light of this, I would do what I could to protect myself, to protect Will and Alan, to keep my mother hanging on. Yet, at the end of the day, I believed we might still kill each other or ourselves.

So perhaps it makes sense that on the day I received the news that someone *actually had* died, my mind went there, to that old, familiar place.

Over and over, it's returned to that place, like revisiting the scene of a crime. In searching for context, the thought changed from *she did this* to *they did this*. They, meaning my mother and Mike. They, meaning the doctors. Sometimes it was they, the drugs. It meant they, the system designed to protect and care for Alan.

Before it releases its grip entirely, the thought serves up one more iteration: *I did this.* Maybe by my inaction, through my failure to intervene, it's my fault too. Maybe I could have done more to protect my brother, to learn about his condition and the possible complications, to advocate on his behalf. Maybe in moving out and saving myself, I shirked my responsibility to my brother.

At the core of all these questions is not culpability, but rather obligation, duty, loyalty. Who was really responsible for Alan? Was it my parents? Or was it me?

I'm not here to tell you that any of us are at fault. Nothing is that simple. It's telling that on that day in the Seattle airport, even as I had these dark thoughts, I had other thoughts too. *Did Alan know I loved him? Did he love me? It's too soon. I wanted to see him one more time.* For as much as my childhood was characterized by fear, there was also deep love. There was joy. There was longing.

This was the paradox.

I thought having answers would soothe my grief. But the relentless pursuit of those answers is only fueling my pain, making it a hot, untenable monster. To give up my quest is to accept the loss for what it is: irretrievable. To admit that I will never fully understand what I lost when Alan died. To admit that the deeper question is not whether Alan could have survived longer, but how did I survive all those years? Maybe his death was no one's fault. Just as the abuse was never our fault, his or mine. Maybe my ambivalent feelings are now (and forever) okay. Because fear and love are not mutually exclusive. The sum of my thoughts, memories, and experiences make that true. So, for now, I put all this away. There's nothing left to distract me from my grief.

Fact: Alan lived for forty-three years.
Fact: Alan is dead.
Unknown: How exactly he died.

Part Seven

The Other Half of the Ashes

Chapter Thirty-Three

Earthquakes happen when pieces of the earth suddenly slip past one another. The location underground where the earthquake starts is called the hypocenter. The location above the surface of the earth, where everyone feels it, is called the epicenter. Sometimes, but not always, an earthquake has foreshocks or little vibrations that happen first, like a warning. Not everyone can feel the foreshocks. Even the most sensitive of machines can't always predict when the earthquake is coming. Many earthquakes have aftershocks, reverberations. More often, people feel the aftershocks, perhaps because after a big shake, they are more alert, sensitive, vigilant.

We blame the cracks where earthquakes occur for the resulting destruction. We call them faults. Earth scientists map and describe three different kinds of fault lines. "Normal" faults happen when two blocks of land pull apart, stretching the earth's crust into a valley or rift. "Strike-slip" faults happen when land masses slide past each other horizontally, with little to no vertical movement. The San Andreas in California is a strike-slip. "Reverse" faults, also called thrust faults, push one block of earth on top of another. These faults are commonly found in collision zones, where tectonic plates push up into mountain ranges like the Himalayas and the Rocky Mountains.

The forces that create faults are compression, movement, expansion, and gravity. In other words, whenever something is under pressure, weighted down, vibrating, or grating against itself, trying to move in opposite directions – things crack. Fractures occur. Destruction. New geographies are formed.

I think about the core attributes of a person, their own personal bedrock. Their personalities, their fundamental traits seem solid unless acted upon dramatically by some outside force. Looking back at my family's history, I can't tell you what constitutes the biggest seismic event, what was merely a foreshock, what was an aftershock. I can't map the fault lines. There are too many. It seems the ground was never really steady. We always struggled to gain our footing.

My parents are shaped by natural forces and unnatural forces. They are weighed down by gravity. They are compressed. They pull apart, a wide valley or rift stretching between their two bodies. Their fault lines are vertical and horizontal and diagonal. They collide. They vibrate. They chafe. They form new geographies within themselves and within our family, fault lines spreading in all directions.

Though I didn't have words for it when I was young, I felt foreshocks. I knew how to brace myself, how to find shelter in the door frames or under my bed. I survived the ensuing earthquakes at the epicenter. I rode the waves of reverberation. I learned how to navigate the new geography, how to find my way out.

A memory from long ago, when I am five, maybe six: My parents are separating their belongings. My father is in the living room, pulling books off a tall, built-in bookcase one at a time, cracking the spine, contemplating, and then sorting it into one of two piles. His. Hers.

In the kitchen, my mother is filling a cardboard box with pots and pans and appliances. Not the good stuff. Not the Corningware or copper-bottom pots they received as wedding gifts. She's giving him the scratched Teflon pan, the picnicware, the spare set of forks and knives. He yells from the other room that he needs measuring cups and spoons. "I plan to cook," he insists.

My mother huffs and rifles through the cupboards. I watch her grab my *Sesame Street* play kitchen set with its Big Bird measuring cup, the teaspoon and tablespoon featuring Burt and Ernie, and a Grover rolling pin. She looks at me, says, "I'll buy you a new set," and tosses them into the box.

Mom keeps the house.
Dad takes the retirement accounts.
She keeps the television.
He takes the green recliner.
An equitable division of assets? Who knows. It's a division, nonetheless.

There are other things my parents will eventually divvy up:

1. Their favorite records. When they couldn't decide who should take them, my mother snaps the vinyl in half over her knee.
2. Custody of their children. Though this is not equitable. We live with Mom full-time and only see

my dad four days a month, sometimes less. Years later Dad will tell me he fought for more time with us, and my mother refused. I wonder if he's just telling me what I want to hear, that he wanted me as much as I wanted him.

3. Holidays and birthdays. Sometimes we celebrate twice. Christmas Eve at Mom's house and Christmas Day at Dad's. Sometimes they alternate – one year with Mom, the next with Dad. There's one year when I'm at my dad's house on my birthday, and Mom forgets to celebrate it at all.

4. Our loyalties. Over the years, when conflicts arise, I tend to side with my Dad while Will sides with Mom. This continues into adulthood.

5. Alan's body.

If Alan's death is an earthquake, then the news that my parents are dividing his remains is the aftershock.

I don't know what my parents' stories are regarding the division of Alan's ashes. I only know how I experienced it as an onlooker, someone who had no say in the matter. In the days following Alan's death, I heard the hushed arguments about funeral arrangements. I saw my father throw up his hands in frustration. I heard them discuss burying him in Minnesota, where my father grew up. I heard my mother suggest New Mexico, where she grew up. I gently suggested that they consider what Alan might have wanted. Neither Minnesota nor New Mexico, in my opinion, is where Alan would have wanted to have been buried. He rarely spoke of places. Instead, he was connected to people – his immediate family, friends, and his dogs. I thought, if he'd had a choice, he'd have liked to have been buried at the dog park that he frequented with Clyde.

I heard Will complain that no decisions were being made. I saw that a minister was brought in to mediate and move my parents toward an agreement. I heard that they agreed to split him up. I was silent, confused. I was angry. I was sad to think my brother could not be kept whole.

Now, some time later, I confess that a small part of me felt vindicated because I realized the fracturing, the brokenness of our family – a brokenness that was for so long hidden beneath layers of denial and secrets – now has a physical manifestation. The hypocenter becomes the epicenter. Anyone can see it. We are divided, just as Alan's body is divided.

The journey of Alan's ashes began shortly after his death in Boulder, Colorado. He was cremated, but before that happened, there was the disagreement over what to do with his remains, whether he would be embalmed for a viewing and then cremated or just cremated. Preserving his body in a casket was an additional step. "No one wants to say goodbye to an urn," I heard my mother say. And if he was buried whole rather than cremated, where would he rest? They couldn't agree, and so in the end, they decided to burn him and split the ashes evenly.

An equal division of assets.

Of course, human ashes are divided all the time. Sometimes families divide ashes into a dozen little vials so that everyone can have a piece of the person they lost. Jewelers make miniature urn necklaces. There is a sharing, a giving, a carrying of this person with you even after they're gone. Sometimes ashes are divided so that they can be spread in multiple geographies that represent places that person loved.

This is not how it goes with Alan's remains. In my assessment, the splitting of his body was not done out of wanting to share him or release him into the wind. The division was born out of confusion and disagreement and anger and conflicting agendas. To me, it felt like he was being ripped apart. The division of the ashes was symbolic not only of Alan's life, but also of our childhood. In pieces, fragmented.

At Alan's funeral, there is no mention of a burial. Those closest to Alan know that the casket on display is not his final resting place, but no one knows what will happen next, if there will be a gravesite or internment, or if my parents will just hold onto their pieces of my brother for themselves. No one knows. Or maybe they do know, but they don't say.

In October 2016, two months after Alan died, I am sitting at my kitchen island in Phoenix, drinking coffee and scrolling through social media when I see a series of posts by Will. He's in New Mexico. He posts a photo of him and my two-year-old nephew next to a landmark near Santa Fe called Camel Rock— a tall, sandstone, balanced-rock formation that is aptly named for its resemblance to a camel. I scroll a few images down and see that he's also posted a diptych. One side is a photo of himself holding my nephew. The other side is a photo of my father in the exact same spot forty years ago holding two-year-old Alan. I thumb down and find a final photo, an image of a headstone bearing Alan's name engraved with a smiling cartoonish cloud and rainbow and an inscription that says, "Alan painted his rainbows with the colors he was given."

I'm confused, but only for a moment. I look closer at the headstone and notice the fresh dirt and flower arrangement below it. I realize my mother must have buried her half of Alan's ashes. I imagine there was a ceremony or memorial of some sort. I assume Will was invited to attend. I was not.

I close the social media app and put my phone down on the

counter. The room starts to sway. I close my eyes and grip my mug of coffee tightly in both hands. I notice its warmth. I bring the mug to my lips and take a long sip.

Today is the first cool morning we've had in Phoenix in months. When I woke up, I imagined dropping the kids off at school and going for a short run, something I haven't been able to bring myself to do since Alan died and my body started aching. I'd gotten dressed in my running shorts and tank top, ushered the kids into the car. I'd driven the fifteen minutes to school in rush hour. I'd driven the fifteen minutes home. Those actions alone had exhausted me. I wasn't sure if I still felt like running, so I'd brewed coffee instead and zoned out with my phone.

Several minutes pass. Maybe it's the caffeine or a surge of anger at seeing Will's posts, but I suddenly feel like running. I lace my shoes tighter, grab my sunglasses and water bottle, and head out the front door. Our house is near a network of multi-use trails that climb up and around Phoenix's South Mountain Preserve. I take off at a sprint down the street toward the mountain and turn onto a singletrack trail. The weather is warmer than I anticipated, maybe 80 degrees, the sun having burned off this morning's chill. I know I'm not in shape to run this fast, but I don't slow down.

I run. Toward something. Away from something. Up and over something. Around something. The trail is rolling and sandy for about a mile, and then it becomes rocky and steep. I climb, willing my legs to move up and down like pistons, over boulders and around sagebrush and prickly pears. My breath becomes shallow. My face is hot. My rib cage burns. I come around a switchback and stop, unable to climb further. It's as if I hit a brick wall. I bend over, unable to catch my breath. My mouth is hanging open, and there's a sound coming out of me like muted screams. I gasp and exhale silent howls.

My legs are heavy. I stomp my feet and kick the sandy dirt. It flies up in a cloud and settles on my sweaty skin. *Leave me alone*, I think. *Get the hell off of me.* But it's just me here on the trail. I brush away the dirt and feel it abrade my skin. I can't get ahead of my breathing. I can't get away from the heat, the sand, from the rage that is chasing me up this trail. I just stand there, head hanging low, panting like a dog, sweating it out.

Why am I so angry? It's not like I wanted to go to my mother's burial service. Had she asked me, I probably would have said no.

It's something else. Something too difficult to describe. Something about seeing the photo of his gravestone and the fresh dirt around it. Something about Will posting the images. The fact that half of Alan was buried without me knowing changes nothing. Alan is still dead.

It also changes everything.

Years from now, I'll wonder if this is irrational, if I'm overreacting. My mother had a right to bury her half of Alan wherever she wants, however she wants, with whomever she wants in attendance. But in this moment, the ground is shaking. I feel like I'm dying, like I'm being buried along with half of Alan in that box.

I try to imagine which pieces of Alan are now underground. His head? His heart? His arms or legs? It doesn't matter. It's the intangible pieces – Alan's story, our ambiguous relationship, the facts of his death. That's what was sent underground, forever out of my reach.

A secret burial isn't all that different from burying secrets.

I stand there on the trail for what feels like an hour, waiting for my chest to stop heaving, for my heart rate to slow down. I take off my shirt so that I'm wearing just a sports bra and shorts. I use the shirt to wipe the dirt and sweat off my arms and legs and fan my face. Though I'm all alone, I feel exposed, vulnerable.

I slowly walk the last few switchbacks up to the ridgeline I had been aiming for, determined to finish what I started. Once I'm there, I can see the Phoenix skyline, a parade of midsize buildings with one or two skyscrapers. Beyond that are more mountains and rolling desert. I can hear the morning rush hour traffic on the streets below. A plane flies overhead, leaving contrails in the sky. The city is breathing. People are coming and going. I am in no more control of their stories as I am Alan's or anyone's. I am an observer. I am someone who needs permission to exhale, to let go.

Chapter Thirty-Four

May 2017.

Travel tip: If you're packing someone's ashes in your carry-on bag, be sure to seal them neatly in a sturdy zipper-lock bag. The rule of thumb, according to crematorium websites and urn catalogs is this: One pound of human body weight typically yields one cubic inch of ash. A gallon-size zipper-lock bag is roughly 230 cubic inches, which theoretically can hold the ashes of a 230-pound human being, which would have been more than sufficient for my brother since we only had half of him.

On a Friday morning in May, ten months after Alan died, my father carries half of my brother in a wooden box through a TSA checkpoint in Atlanta. He is stopped, searched, and questioned at length. Traditional urns made of metal, wood, or stone thwart the X-ray machine and cause commotion, he learns. An urn containing your loved one doesn't appear all that different from a homemade bomb. Add to that, they require some documentation certifying that the ashes are human – a death certificate or certified letter from the crematorium. Ashes look like explosive powder. A clear plastic bag would have been better, the officers say.

I am across the country, sitting in the Phoenix Airport, waiting for my flight to board. I too was stopped at security, but much less dramatically. I'd packed an aromatherapy gel eye mask, anticipating a need to relax, not considering that the beads of silicone in the mask would exceed the three-ounce limit on liquids or gels.

The story about Dad and the ashes is being relayed to me over group text by my half-sister, Emma. She and my step-mother are there in Atlanta with Dad, trying to calm him down. In yet another airport, Will is preparing to depart. Also on their way are my aunt and uncle, my dad's siblings. I'm watching their texts roll in, like threads tethering us to my father's dilemma:

> This is ridiculous.

> Heartless bastards. You'd think they'd be more compassionate.

> Can you just put the box in your checked luggage?

> Why don't they just examine the ashes? They can tell they're not explosive.

> It's against policy for them to touch human remains.

I'm cringing as I read. I can feel Dad's tension from here, his blood pressure rising. He's a stoic man, restrained. I didn't see him cry at Alan's funeral, but I could sense his pain, like a radio frequency I've been tuned to since I was a child. My father is adept at containing his feelings. I believe it's this ability to compartmentalize that allowed him to leave my brothers and me when we were kids. But under great strain, his body vibrates, twitches, sends out ripples into the atmosphere.

In between reading texts, I open my laptop and google *traveling with human remains* and *how to pack human ashes in your carry-on bag.*

My dad had received his half of the ashes from my mother, but none of the documentation to go with it. He bargains with the TSA. He pulls up the obituary for them to see. In the end, they let him – and Alan – through the terminal and onto the plane.

Dad called us all weeks ago – me, Will, Emma, my aunt and uncle – and said that May would be the month. He wanted to bury his half of Alan in his hometown of Hibbing in northern Minnesota next to his parents. He wanted to do it as soon as possible but was told by the cemetery manager that he'd have to wait until the ground thawed. He told us he has permission to use the same burial plot as my grandparents. He could even inscribe the backside of their tombstone with Alan's name.

"It'd mean a lot if you could be there," Dad told me.

"Of course," I said. "I'd be happy to go."

This was a lie. Though I feel honored that my father has included me – my mother didn't invite me to her burial, after all – I'm not happy about going. I feel some warmth at the invitation. I can hear in my father's voice that this is important to him. He had so little influence over Alan's funeral or the gatherings at my mother's house in the week following Alan's death. But this. This is something he's thought about and planned. And as much as I believe Alan did not feel connected to Minnesota, my dad believes it's an appropriate resting place, next to his parents, surrounded by our ancestors. I tell myself I will go, that I'm doing it for my father, to support him, to honor his wishes, if not Alan's.

In the nights leading up to this trip, I awaken several times with the same nightmare. A weight is pressing down on my shoulders. Something is pinching my neck like a clamp closing tighter and tighter. I feel it gripping and squeezing my throat until I cannot breathe. I sit up straight in bed sweating and gasping for air. I can't tell if I really stopped breathing or if it was just the dream. I press my hands to my chest and feel my heart pounding. I cross my arms and hug myself, rocking back and forth until my heart slows down. "You're okay," I whisper. "You're breathing. You're safe." I'm too terrified to cry.

I have the same nightmare in the pre-dawn hours of May 20th, 2017, the day we bury half my brother in northern Minnesota. "You're safe," I whisper, rocking back and forth. "You're okay."

I am unsure if I'm telling this to myself or to Alan.

After navigating airline security and flying from various points across the country, we all arrived in Hibbing last night and went straight to the only bar that was open: a dark, wood-paneled building with sticky floors that smelled like stale cigarette smoke. Several men with white hair wearing work boots and flannel shirts were stooped over the bar drinking light beer. They glared at us as we walked in. Already conspicuous out-of-towners, we sat at the only high-top table in the center of the room. Why not?

I drank watered-down gin and tonic while Will programmed a jukebox to play rap songs, a practical joke for the locals who clearly weren't in the mood. Emma and I scrolled through our phones. I showed her the latest pictures of the kids. She showed me some recent travel photos. Meanwhile, my dad and his siblings sipped beer and reminisced about Hibbing, what it was when they were kids and what it has become.

When they were young, Hibbing was a bustling town full of Italian and German immigrant families who were drawn to the "Iron Capital of the World." A huge open-pit iron mine was the lifeblood of the area during World War I and World War II. At its height, the mine provided one-fourth of the iron ore that was produced in the U.S. The Greyhound Bus Line started here, offering reliable transportation to and from the area towns to the mine. Downtown Hibbing included elaborate stone architecture and numerous parks and schools. It was also the hometown of Bob Dylan, or Bobby Zimmerman, as my grand-mother used to call him. "That Bobby Zimmerman, he sure has made a name for himself," she'd say. "I don't care for his music, though. You can't understand a word he's saying."

In recent decades, the town infrastructure and its residents have aged. People have either moved away or died. The population has steadily declined since 1980. Wandering the historic district feels akin to visiting a ghost town.

It's like this on the morning of Alan's burial as we drive around the cemetery and my dad points out how many more graves there are than the last time he was here. "They're running out of room to bury people," he says. I suddenly wonder if the choice to inter Alan in the same exact plot with my grandparents is because there wasn't anywhere else for him to go.

The weather is gloomy, like winter hasn't fully loosened its grip. It's fifty degrees with a low ceiling of gray clouds and mist. We pull our jackets around ourselves as we walk through the cemetery. My dad points out the gravesites of my grandfather's extended family, Italians who arrived on Ellis Island in New

York and immediately took a train to Minnesota for the promise of work in the mine. They knew nothing of this upper midwestern climate, how different it would be from their Mediterranean home.

Eventually, we turn a corner and find a row of gravestones where a priest is standing in full clerical robes. Next to him is a man in jeans and work boots carrying a shovel. The priest introduces himself to my father, and they exchange pleasantries. Then, he goes around the group and shakes each of our hands. As he does, we each say our name and our relationship to Alan. "My name is Gina, and I was Alan's younger sister."

My father arranged this in advance – the priest, a small memorial ceremony, prayers and blessings to be given before Alan is placed underground. The priest begins by asking us about Alan, what he was like, how he died. My father talks about Alan's love of dogs and cars and music. He explains that Alan had developmental disabilities and died suddenly, but doesn't elaborate. The priest nods and says, "It sounds like Alan was a remarkable young man. I know he'll be missed."

Then, the memorial begins. The priest flips open a book and reads a short rite. We bow our heads to pray. Instead of closing my eyes, I stare at a patch of brown grass beneath my toes. As I shift my weight, the saturated ground makes a squishing noise. The wind picks up. I'm shivering. I focus on the priest's words; his steady deep voice is soothing. I glance down at the headstone that bears my grandparents' names, Lorraine and Herman. Lorraine died of cancer in 1997, when I was in college. Herman died of Alzheimer's in 2008, nine months after my daughter Bronwynn was born. He never got to meet his great-granddaughter.

My memories of my grandparents are sparse. We didn't see them often after my parents divorced. But I do vividly recall how much they adored Alan. My grandfather was a barber who loved to tell stories. We'd take turns sitting in his barber chair and getting our hair cut while he'd chat away about his bocce ball league or the Italian village his family emigrated from. Alan sat so quietly. He loved having his hair combed. I think he also liked the cadence of my grandfather's voice. After our haircuts, Grandpa would take us to the corner store and let us pick out a comic book or candy bar.

My grandmother believed Alan was capable of anything. She doted on him, her first grandchild, buying him patent leather shoes and bowties and black licorice, his favorite candy. She wanted him to look and feel his best. He's just like any other child, she used to say. But he wasn't. We all knew he wasn't. Still, she bought him chapter books and games that were age-appropriate, but too advanced for his intellectual ability. This angered my mother, who would call my grandmother and complain, "It's too hard! You'll just frustrate him." But my grandmother was stubborn. She insisted Alan should be treated the same as Will and me. Why not present him with options and see if he rises to the challenge?

Looking back, I can see that my grandmother's intentions were good, if misguided. In the 70s and 80s, kids with disabilities were marginalized, dismissed. I like to think she was trying to combat the stigma, trying to help Alan fit in and feel "normal." She didn't see his limitations the same way the rest of us did. She saw only her precious grandson who deserved the best life had to offer.

When I look up from the prayer, a small, square hole has been dug, maybe two feet wide. The priest reaches out his hands to my father, and my dad gives him the wooden box. The priest carefully lowers it into the hole, grabs a handful of wet dirt in his hand, and gently sprinkles it atop the box. He invites us to do the same. My dad crouches down and grabs some wet earth and spreads it like salt over Alan. My stepmom, aunt, and uncle all follow. Then Will and Emma. Last, I sink my hand into the pile of dirt, feel it seep beneath my fingernails. I squeeze it, coating my palm in mud. I hold my fist over the box and release it with a thud. I wipe my palm on my pant leg, creating a stain that will never wash out.

There's silence for a moment as we all stare at the box in the ground. I hadn't expected to feel anything, but as I glance again at the nearby headstone and see my grandparents' names, I'm overcome by something, like a jolt. My legs tremble. Tears spring to my eyes, and as I close them, I feel warmth wash over my body.

I have a vision of my grandmother standing with her arms outstretched. She is just as I remember her as a child, with tight white curls, plump rosy cheeks, and thick, round frameless eyeglasses. I look down and see myself holding Alan like an infant. I see my grandfather next to my grandmother, smiling and nodding at me as if to say, *Go ahead, it's fine.* I look down at the baby with the gentleman's face and slick dark hair. I hear my grandmother's lilting voice saying, "It's okay, Gina. It's all going to be okay. We've got him now." The voice is so real that I open my eyes to see if anyone else has heard it, but they're all still staring down at Alan's ashes in the ground. My arms are empty. The priest is reciting another prayer.

I close my eyes again, feel the warmth, and hear my grandmother's voice. "We'll take him from here," she says. "You've done enough." I see myself reaching out my arms, gingerly handing over the baby, my precious older brother. My grandmother takes him in her arms and begins to rock back and forth, shushing him. My grandfather puts an arm around her shoulder. They look like proud new parents.

I see it and feel it simultaneously, the relinquishing of my burden. "He was never yours to hold," I can hear my grandmother say. "Let us take care of him."

I am weeping, trembling. I feel something strange, like courage and despair coming together, intertwining, forming an amalgam of emotion that resembles peace. I am wrapped in a blanket of peace. It's not unlike the moment I left the stone at the center of the labyrinth. But deeper and sadder. A much bigger weight left behind.

As the priest closes the ceremony, I open my eyes and look around. Everything looks the same, but also completely different. I notice a weird quality to the light as the sun fights for space from behind the clouds, casting long beams across the headstones and reflecting in puddles of water on the road. I notice the trees, still leafless, swaying in the wind. The green blades of grass fighting with the mud. Everywhere I look there are beginnings and endings. Knowns and unknowns. Beauty and gray.

Early the next morning, I'm back on an airplane, sitting in a window seat, eager to get home to Kris and the kids. As the plane lifts off the tarmac, it makes a northerly arc, skirting the edge of the Boundary Waters, a wilderness area that spans more than a million acres. The wilderness is a patchwork of lakes, rivers, woods, and wetlands that act as a buffer zone between the U.S. and Canada. Pink dawn light illuminates the watery surfaces, putting them in sharp relief against the trees. This is a place where harsh geologic forces – fracturing, abrasion, flooding, the pooling and splitting of bodies of water – have resulted in a geography that is marvelous, beautiful, peaceful. The lakes are framed with green rolling hills and cliffs that were carved by glaciers ages ago.

I stare out the window, unable to take my eyes off the shimmering pink water, the ribbons of blue and green. There's a kind of perspective that comes from looking at something so complex from a great distance. It occurs to me that soaring 30,000 feet above the Boundary Waters, the landscape makes sense in a way that it can't when you're on the ground, deep inside of it. On the ground, it's difficult to navigate. People travel from all over the world to this tangled wilderness, seeking the challenge. They spend weeks in their canoes, tracing paths that are broken by dense forests and long, grueling portages. The complexity is its beauty.

Above, from this height, the landscape forms a complete picture, even with its holes and valleys and rifts and green and blue debris. It is both solitary and communal. It is at once broken and completely whole.

Acknowledgments

I owe enormous thanks to many people, but above all Kris, Bronwynn, and Miles, my whole heart and home. Thank you for giving me the space to write and for bringing unending joy, love, adventure, and laughter to my life. I love you.

Thank you to Nicole Cunningham, my wonderful agent, trusted reader, advocate, fellow nature-lover, and friend. This book wouldn't exist without your support. I feel honored to know you and lucky to work with you.

To everyone at Running Wild, especially Lisa Kastner and Aimee Hardy: Thank you for seeing the value in this story and helping launch it into the world. Your collective wisdom, insight, and collaborative spirit make the publishing industry a better, more inclusive space.

Thank you, Claire Bidwell Smith, for your mentorship, encouragement, and abiding friendship. You believed in this book wholeheartedly from the very beginning, even when I doubted. Thanks for cheering me on.

The advice and support of many teachers and fellow authors is etched on these pages. Among them Alexander Chee, Rebecca Woolf, Hannah Beresford, Nora McInerny (and the TTFA team), Annette McGivney, Matt Logelin, Rachel Walker, Buzzy Jackson, Katherine Sleadd, and the faculty and fellow workshoppers at Lighthouse Writers and the Squaw Valley Community of Writers.

Thank you to Rachel Walker and Evelyn Spence for being

there on one of the worst days of my life and for supporting me in the aftermath. You have offered me templates for what it means to be a dedicated writer and a compassionate, courageous, authentic human in this wild world.

To Sarah Fonder-Kristy, Katie Grice, Sara Hougan, Jeanette Chian Brooks, and Alisa Marzilli: Your collective brilliance and thirty-plus years of friendship has been one of the greatest miracles in my life. I'm weeping as I think about all the ways you show up to support me (and one another). I love you all.

To Louise: You heard and honored this story long before I ever typed a word of it. Thank you for your unwavering ability to witness the darkest moments and guide me to the light. You've shown me how it feels to be seen and accepted – and to see and accept myself.

Thanks to all my friends who have lifted me up and kept me sane as I worked on this book. Many of you have felt like sisters and brothers over the years. An incomplete list : Hilary Anderson (MFH!), Sara Ellison, Katherine Sleadd, Annette McGivney, Jessica Hulse, Jen and Dennis Lewon, Laurel Justice, Elizabeth Turnage, Lisa Pivin, Angel Jannasch-Pennell, Alyssa Albertone, Audrey Butters, Theresa Caldwell, Carri Grimditch, Dana Myers, Nancy Christensen, Jennifer and Jonathan Fenske, Andy and Jane Hathaway, Gen Grant, Heather Bingham, Susan Sweet, Alissa Dodson, Robyn Woodman, Whitney Logan, Jen Sinkler, Tim and Audre Shisler, JB Brockman, Jessica Bell, and Jennifer Baker.

I'm grateful to my family—especially Suzie, Nick, Rob, Liz, Abby, Don, Cara, Dad, Ronnie, Amanda, Ted, Hilary, and Andrew—for supporting my work and sharing your memories of Alan.

To the readers of my *New York Times* essay about Alan: Thank you for the kind emails and comments and for asking me to write more. And thank you, Roberta Zeff, for giving that essay a home.

Thank you to Liz, Nina, and the team at Know Rare for your work spreading hope not only to people living with rare disease, but also their caregivers and siblings. Thanks also to the Sibling Support Project and SibNet for creating a safe place for siblings to share honestly and find validation.

To my local Colorado community, for all the ways you reminded me this book is important: Ling TeBockhorst, Ann Swan-Evans (and everyone at CP Waneka), and Teresa Doherty for helping move the story through my body and onto the page. Everyone at Ozo Coffee and OTIS Craft Collective, for providing a safe space to write (and keeping me caffeinated). Hana and William at Thalken, for treating me like an old friend, spreading joy, and supplying me with candles and cozy socks. And Bethany Sartell for easing our transition back home.

Finally, dear reader: Writing a memoir is both solitary and communal. It's easy for an author to feel alone with a blank page and a pile of documents or memories to untangle. But throughout the process, I held your faces in my mind. I imagined your hands holding this book and perhaps finding some comfort and validation within. Which is to say, we are never alone. Thank you for reading.

Copyright permissions

About the Author

Gina DeMillo Wagner is an award-winning journalist and author. Her writing has appeared in *The New York Times*, *The Washington Post*, *Memoir Magazine*, *Modern Loss*, *Self*, *Outside*, *CRAFT Literary*, and other publications. She is a winner of the CRAFT Creative Nonfiction Award, and her memoir was longlisted for the 2022 SFWP Literary Award. She lives and works near Boulder, Colorado.

Website: ginadwagner.com

Loved these stories and want more? Follow us at www.runningwildpress.com, www.facebook.com/running-wildpress, on Twitter @lisadkastner @RunWildBooks @RwpRIZE